Writing otherwise

Manchester University Press

Writing otherwise

Experiments in cultural criticism

Edited by

Jackie Stacey and Janet Wolff

Manchester University Press
Manchester and New York

Distributed in the United States exclusively
by Palgrave Macmillan

Published by Manchester University Press
Oxford Road, Manchester M13 9NR, UK
and Room 400, 175 Fifth Avenue, New York, NY 10010, USA
www.manchesteruniversitypress.co.uk

Distributed in the United States exclusively by
Palgrave Macmillan, 175 Fifth Avenue, New York,
NY 10010, USA

Distributed in Canada exclusively by
UBC Press, University of British Columbia, 2029 West Mall,
Vancouver, BC, Canada V6T 1Z2

British Library Cataloguing-in-Publication Data
A catalogue record for this book is available from the British Library

Library of Congress Cataloging-in-Publication Data applied for

ISBN   978 07190 8942 8   *hardback*

First published 2013

Typeset in Caslon with Myriad display by
by Special Edition Pre-press Services

Printed in Great Britain
by TJ International Ltd, Padstow

Contents

Contributors

Margaret Beetham retired in 2005 from Manchester Metropolitan University where she had taught for many years, been course leader for the MA in women's studies, and held the position of reader in the Department of English. She is now an honorary research fellow in the School of Humanities, Languages and Social Science at Salford University. Her research interests are in histories of women's popular reading, recipe books, Lancashire dialect writing, and feminist criticism and teaching. Publications include: *A Magazine of her Own?: Domesticity and Desire in the Woman's Magazine 1800–1914* (1996), *The Victorian Woman's Magazine: An Anthology*, with Kay Boardman (2001), and several edited volumes, together with articles and chapters in English, Italian and German publications. She was an associate editor of the *Dictionary of Nineteenth Century Journalism* (2009). She has just completed a book-length work of memoir and reflection entitled *Home is Where*.

Mary Cappello has been interested for over a decade in testing the boundaries of scholarly and poetic practice, bringing incompatible knowledges into the same space and creating forms of disruptive beauty. Her numerous essays and experimental prose appear in such venues as *The Georgia Review*, *Salmagundi* and *Cabinet Magazine*, and she is the author of four books of literary non-fiction, including *Called Back* (2009), which won a Foreword Book of the Year Award, and Independent Publishers Prize, and *Awkward: A Detour* (2007), a *Los Angeles Times* Bestseller. A recipient of the Bechtel Prize for Educating the Imagination from Teachers and Writers Collaborative, the Dorothea Lange–Paul Taylor Prize from Duke University's Center for Documentary Studies, and a Guggenheim Fellowship, Cappello is a former Fulbright Lecturer at the Gorky Literary Institute (Moscow) and currently professor of English and creative writing at the University of Rhode Island.

Contributors

Brenda Cooper is an emeritus professor at the University of Cape Town, where she was the director of the Centre for African Studies. In 2009 she moved to Salford and is now an honorary research associate at the University of Manchester. She also runs an academic writing mentoring consultancy called *Burnish*. She has published four academic books – *To Lay These Secrets Open* (1992); *Magical Realism in West African Fiction* (1998); *Weary Sons of Conrad* (2002); and *A New Generation of African Writers* (2008) – and many journal articles and book chapters on African and diasporic fiction and literary theory. She is currently writing a cross-genre book that includes art, literature and her own life story, entitled *Floating in an Anti-bubble from South Africa to Salford*.

Marianne Hirsch is the William Peterfield Trent Professor of English and Comparative Literature at Columbia University, as well as professor in the Institute for Research on Women and Gender. She is the 2013 president of the Modern Language Association of America. Her most recent publications are *The Generation of Postmemory: Writing and Visual Culture After the Holocaust* (2012) and, as co-author with Leo Spitzer, *Ghosts of Home: The Afterlife of Czernowitz in Jewish Memory* (2010). Other works include *Family Frames: Photography, Narrative, and Postmemory* (1997), *The Mother/Daughter Plot* (1989), and the (co-)edited volumes *Rites of Return: Diaspora Poetics and the Politics of Memory* (2011), *The Familial Gaze* (1999) and *Conflicts in Feminism* (1991).

Judy Kendall is a senior lecturer at Salford University where she has led the BA and MA programmes in English and creative writing. An award-winning poet-academic, she has produced three books on Edward Thomas and three collections of her own poetry. She also writes plays and short fiction, and she works as a collaborative translator in several languages. She was guest editor of the 2013 *European Journal of English Studies* (17.1) on 'visual text', and lectures on visual text at undergraduate and graduate level at Salford. As well as publishing several articles on the subject, she has worked creatively on projects in this area, including exploratory films, visual translations and interactive and kinetic digital poetry.

Lynne Pearce is professor of literary theory and women's writing at Lancaster University. Her books include: *Woman/Image/Text: Readings in Pre-Raphaelite Art & Literature* (1991); *Reading Dialogics* (1994); *Feminism and the Politics of Reading* (1997); *Devolving Identities: Feminist Readings in Home & Belonging* (as editor) (2000); *The Rhetorics of Feminism* (2004); *Romance Writing* (2007). From 2006 to 2010 she was principal investigator for the AHRC-funded project, 'Moving Manchester: how the experience of migration has informed writing in Greater Manchester from 1960 to the present', culminating in the publication (by Manchester University Press in 2013) of *Postcolonial Manchester: Diaspora Space and the Devolution of Literary Culture*. She is now working on a new book on driving, provisionally entitled *Driving: A Journey Through Twentieth-Century Consciousness,* and her previous work on this topic includes 'Driving north / driving south' (*Devolving Identities*, 2000) and 'Automobility in Manchester fiction' (*Mobilities*, 7:1, 2012).

Contributors

Monica B. Pearl is a lecturer in twentieth-century American literature at the University of Manchester. Her work addresses the construction of subjectivity in cultural texts, with recent focus on AIDS and its written and visual representation. She is the author of *AIDS Literature and Gay Identity: The Literature of Loss* (2013) and, most recently, of essays on Alison Bechdel's graphic memoir *Fun Home*, Audre Lorde's biomythography *Zami*, the writing of W. G. Sebald, and the play and film *Angels in America*.

Griselda Pollock is the director of the Centre for Cultural Analysis, Theory and History at the University of Leeds, where she is professor of social and critical histories of art. Recent publications include *Encounters in the Virtual Feminist Museum: Time, Space and the Archive* (2007), *Digital and Other Virtualities: Renegotiating the Image* (2010, with Anthony Bryant), *Bracha L. Ettinger: Art as Compassion* (2011, edited with Catherine de Zegher), *Concentrationary Cinema: Aesthetics as Resistance in Alain Resnais's Night and Fog* (2011, with Max Silverman), which won the Kraszna-Krausz Award for Best Book on the Moving Image 2011. Forthcoming are *After-affect /After-image: Trauma and Aesthetic Transformation* (2013), *The Nameless Artist and the Invention of Memory: Charlotte Salomon's Orphic Journey in Life? or Theatre? 1941–42* (2013) and *From Trauma to Cultural Memory: Representation and the Holocaust* (2014).

Carol Smart is professor of sociology and co-founder of the Morgan Centre for the Study of Relationships and Personal Life at the University of Manchester. She has just completed a project on civil partnership and is currently working on a new project on donor conception called 'Relative strangers'. Her publications include *Personal Life: New Directions in Sociological Thinking* (2007); *Family Fragments?* (1998, with B. Neale); and *Feminism and the Power of Law* (1989). Her recent article in *Sociology* (2011), 'Families, secrets and memories', won the Sage Prize for Innovation and Excellence. She is working on a new edited book, *The Craft of Knowledge* with Allison James and Jenny Hockey to be published in 2013 by Palgrave. In 2009 she was awarded an honorary doctorate in law from the University of Kent. Further information can be found at www.manchester.ac.uk/morgancentre.

Leo Spitzer is the Kathe Tappe Vernon Professor of History emeritus at Dartmouth College, New Hampshire, and visiting professor, Oral History Research Center, Columbia University, New York. His most recent book, co-authored with Marianne Hirsch, is *Ghosts of Home: The Afterlife of Czernowitz in Jewish Memory* (2010). He is also the author of *Hotel Bolivia: The Culture of Memory in a Refuge from Nazism* (1998); *Lives in Between: Assimilation and Marginality in Austria, Brazil and West Africa* (1990 and 1999); *The Creoles of Sierra Leone: Responses to Colonialism* (1974); and co-editor, with Mieke Bal and Jonathan Crewe, of *Acts of Memory: Cultural Recall in the Present* (1999). He is currently working on a book of stories about German-Jewish refugees in New York in the decade of the 1950s and, with Marianne Hirsch, on a book of essays on school photos.

Contributors

Jackie Stacey is professor of media and cultural studies at the University of Manchester where she is currently director of the Centre for Interdisciplinary Research in the Arts and Languages. Running across her research interests (which have ranged from gender and sexuality in the cinema to the visualising technologies of medical science) has been a concern with changing formations of fantasy, processes of subjectivity and modes of embodiment. Her publications, some of which have been written more 'otherwise' than others, include: *Star Gazing: Female Spectators and Hollywood Cinema* (1994); *Teratologies: A Cultural Study of Cancer* (1997) *Thinking Through the Skin* (2001, co-edited with Sara Ahmed) and *Queer Screens* (2007, co-edited with Sarah Street). Her most recent book, *The Cinematic Life of the Gene*, was published by Duke University Press in 2010.

Vron Ware has worked as a journalist, editor, photographer, campaigner and academic. Her publications include *Beyond the Pale: White Women, Racism & History* (1992); *Out of Whiteness: Color, Politics & Culture*, with Les Back (2002); *Who Cares about Britishness? A Global View of the National Identity Debate* (2007); and *Military Migrants. Fighting for YOUR Country* (2012). She is currently based in the Department of Sociology at the Open University, but has also taught at the University of Greenwich and at Yale University. Her contribution is based on an unpublished book, entitled *Where Was I? The World in an English Village*, which was written during the Connecticut years, from 1999 to 2005.

Janet Wolff is professor emerita of cultural sociology at the University of Manchester, where she directed the Centre for Interdisciplinary Research in the Arts from 2008 to 2010. She returned to Manchester, her home town, in 2006. Before that, she taught at the University of Leeds; the University of Rochester, New York, where she was director of the Program in Visual and Cultural Studies; and Columbia University, New York, where she was associate dean for academic affairs in the School of the Arts. Her books include *The Social Production of Art* (1981 and 1993), *Aesthetics and the Sociology of Art* (1983 and 1993), *Feminine Sentences* (1990), *Resident Alien* (1995), *AngloModern* (2003) and *The Aesthetics of Uncertainty* (2008). She is currently working on a book combining memoir, family history, trans-Atlantic reflections, and visual imagery, and is co-editing (with Mike Savage) a book about Manchester's cultural history.

Writing otherwise

Jackie Stacey and Janet Wolff

The essays in this collection all share a desire to write otherwise. Emerging from an event of the same name, this project carries with it a number of aspirations.[1] Foremost among these is the intention to bring together a series of contributions which push against conventional academic modes of writing in a number of different ways. The idea behind this book was to invite contributors to move their writing into more exploratory registers. Our aim is to expand some of the traditional boundaries of academic practice and generate a series of essays that step slightly to the side of its familiar conventions. *Writing Otherwise* reflects upon the occasions for our departure from the usual scholarly genres of expression and asks what else we might want to say about our subjects and about ourselves if we were to move beyond the expected forms through which our thinking and writing as academics have previously flourished.

The boundary between our usual academic writing and these more experimental modes is a porous one. There is a long tradition of academics (especially in literary studies) producing fiction alongside their academic work, and teachers of creative writing, of course, also publish it, as well as doing their own critical scholarship.[2] At the same time, there has been a long-standing attempt by academics to combine autobiographical with scholarly writing.[3] Here we have no ambitions to combine fictional and academic writing, or to move from the latter into straightforwardly autobiographical or memoir essays. This would be a slightly different kind of book.[4] Instead, all the contributors to *Writing Otherwise* are invested in exploring how to write otherwise *as* academics. Exactly what this means for our contributors takes us in some interestingly different directions. Some essays combine academic style with a more poetic or personal one; some work in dialogue or reflect on the collaborative possibilities of writing otherwise. Some use creative non-fiction as a route into long-standing academic questions; some mix visual and textual elements or read the one through the other; some rethink academic debates through influences beyond their usual remit; and some engage with the more elusive (intangible, ephemeral) things in life that academics have struggled to put into words.

Running across a number of essays is the question of the personal and its place in academic writing.[5] This relationship has been of particular interest in feminist criticism but is by no means restricted to this agenda.[6] All the contributions in this volume could be read through the lens of more personal writing in some senses, but this is a deceptively unifying category which obscures the innovative ways in which they also undercut what the idea of the personal so often promises. The autobiographical register may be used in search of a more discursive understanding – a form of creative non-fiction writing with broader implications.[7] Influenced as they are by the kind of critical thinking of the past decades that disturbs any expectation that the personal (or what some might call the experiential) can be straightforwardly conveyed to others through language, these essays all move into more intimate spaces with caution.[8] If a number of contributions play with memoir, they do so with an awareness of the elliptical presence of both the past and the self in this form. Refusing its conventional pleasures, a number of essays take a more oblique approach to self-narration.

In contrast to the academic voice of the lone scholar still typical of most humanities research, a number of essays in this volume move beyond the singularity of authorship and experiment instead with both explicit and implicit collaborative modes. Mourning the death of a life-long beloved collaborator, Griselda Pollock's essay commemorates the ways that writing otherwise (with others, across genres, for different readerships, in the name of social and cultural change) has been part of a feminist politics intent on crossing the usual divide between intellectual and political practices. Just as this opening contribution undercuts the individualised academic voice, so other essays experiment with various dialogic registers; for example, Janet Wolff decentres the individualised self of the memoir in her piece, as she traces the fragments of a life mapped out through the stories of other, sometimes loosely connected, biographies and histories. In related ways, Vron Ware combines personal history with ethnography to explore the past through dialogue; Brenda Cooper borrows images from elsewhere to renarrate a personal but highly political history; and Margaret Beetham invents a persona in order to return to childhood memories – the third-person memoir. Whilst co-authorship as such is nothing new, there are surprisingly few conceptualisations of such collaborative work. Marianne Hirsch and Leo Spitzer's contribution combines co-authorship with a critical account of the processes of collaboration.

If the *otherwise* of our title gestures towards a refusal of more conventional authorial dispositions, then it also expresses something of the elusive character of some topics addressed in this collection. A number of contributions reflect upon the difficulty of finding a language for the ghostly, the affective and the ineffable – those elements that seem the least tangible and yet may make the most powerful impression upon us. To the extent that language (including, but not only, academic language) fails to capture so much that may drive our intellectual appetites, the authors of these essays write in search of something that may seem to escape discourse and yet whose affective presence persists. These are matters of mood, of touch, of pleasure and of gesture. They may be lingering memories or seductive anticipations. They may be unanswerable speculations or unconscious repetitions. They may be fleeting thoughts which leave significant traces. Here they take the form of the awkward intimacy of professional touch in Mary Cappello's essay, and the affective transformations in a group of relative strangers in Jackie Stacey's. They also appear as research encounters that touch us, as in Carol

Smart's contribution, and as modes of thinking while driving, as in Lynne Pearce's. And in Monica Pearl's essay, we encounter pleasures so thrilling they almost seem beyond words.

A final mode of writing otherwise includes those essays which interrogate the dynamic play between written and visual languages. In Judy Kendall's contribution, the visuality of text itself – layout, font, composition – is the point of a poetic exploration of how attention to the graphics of writing might newly animate us as readers. The relationship between words and images in other essays is not necessarily reiterative, or illustrative. Instead, a photograph might interrupt the flow of a narrative or a textual fragment might be left as an enigmatic trace of a past correspondence. It may also be that something in a photograph belonging to someone else might inspire a tangential story or precipitate the desire to possess or even purloin something for one's own purposes.

The essays in this book vary considerably with respect to formal experimentation. If graphic experimentation dislocates the reader in an instructive or imaginative way, then the shifts in register employed in so many of the essays may have a varying impact on the familiar pleasures of reading practices more generally. Voyeuristic desires for confessional disclosure may be aroused and then thwarted; and the reassuring closures of narrative may be promised but not delivered. Diary entries may be treated as data and subjected to rigorous textual analysis. Tolerance for incomplete stories may be tested. And when linearity precipitates the expectation of resolution, the reader may nevertheless be left feeling dissatisfied by an abrupt break or something that feels like a premature ending. Loss and bereavement may linger uncomfortably; the return to places of childhood or countries of the past may not deliver the desired answers to the questions about which readers have been invited to feel curious.

Unlike the experimentation of more avant-garde writing, these innovations tend towards something unconventional and yet are still easily legible within an academic frame. The *otherwise* in question operates through register, mode of address and tone, often drawing us into familiar territory and yet leaving us somewhere slightly unexpected. Even at their most poetic or inventive, all the essays in this book offer some kind of cultural criticism.[9] Shifting across and between the disciplines of history, literature, art history, music and sociology and working within the interdisciplinary fields of feminist studies, cultural and visual studies and postcolonial studies, this collection challenges us as academics, through both formal and thematic interventions, to think and write otherwise.

The kinds of writing represented in these essays often establish a rather different relationship to the reader. Some of the pieces invite the reader to imagine new spaces of intellectual work; others combine genres and styles in an attempt to animate a very different kind of academic reading. Sometimes drawing readers into a more intimate space or into a consideration of the reading and writing practices themselves, a number of pieces place the dynamics between authors and their subjects centre stage. In this way, we hope that the collection as a whole speaks to an interest in relationality both as process and as topic. A concept that in many ways is grounded in the idea of process, it opens up the dynamics not only of readers and authors but also of self and other (and of self as other), which many contributions seek to put in the place of the individualised self of personal narration, autobiography and memoir.

A preoccupation of a cultural criticism informed by psychoanalysis and post-structuralism, the relational dynamics of subjectivity are the focus of a number of chapters. Feminism has had a particular investment in refusing the individualising imperatives (often associated with masculine ideals of autonomy), and in imagining other ways not only of working collaboratively but also of theorising how culture works to privilege certain genres of self-presentation.[10] Celebrating the intellectual and political contributions of feminist work, some essays mark out imaginative spaces for writing that history anew: perhaps to write of the limits to academia's tolerance for more personal modes; perhaps to test the ethics of borrowing from histories that are not our own. Others reflect on their previous research to push towards something that has transformed their thinking, be it a poignant interview or an ontological switch in how we approach academic subjects.

Another aspect of thinking relationally that is important here is the way a number of essays are concerned with how to write about the body. If subjectivity is never fully available to us, as many have argued, or indeed is never exclusively 'our own' in any kind of possessive way, then our bodies might also be thought about less as singular biological entities and more as potential collaborations constituted through our encounters with others.[11] Finding ways to articulate that place between the substantial physicality of the body and its nonetheless uncanny ephemeral affects, some of these modes of writing continue this longstanding feminist focus.[12] Here psychoanalytic approaches meet more phenomenological influences, as authors experiment with a new language of embodied perception and somatic experience. Be it the touch of healing hands, the smell of a stranger, or the sound of a voice singing at its most powerful, our sense of ourselves comes from the ways that our bodies are animated by the presence of other people's. Sometimes this involves intimacies, welcome and unwelcome, both with those with whom we live and work and with strangers. How do we navigate the awkwardness of a stranger's touch that we have invited, or the mood of a group we belong to that has failed to support someone in distress? How are memories of childhood triggered through the senses and why is it sometimes impossible for us to own these as ours? And how might other people's physical capacities thrill us so intensely we can hardly bear their impact on our own bodies? These are some of the questions that are addressed here about affect, intimacy and the senses in ways that seem to demand something beyond the usual academic modes of writing.[13] Perhaps they require us to think about ourselves through the 'transpersonal', a category that indicates how deeply social and historical we are, even as we feel the burdens of particular lives to be ours alone.[14]

But bodies are not abstractions here; rather, they are always located. Our relationship to place thus also comes under frequent scrutiny in this volume. For relationalities between subjects involve the negotiation of our changing feelings about the places we inhabit. In trying *both* to write about *and* to generate a sense of subjects and bodies in process, some of these essays take the reader on journeys between different locations, across borders and back into the imaginative and geographical memories of past lives. Whether literal or metaphorical, journeying is the focus of how and why place comes to really matter to us. The return to past places is a move made by a number of contributions. Interviews and oral histories are sometimes combined with autobiography, diary entries and memoir, yet never straightforwardly. Writing in search of a sense of belonging is often interrupted by the losses and fractures brought by the return to places from the past. Narrations of origins and connections are sometimes disturbed by the vicissitudes of memory or the shame of privilege. Fragments of family history are threaded together to produce stories of uncertainty.[15]

Place can seem a very static concept. But in this collection, a number of contributions try to mobilise it through their writing practices. Space here becomes 'practiced place'.[16] A city, for example, becomes the focus for the comings and goings of different generations, enabling us to imagine its fluid nature in processes of narration. A drive between two locations that has been repeated over the years becomes the route to thinking about somatic perception and how thoughts make us feel while we move between places. A village is returned to as the site of social processes and indicator of a nation's fading claim on its pastoral self-image. A nation, formed through a history of violent colonial repressions, becomes the force through which possession is mediated. Whether expansive or depleting, inviting or alienating, the return to place is a generative moment of personal and political history that often defies conventional expression.

A sense of belonging is central here but so too are stories of displacement, departure and mobility. Reflections upon movements in particular directions reveal the sometimes paradoxical nature of our desires and aversions in relation to place. Both generating and refusing identity claims, place is scaled up and down according to our memories and aspirations. Like the body, it seems to be of a certain physical substance that should have a determining force; and yet, there is so often something transient about its significance. If there is sometimes a contest over the ownership of words, images, documents, and memories in the pieces in this book, then it is worked out through processes of writing that illuminate the indeterminacy of many such claims. Across a number of these essays, we find contested loyalties and uncertain relationships: how do we connect a sense of who and what we think we are to where we have lived and worked, and to the places we have left?[17] Many of these accounts of geographical mobility tell of displacement and migration. Imagining another country or city might generate a new version of oneself (less bound by history, more open to the future), and the desire to relocate might get caught up in psychic investments in personal transformation. Moving to another country to become someone else might have the effect of giving up custody of the past to place and location.

Belonging obviously always speaks of a deeply invested relationship to location. Embedded within the orientational dynamics between people and places conjured here is the history of (often violent) appropriations. Colonialism and its legacies surface repeatedly through these discursive explorations of where we feel at home. Finding ways to articulate a balance between shameful personal responsibility for a nation's violent political practices and adult reflections on the consequent childhood of privilege, for example, poses the question of how indirect narration might work as a form of cultural critique. Similarly, a white critic's appropriative use of an image from a postcolonial artist, whose work has sought to challenge dominant historical accounts, may seem to run the risk of an inappropriate colonial repetition.

Alongside modes of writing otherwise about colonial and postcolonial histories, a number of essays explore new forms through which to consider how anti-semitism has been played out across generations. The post-memory of survivorship, as Holocaust legacies continue to shape present lives, is approached through a collaborative return to a place of family origin, a return that refuses to bring the desired closure.[18] The incommensurability between genealogy and place across time lingers, as the only history available is one of erasure and disjuncture. Moments of recognition of Jewish identity, and of the inheritance of Holocaust suffering, interrupt a narrative of art-historical reflection. In a rather different way, two generations of Jewish migration are mapped through personal, sometimes accidental, connections. Only in retrospect does the gratitude of refugees appear touchingly naïve, in the context of continuing anti-semitism and a somewhat compromised welcome by the 'saviour' countries. Working with (instead of against) these fragments, the autobiographical, biographical and memoir writing here pushes towards a sense of how to connect the personal stories with political histories in ways that resist the closures of linearity and transparency.

Feeling at ease in a place is always a relational matter. Who belongs where and when is partly to do with very concrete experiences that locate us in (or in between) villages, cities, nations or continents, and is partly to do with something much less tangible, like atmosphere or mood, sensation or perception. Whether people feel they fit into the places where they live and work is often a question of an affective dynamic that is hard to put into words. If some places make some people feel they belong on arrival but others that they must escape to save their lives, then what is it that charges these responses to ways of living with each other in specific locations? The particular configuration of subjectivity, identity and a sense of belonging (or its absence) is often hard to articulate. Finding ways to think and write about what makes us feel at ease may mean exploring psychic investments or somatic modes of perception that seem highly individualised but that often carry familiar patterns – as described over the years by various strands of psychoanalysis and phenomenology. The question is how we can put into an academic language some of the subtleties of how and why we might be drawn to some people and places, and not others. And how might this shift around as a new sense of subjectivity emerges in relation to our location? What new languages of interiority might we want to invent, even as we acknowledge the phantasmatic nature of our connection to people and places?[19] Do we really only feel at ease with what feels familiar or do particular differences draw us, even as they shift into something that feels more potentially threatening? And how might we think about our shameful aversions to some of the more disturbing differences we imagine others to represent?

In the context of challenging colonial racism and anti-semitism, discussed in some of the essays, a cosmopolitan ethos of openness to strangers and foreigners might seem like an obviously desirable political goal where the multi-cultural project might need reinvigorating; but perhaps such easiness cannot be trusted to endure, and may not even be reliably legible.[20] We need to explore the connections between individualised responses and the wider sociological and historical questions of belonging. In this way, we might begin to articulate those more personal registers that have haunted subjects like sociology as they have tried to produce generalised models of our lives. Some of the limits of existing academic frameworks and disciplines are tested through the essays in this volume, which attempt to answer some of these lingering questions by experimenting with new combinations of the personal and the theoretical.

Writing about the powerful dynamics of belonging and displacement brings with it inevitable issues about temporality. A sense of the past (welcome and unwelcome) pervades these stories of migration and resettling. Places we couldn't wait to leave but to which we have returned; places by which we have always been haunted. Places we travel between, when belonging is primarily found in the sense of journeying. The enduring atmosphere of a building (like a school or a house), the survival of village farms or hedgerows, the history of a city and its inhabitants – these become the focus of writing otherwise about the past and its relationship to the present. The family histories here are not searched for as self-evident facts (though those may have their thrilling appeal when discovered); rather, genealogies are traced in order to explore the unexpected stories or indirect connections that emerge, or the elliptical relevance of trivia that turn out to be evidence of lasting significance. Cautious approaches to the seductive continuities and causations promised by teleological narratives run across a number of the essays collected here. There is something ungraspable about time passing and about the processes of change it seems to impose upon us. In the light of our inevitable mortality and our eventual insignificance in the future, our lack of agency over time has been the subject of much philosophical theorising.[21] Across the historical work that has been carried out well beyond the discipline of history itself runs a set of tensions between material objects and their compelling traces, and between a belief in a retrievable past and a sense of it as necessarily already lost. A great deal has been written about the uncanny nature of modern time, not least its own apparent 'refusal to submit to a temporal logic'.[22] The modern imperatives towards linearity and sequence promise an orderly sense of directional flow. But time is more unruly and beyond such modern regulatory disciplines. The past will not remain behind us;[23] we struggle to remain present in the present;[24] and the future necessarily eludes us.[25]

A number of essays here navigate the particular temporal paradoxes of writing. Just as processes of reading bring us into a delayed temporal relation with the author who both is and is not present in the text, so textuality itself further complicates intention, and the structures of language in turn undermine the very idea of fully 'making sense'. The inevitable gaps and fissures of the writing process generate a longing for stable meanings and satisfactory closures. Our desire to narrate, to capture, to conjure, to thrill – all of these become the uncertain intentions of academic as well as creative authorship. Some contributions both perform and reflect upon writing's temporal aspects. In their narrations of returning to past events, people and places, they evoke the powerful attachments that have been lost or have faded, but they also find new ways of disturbing conventional sequences and undoing singular life stories. Ranging across oral history, art history and family history, a number of essays invent new lenses through which to view the traces of lived lives. Stories and anecdotes remain stubbornly structured according to modern principles of temporal linearity, but those told here move in and out of such conventions, investigating their pull whilst continuing to deliver many of their pleasures.

Other essays explore the challenge of 'staying in the moment'.[26] How can we write about the difficulty of staying in the presence of something that moves us, when its thrill feels too intense for words? And what if movement itself generates an experience of the present governed by feelings of departure and arrival or by memories of lost love? What do these encounters with places and people feel like and how might we write about them? What kinds of creative accounts enable us to think better about the intimacy of touching and being touched? The boundaries between pleasure and its opposites are delicate and fragile in these reflections, sometimes because pleasure itself can feel unbearable, at other times because moods can shift so quickly in and out of its warm glow. The mood of a group of people has a certain kind of presence, but, when the affects are too disturbing, we are quick to defend against them by absenting ourselves in our customary ways. Articulations of these shifts sometimes bring everyone back into the room, just as modes of address can rewrite readership afresh. Changes in tone and register ask for our attention in a way that brings us into the present of the textual encounter; changes in the appearances of the text adjust our awareness as readers. Reading becomes an activity that requires our active participation and our full attention.

Finally, we return to the essays themselves. We have grouped them under three section headings: affects; displacements; poetics. The volume opens with Griselda Pollock's essay, which is, above all else, a eulogy for her friend and colleague, Rozsika Parker. Looking back on their years of collaboration as writers and curators leads her into other kinds of reflection: on the early years of the women's art movement and feminist art history; on how we respond to the death of those close to us, and how this response itself might be translated into an art practice; and, central to all of this, how 'writing from the heart', characteristic of Rosie Parker's own work, can now inform this moving tribute to her. The second essay in this group on 'affects' is Mary Cappello's exploration of contact – of what actually goes on in bodily encounters between two people, in this case between people who are not otherwise intimate. The occasion of a massage session evokes a range of feelings and leads to a sequence of reflections on touch, talk and – connected in a number of ways to this theme – writing itself. For Jackie Stacey, as for Griselda Pollock, the psychoanalytic is a crucial aspect of understanding affect, in her discussion of two rather different social groups: an academic centre for the study of cosmopolitanism and a course on analytic approaches to group work. The complex interactions played out in the latter, it transpires, offer important insights for the former, and especially with regard to the cosmopolitan ideal of being open to others. In the next essay, Carol Smart looks back on her work as a sociologist of family relations, challenging the academic requirement to retain distance and objectivity, and exploring how the personal connection intervenes, despite oneself, in the encounter with some of those studied. In a rather different example of openness to others, she too comes back to questions of affect in her account of being touched by the stories she uncovers.

The essays in the next section are concerned in different ways with place, including, too, the experience of being *dis*placed and the sense of being between places. Janet Wolff's piece is structured around the move from England to the United States, with the dislocation of perception that comes with that shift. It operates as part memoir and part family history, these strands also intersecting with other people's stories. In Lynne Pearce's essay, movement between two places (the north of England and rural Scotland) is also the focus of a piece combining the personal with the more conceptual; but here phenomenology inspires the study of diary extracts of driving the same route regularly over a period of more than ten years. Her account of these road trips in her own 'driving diaries' becomes the 'data' in this perceptual exploration of what we're thinking when we're driving. Movement between countries, and also into the countryside, is central to Vron Ware's paper, which is another personal account mediated to some extent by other people's stories. Her focus is the village in which she was born, and the transformations it has undergone over half a century. The central concern in this return to place is to try to ascertain how one's sense of self also changes, and – crucially – how one can write about this. Brenda Cooper – another trans-continental traveller – writes about her current, displaced, view of her place of origin (South Africa), her long-term academic concerns (African diasporic writing) and, most of all, her revised understanding of herself and of her own family history. Lastly, Margaret Beetham, in a fragment of a memoir written 'otherwise' (namely in the third person) creates a collage of memory about growing up in India, moving back and forth between her childhood self and the present moment.

The three remaining essays are in fact very different from one another, and yet each speaks, we think, to a more general concern with 'poetics'. Monica Pearl discusses the pleasures of opera, exploring through her own long immersion as an aficionado a new poetics through which we might understand the experience of bliss which is peculiar to this art form. Here language is somehow not enough, or not adequate. And yet, of course, we must employ language to talk about this intense experience. Judy Kendall's poetics concern a more fundamental aspect of writing: namely, what the written page looks like. Her essay obliges us to look closely at the visual materiality of the text, and at how such things as font, layout and other textual effects, normally invisible to the reader, in fact produce meanings of their own, confirming or contesting the actual sense of words. In the last essay in this volume, Marianne Hirsch and Leo Spitzer use the occasion of a retrospective look at their recent co-authored book to think about writing, and especially the project of writing together. The fact of co-authorship turns out to facilitate an important aspect of their study of the history of Czernowitz before, during and since the Holocaust: namely, the ability to hear, and to present, the many different voices and perspectives of those implicated in that history. Here questions of poetics also open into questions of ethics and politics.

The academics writing otherwise here are all in dialogue with academic writing (their own, each other's, other people's), however indirectly. Not seeking to abandon the academic, these pieces find new routes through to some of the same old questions, as well as setting new agendas. To write as an academic (reflectively, critically, dialogically, theoretically), but to approach cultural criticism as an opportunity for innovation – this is the space this volume seeks to open up.

Our thanks to Rosemary Deller for her excellent work as editorial assistant in preparing the essays in this book for publication.

Notes

1 'Writing Otherwise' was the title of a conference organised by Jackie Stacey for Janet Wolff's retirement and held on 28 June 2010 at the University of Manchester. We would like to thank Hilary Hinds for suggesting this title and also for helpful comments on this introductory essay.

2 These are too numerous to detail here, but see, for example: Patricia Duncker, *Hallucinating Foucault* and *The Strange Case of the Composer and His Judge*; Carolyn Heilbrun and her many detective novels written under the name Amanda Cross, including *Death in a Tenured Position*; Frank Lentricchia, *The Sadness of Antonioni*; Ann Oakley, *The Men's Room*; Jacqueline Rose, *Albertine: A Novel*.

3 Some of the most significant examples of such combinations include: Janet Catherine Berlo, *Quilting Lessons: Notes from the Scrap Bag of a Writer and Quilter*; Annette Kuhn, *Family Secrets: Acts of Memory and Imagination*; Alice Kaplan, *French Lessons: A Memoir*; Ann Oakley, *Fracture: Adventures of a Broken Body*; Carolyn Steedman, *Landscape for a Good Woman: A Story of Two Lives*; Valerie Walkerdine, *Daddy's Girl: Young Girls and Popular Culture*.

4 There are now numerous memoirs by feminists, including: Susan Rubin Suleiman, *Budapest Diary: In Search of the Motherbook*; Alessandra Comini, *In Passionate Pursuit: A Memoir*; Sara Suleri, *Meatless Days: A Memoir*; Marjorie Perloff, *The Vienna Paradox: A Memoir*; Lynne Segal, *Making Trouble: Life and Politics*. In addition to individual memoirs, two edited collections also stand out: Liz Heron's *Truth, Dare or Promise: Girls Growing up in the Fifties* and *The Feminist Memoir Project: Voices from Women's Liberation*, edited by Ann Snitow and Rachel Duplessis.

5 This question has been addressed by numerous scholars, including Nancy K. Miller, *Getting Personal: Feminist Occasions and Other Autobiographical Acts*; Lynne Pearce, *Feminism and the Politics of Reading*; Eve Kosofsky Sedgwick, *Touching Feeling: Affect, Pedagogy, Performativity*; Elspeth Probyn, *Sexing the Self: Gendered Positions in*

Cultural Studies and Carol Smart, *Personal Life: New Directions in Sociological Thinking*. The question has also been considered specifically in the case of illness: for example, by Mary Cappello, *Called Back*; Jackie Stacey, *Teratologies. A Cultural Study of Cancer*; Sandra Butler and Barbara Rosenblum, *Cancer in Two Voices*; Gillian Rose, *Love's Work: A Reckoning With Life*; and Eve Kosofsky Sedgwick, *A Dialogue on Love*.

6   There have been a number of reflective memoirs by academics engaging with questions of class and masculinity, including Ronald Fraser's *In Search of a Past: The Manor House, Amnersfield, 1933–1945;* Derek Sayer's *Going Down for Air: A Memoir in Search of a Subject*; Frank Lentricchia's *The Edge of the Night*.

7   Cappello, one of the contributors to this volume, has introduced the suggestive term 'discursive autobiography' to describe this kind of writing. For details, see: www.swallowthebook.com/awkward-autobiography.html.

8   Central to this development have been the insights of poststructuralist and psychoanalytic theory. Foundational texts in this kind of cultural criticism include Rosalind Coward and John Ellis *Language and Materialism: Developments in Semiology and the Theory of the Subject*; Julian Henriques *et al.*, *Changing the Subject: Psychology, Social Regulation and Subjectivity*; and Chris Weedon *Feminist Practice and Poststructuralist Theory*.

9   Other collections of cultural critics 'writing otherwise' include: John Schad and Oliver Tearle (eds), *Crrritic! Sighs, Cries, Lies, Insults, Outbursts, Hoaxes, Disasters, Letters of Resignation, and Various Other Noises Off in These the First and Last Days of Literary Criticism, Not to Mention the University*; H. Aram Veeser (ed.), *Confessions of the Critics*; and Angelika Bammer and Ruth-Ellen Boetcher Joeres' forthcoming collection *Rigor & Beauty: The Art of Scholarly Writing*.

10   Two important early studies on the construction of masculinity as a firmly bounded identity are Nancy Chodorow's *The Reproduction of Mothering* and Dorothy Dinnerstein's *The Mermaid and the Minotaur*. See also R. W. Connell, *Masculinities*.

11   See Judith Butler, *Giving an Account of Oneself* and Adriana Cavarero, *Relating Narratives: Storytelling and Selfhood*. Earlier texts exploring the ways in which writing constructs the self include: Charlotte Linde's *Life Stories: The Creation of Coherence*; Tess Cosslett, Celia Lury and Penny Summerfield's edited collection, *Feminism and Autobiography: Texts, Theories, Methods*; Domna C. Stanton's edited collection, *The Female Autograph: Theory and Practice of Autobiography from the Tenth to the Twentieth Century* (which introduces the idea of 'autogynography'); and Leigh Gilmore's *Autobiographics: A Feminist Theory of Women's Self-Representation*.

12   The insistence on the body was an important contribution of French feminism of the 1980s – in particular Luce Irigaray's *This Sex Which Is Not One*. More recent work includes: Rosi Braidotti, *Nomadic Subjects: Embodiment and Sexual Difference in Contemporary Feminist Theory*; Judith Butler, *Bodies that Matter: On the Discursive Limits of Sex*; Elizabeth Grosz, *Volatile Bodies: Toward a Corporeal Feminism*; Donna Haraway *Simians, Cyborgs and Women: The Reinvention of Nature*; and Emily Martin, *The Woman in the Body: A Cultural Analysis of Reproduction*.

13   There is growing literature in the humanities, and to some extent in the social sciences, on the nature and role of affect in personal and social life, and in aesthetic encounters. See for example, Sara Ahmed, *The Cultural Politics of Emotion*; Lauren Berlant (ed.), *Compassion: The Culture and Politics of an Emotion*; Patricia Ticineto Clough, *The Affective Turn: Theorizing the Social*; Melissa Gregg and Gregory J. Seigworth (eds), *The Affect Theory Reader*; Sianne Ngai, *Ugly Feelings*; Eve Kosofsky Sedgwick and Adam Frank (eds), *Shame and Its Sisters: A Silvan Tomkins Reader*; Janet Staiger, Ann

Cvetkovitch and Ann Reynolds (eds), *Political Emotions*; Kathleen Stewart, *Ordinary Affects*.

14 The concept of the 'transpersonal', raised in Marianne Hirsch and Leo Spitzer's essay in this volume, is a fascinating one. See Nancy K. Miller, 'Getting transpersonal', in which the transpersonal is understood as 'the links to others that we establish with generations past and present', p. 166.

15 For a discussion of how geographical dislocations may provide new points of view see Wolff, 'The female stranger: marginality and modes of writing'.

16 Michel de Certeau, *The Practice of Everyday Life*, p. 117.

17 See Cavarero, *Relating Narratives* in which her point of departure is the discursive distinction between the philosophical question, '*what* is Man?' and the biographical narration of a particular life in answer to the question, '*who* is s/he?', p. 13.

18 The concept of 'postmemory' has been proposed by Hirsch, as a way of conceptualising the inherited narratives of the children of Holocaust survivors. Hirsch, *Family Frames: Photography Narrative and Postmemory*, pp. 21–3.

19 The term phantasmatic refers to the imaginative activity which underlies all conscious thought and feeling and gives associations and manifestations a psychic reality with material consequences, see Charles Rycroft, *Critical Dictionary of Psychoanalysis*, p. 131.

20 On cosmopolitanism and the problem of the legibility of identity, see Stacey, 'The uneasy cosmopolitans of *Code Unknown*' (forthcoming 2014), and in this volume.

21 There is a vast philosophical literature on temporality; good examples of books that offer some lead into this literature include: Grosz, *Space, Time and Perversion: Essays on the Politics of Bodies* and Grosz, *The Nick of Time: Politics, Evolution and the Untimely*; see also, Scott Lash, Andrew Quick and Richard Roberts (eds), *Time and Value*.

22 Lee Edelman makes this argument in the context of a roundtable debate on queer sexuality and time: see Carolyn Dinshaw *et al.*, 'Theorizing queer temporalities: a roundtable discussion' in the special issue of *GLQ* on 'Queer temporalities', p. 188.

23 This phrase is taken from Sheila Rowbotham, *The Past Before Us: Feminism in Action since the 1960s*. See also Adam Phillips, *Missing Out: In Praise of the Unlived Life* for a discussion of our discomfort with the sense of our 'unlived lives'.

24 For one of the more interesting books in the current wave of publications on being present in the present (often captured by the term mindfulness) see Tim Parks, *Teach Us To Sit Still: A Sceptic's Search for Health and Healing*.

25 For a discussion of the heterosexual imperative to invest in reproductive futurism, see Edelman's *No Future: Queer Theory and the Death Drive*.

26 See Claire Bacha, 'The courage to stay in the moment'.

Bibliography

Ahmed, Sara, *The Cultural Politics of Emotion* (Edinburgh: Edinburgh University Press, 2004).

Bacha, Claire S., 'The courage to stay in the moment', *Psychodynamic Counselling*, 7:3 (2001), 279–95.

Bammer, Angelika, and Ruth-Ellen Boetcher Joeres, *Rigor & Beauty: The Art of Scholarly Writing* (in progress/forthcoming).

Berlant, Lauren (ed.), *Compassion: The Culture and Politics of an Emotion* (New York: Routledge, 2004).

Berlo, Janet Catherine, *Quilting Lessons: Notes from the Scrap Bag of a Writer and Quilter* (Lincoln, NE, and London: University of Nebraska Press, 2001).

Braidotti, Rosi, *Nomadic Subjects: Embodiment and Sexual Difference in Contemporary Feminist Theory* (New York: Columbia University Press, 1994).

Butler, Judith, *Bodies that Matter: On the Discursive Limits of Sex* (New York: Routledge, 1993).

Butler, Judith, *Giving an Account of Oneself* (New York: Fordham University Press, 2005).

Butler, Sandra, and Barbara Rosenblum, *Cancer in Two Voices* (San Francisco, CA: Spinsters Book Company, 1991).

Cappello, Mary, *Called Back: My Reply to Cancer, My Return to Life* (New York: Alyson Publications, 2009).

Cavarero, Adriana, *Relating Narratives: Storytelling and Selfhood* (London and New York: Routledge, 2000).

Certeau, Michel De, *The Practice of Everyday Life* (Berkeley and Los Angeles, CA: The University of California Press, 1984).

Chodorow, Nancy J., *The Reproduction of Mothering* (Berkeley and Los Angeles, CA: The University of California Press, 1978).

Clough, Patricia Ticineto, with Jean Halley, *The Affective Turn: Theorizing the Social* (Durham, NC: Duke University Press, 2007).

Comini, Alessandra, *In Passionate Pursuit: A Memoir* (New York: George Braziller, 2004).

Connell, R. W., *Masculinities* (Cambridge: Polity Press 1995).

Cosslett, Tess, Celia Lury and Penny Summerfield (eds), *Feminism and Autobiography: Texts, Theories, Methods* (London and New York: Routledge, 2000).

Coward, Rosalind, and John Ellis, *Language and Materialism: Developments in Semiology and the Theory of the Subject* (London: Routledge & Kegan Paul, 1977).

Dinnerstein, Dorothy, *The Mermaid and the Minotaur: Sexual Arrangements and the Human Malaise* (New York: Harper Colophon, 1976). Published in the United Kingdom as *The Rocking of the Cradle and the Ruling of the World* (London: The Women's Press, 1987).

Dinshaw, Carolyn, Lee Edelman, Roderick A. Ferguson, Carla Freccero, Elizabeth Freeman, Judith Halberstam, Annemarie Jagose, Christopher Nealon and Nguyen Tan Hoang, 'Theorizing queer temporalities: a roundtable discussion', *GLQ: A Journal of Lesbian and Gay Studies*, 13: 2–3 (2007), 177–95.

Edelman, Lee, *No Future: Queer Theory and the Death Drive* (Durham, NC: Duke University Press, 2007).

Fraser, Ronald, *In Search of a Past: The Manor House, Amnersfield, 1933–1945* (London: Verso Editions and NLB, 1984).

Gilmore, Leigh, *Autobiographics: A Feminist Theory of Women's Self-Representation* (Ithaca, NY, and London: Cornell University Press, 1994).

Gregg, Melissa, and Gregory J. Seigworth (eds), *The Affect Theory Reader* (Durham, NC: Duke University Press, 2010).

Grosz, Elizabeth, *Volatile Bodies: Toward a Corporeal Feminism* (New York: John Wiley & Sons, 1994).

Grosz, Elizabeth, *Space, Time and Perversion: Essays on the Politics of Bodies* (New York and London: Routledge, 1995).

Grosz, Elizabeth, *The Nick of Time: Politics, Evolution and the Untimely* (Durham, NC: Duke University Press, 2004).

Haraway, Donna, *Simians, Cyborgs and Women: The Reinvention of Nature* (New York and London: Routledge, 1991).

Henriques, Julian, Wendy Hollway, Cathy Urwin, Couze Venn and Valerie Walkerdine, *Changing the Subject: Psychology, Social Regulation and Subjectivity* (London: Routledge, 1998 [1984]).

Heron, Liz (ed.), *Truth, Dare or Promise: Girls Growing up in the Fifties* (London: Virago Press, 1985).

Hirsch, Marianne, *Family Frames: Photography Narrative and Postmemory* (Cambridge, MA, and London: Harvard University Press, 1997).

Irigaray, Luce, *This Sex Which Is Not One* (Ithaca, NY: Cornell University Press, 1985).

Kaplan, Alice, *French Lessons: A Memoir* (Chicago, IL, and London: University of Chicago Press, 1993).

Kuhn, Annette, *Family Secrets: Acts of Memory and Imagination* (London and New York: Verso, 1995).

Lash, Scott, Andrew Quick and Richard Roberts (eds), *Time and Value* (Oxford: Blackwell, 1998).

Lentricchia, Frank, *The Edge of Night* (New York: Random House, 1994).

Linde, Charlotte, *Life Stories: The Creation of Coherence* (New York and Oxford: Oxford University Press, 1993).

Martin, Emily, *The Woman in the Body: A Cultural Analysis of Reproduction* (Boston, MA: Beacon Press, 1992).

Miller, Nancy K., *Getting Personal: Feminist Occasions and Other Autobiographical Acts* (New York and London: Routledge, 1991).

Miller, Nancy K., *But Enough About Me: Why We Read Other People's Lives* (New York: Columbia University Press, 2002).

Miller, Nancy K., 'Getting transpersonal', *Prose Studies*, 31: 3 (December 2009), 166-80.

Ngai, Sianne, *Ugly Feelings* (Cambridge, MA, and London: Harvard University Press, 2005).

Oakley, Ann, *Fracture: Adventures of a Broken Body* (Bristol: The Policy Press, 2007).

Parks, Tim, *Teach Us to Sit Still: A Sceptic's Search for Health and Healing* (London: Harvill Secker, 2010).

Pearce, Lynne, *Feminism and the Politics of Reading* (London: Arnold, 1997).

Perloff, Marjorie, *The Vienna Paradox: A Memoir* (New York: New Directions, 2003).

Phillips, Adam, *Missing Out: In Praise of the Unlived Life* (London: Hamish Hamilton, 2012).

Probyn, Elspeth, *Sexing the Self: Gendered Positions in Cultural Studies* (London: Routledge, 1993).

Rose, Gillian, *Love's Work: A Reckoning With Life* (New York: Schocken Books, 1995).

Rowbotham, Sheila, *The Past is Before Us: Feminism in Action since the 1960s* (London: Pandora, 1989).

Rycroft, Charles, *Critical Dictionary of Psychoanalysis* (London: Penguin, 1995).

Sayer, Derek, *Going Down for Air: A Memoir in Search of a Subject* (Boulder, CO, and London: Paradigm Publishers, 2004).

Schad, John, and Oliver Tearle (eds), *Crrritic! Sighs, Cries, Lies, Insults, Outbursts, Hoaxes, Disasters, Letters of Resignation, and Various Other Noises Off in these the First and Last Days of Literary Criticism, Not to Mention the University* (Brighton: Sussex Academic Press, 2011).

Sedgwick, Eve Kosofsky, *A Dialogue on Love* (Boston, MA: Beacon Press, 1999).

Sedgwick, Eve Kosofsky, *Touching Feeling: Affect, Pedagogy, Performativity* (Durham, NC, and London: Duke University Press, 2003).

Sedgwick, Eve Kosofsky, and Adam Frank (eds), *Shame and its Sisters: A Silvan Tomkins*

Reader (Durham, NC: Duke University Press, 1995).

Segal, Lynne, *Making Trouble: Life and Politics* (London: Serpent's Tail, 2007).

Smart, Carol, *Personal Life: New Directions in Sociological Thinking* (Cambridge: Polity Press, 2007).

Snitow, Ann, and Rachel Duplessis (eds), *The Feminist Memoir Project: Voices from Women's Liberation* (New York: Three Rivers Press, 1998).

Staiger, Janet, Ann Cvetkovitch, and Ann Reynolds (eds), *Political Emotions* (London: Routledge, 2010).

Stacey, Jackie, *Teratologies: A Cultural Study of Cancer* (London and New York: Routledge, 1997).

Stacey, Jackie, 'The Uneasy Cosmopolitans of *Code Unknown*', in Nina Glick-Schiller and Andrew Irving (eds), *Whose Cosmopolitanism?* (New York: Berghahn, forthcoming, 2014).

Stanton, Domna C. (ed.), *The Female Autograph: Theory and Practice of Autobiography from the Tenth to the Twentieth Century* (Chicago, IL, and London: The University of Chicago Press, 1987).

Steedman, Carolyn, *Landscape for a Good Woman: A Story of Two Lives* (London: Virago Press, 1986).

Stewart, Kathleen, *Ordinary Affects* (Durham, NC, and London: Duke University Press, 2007).

Suleiman, Susan Rubin, *Budapest Diary: In Search of the Motherbook* (Lincoln, NE, and London: University of Nebraska Press, 1996).

Suleri, Sara, *Meatless Days: A Memoir* (Chicago, IL: University of Chicago Press, 1989).

Veeser, H. Adam (ed.), *Confessions of the Critics* (New York and London: Routledge, 1996).

Walkerdine, Valerie, *Daddy's Girls: Young Girls and Popular Culture* (New York: Harvard University Press, 1998).

Weedon, Chris, *Feminist Practice and Poststructuralist Theory* (Oxford: Blackwell, 1987).

Wolff, Janet, 'The female stranger: marginality and modes of writing', in *Resident Alien: Feminist Cultural Criticism* (Cambridge: Polity Press, 1995).

I
Affects

Writing from the heart

Griselda Pollock

Because trauma cannot be simply remembered, it cannot simply be 'confessed';
it must be testified to, in a struggle shared between a speaker and a listener to
recover something the speaking subject is not – cannot be – in possession of.
Insofar as feminine existence is in fact a traumatized existence, feminine autobiography *cannot be* a confession. It can only be a testimony to survival. And like
other testimonies to survival, its struggle is to testify at once to life and to the
death – the dying – the survival has entailed.

(Shoshana Felman[1])

Preface

In the early 1990s, I experimented with performance, video and book design,
to put into practice what I retrospectively recognise as the radical innovations
of Rozsika (Rosie) Parker, who initiated feminist art history in Britain. She had
invented for herself and others a way of writing and reading with life, death and
survival. This is what constituted a *feminist writing otherwise.*

Rozsika Parker taught me that art can, must matter, and art that matters is
often about what is most serious in women's lives. Thus 'writing from the heart'
concerns affects, traumas and their histories that, in being lived, are, in effect, survived. Although aesthetic practices – and I shall place *art writing* alongside more
formal art making practices – are not therapeutic as they do not aim at a cure, they
can contribute to cultural transformation both subjectively and collectively.

In 'The question of autobiography and the bond of reading', Shoshana Felman
explores the feminist search for a voice that is at once singular – this woman's voice
– while generating solidarity among women, who in a sense become 'women' only
in the reciprocal bond of reading the voiced woman/the story of the other. A community is formed by transgressing social and psychological boundaries policed by
silencing women's voices or never giving women access to the instruments of self-
inscription and hence mutual discovery. Felman argues, however, that the personal
is pre-formed by the psycho-social assumption of identities and formations of
subjectivity shaped by the cultures in which we come to be 'women' and which
offer no spaces prepared for the selves 'we' may wish otherwise to become. Thus to
find our own narratives or form our own voices is a continuing work because 'none
of us, as women, has as yet, precisely, an autobiography'.[2]

In Felman's wake, I have constantly worked on the assumption that we lend our own lives to the reading of cultural or visual texts which, in turn, provide forms and figures through which we come to grasp the present, but shapeless, nature of affects and as-yet-unfigured memories. Felman's epigraph provides a belated, more theoretical formulation of what I realised I had learnt through working with Rosie Parker.[3]

Testifying to survival, or matters of life and death

It was the first week of November 2010. I was in Lodz, Poland. A survey of hitherto little exhibited or unknown works by Polish women artists had been assembled by a curator at the Museum of Modern Art in Lodz. A small symposium was being held in a beautiful villa. I was invited to speak about the gaze, seeing, looking, being seen, performed by this collection of little known paintings by women from the nineteenth to early twentieth centuries in Poland.

To speak about feminism's project in art history thirty years after Rozsika Parker and I had finally brought into the world our long-term project titled *Old Mistresses: Women, Art and Ideology* was a stark reminder of the slow, often uneven but steady elaboration of feminist engagements in art history worldwide.[4] My reading of this 2010 assemblage of paintings that had been stored, hidden and ignored in basements across Poland would be enriched by thirty years of feminist insights, methodologies and theories begun in the early 1970s when I first met Rozsika Parker.

It was on my return from Lodz on 6 November that my husband informed me of her tragic death on 5 November, aged sixty-four. It was a terrible shock because the possibility that she could die, despite having been diagnosed with a virulent cancer, had been firmly put out of my head. She could not. When she first told us of her illness, I felt obliged to make every effort to see her, despite our living in different cities and having followed different paths over several decades. In the last few years, we would more often than not meet, though still rarely, at conferences on psychoanalytical subjects, or on maternal studies rather than in art or art historical circles. Since the end of our fourteen-year writing collaboration in which we worked on three publications together, Rozsika Parker had become a psychotherapist and novelist, I a full-time professional academic.[5] We each had children, and had become caught up in different worlds of work and family. Visiting someone with a diagnosis of a terminal cancer meant risking acknowledging potentially imminent death, even imposing my anxiety upon her, while wishing to deflect such an idea by continuing to talk about shared issues, new books, old questions, as if nothing was happening. Rosie was frank and realistic but necessarily hopeful that this particular enemy within might be controlled, shrunk, excised. Treatment had been going well. It was possible to hope and focus on immediate activities. She managed to finish her new book on body dysmorphia that summer. We talked as of old about how to make sense of images, bodies, psyches and societal pressures, she soliciting my reflections on her ever astute reflections on contemporary body issues.

When my friend and colleague Judith Mastai phoned from Vancouver in December 2000 to tell me that the pain in her legs was now thought to be an indication of cancer, I almost jumped on a plane immediately. But would my arrival not simply signal my assumption that it was time to say goodbye? I did not go. I always regretted not doing so. With Rosie, I made sure I did visit. But pressure of a new semester at university and anxiety about overburdening her with visits, meant that October went by without one. Then she was dead.

I have to admit that I run into trouble confronting cancer. Any encounter with imminent death swerves me back, unwilling but unable to resist, to the traumatic moment when I saw my mother a month before she died from cancer. It was three months after I had last seen her, in pain, but still my mother. But now, the fragile, emaciated and drugged patient I encountered when I was taken to visit my mother in her last months was more shattering in its immediate traumatic impact than the utterly undigestible news, delivered far away from her hospital bed, a month later that she had died the night before. At that moment, my mind snapped shut, sealing me against a statement impossible to digest, isolating the unassimilable pain.

For many years, I could not speak those words. At school, if my teachers, knowing of my mother's prolonged illness, asked how she was, I told them she was fine. I feared to utter the truth, not it seemed because I could not say she had died or denied the fact, but because I felt that *they* could not bear to hear it. In retrospect, it is clear that I was projecting away from my numbed self the deadly impact of the word 'died' that might, if uttered, shatter the hard protective shell of initial shock. I tried to protect others from what seemed to me, but could not yet be acknowledged as, so terrible that the very admission of the truth might 'kill' them, which means, kill me.

I have long remained in revolt against the trite finiteness of the phrase: 'My mother died…' Lots of people lose one or other or even both parents in childhood or early adulthood. The words 'Her mother/father died when she was…' become part of the biographical narrative in which the past tense fixes an event in time past. I never felt that. Death enters into the life of the survivor, making the latter the long-term subject of death, the continuous subjective locus of that which has happened to another but which now 'lives' in the permanently bereaved. The bereaved child is inhabited by the loss of the parent, her life redirected henceforward in ways that radically reorient her future. She will never know who she might have been but the person she will become is forever inflected by the trauma of the dead mother's absence and, paradoxically, by its constant presence. Indeed death is lived as the accumulation of absence, the endlessness of a failed return, a permanent susceptibility to falling into the hole of loss at any time, any place, pricked by so many chance images, stories, sounds. Through endless films about lost or returning parents, my children watched me for the signs. 'Are you crying, Mummy?' they would tenderly ask. When my daughter and I went to see a film *Stepmom,* with Julia Roberts and Susan Sarandon, and the unfolding narrative revealed the imminent death of the Sarandon's character, the mother, from cancer, I fled the cinema half-way through the movie, afraid of what might viscerally and noisily well-up from within as unmediated grief, again. Even mediated by Hollywood *schmaltz,* it was literally unbearable to be taken narratively towards a dying mother.

In 1992, I was invited to a conference to launch a book by Elisabeth Bronfen on the intimate cultural entwining of fear of death, femininity and the aesthetic in Western literature, music and art.[6] Could this be an occasion to break my silence, to speak the words, in public, to testify to survival and the dying involved? But what form would allow me to write or speak otherwise than in professionally authorised academic terms?

I sat down and wrote, in one single writing session, a text titled 'Deadly tales', the like of which I had never imagined nor dared to imagine writing, let alone speaking out loud.[7] It could only be presented as a kind of performance, inviting another way of listening from the audience, a bond of hearing rather than reading. I do not know how I found the courage to breach the protocols of the academic discussion of representations of death in order to represent, by means of my own aesthetically fashioned seven-part text, a series of tales of my own encounters with, and failed mourning before, the deaths of others including my mother, my father-in-law and an unborn child. It felt extraordinarily daring and liberating to speak 'from the heart' in public. Art-savvy audiences attending, for instance, a performance might be prepared, by the framing of such encounters as 'art', for forms of personal narration; artists are expected, if not required, to speak in the first person. (Indeed politically charged art is condemned for being too much the opposite.) But academic audiences are disturbed by intrusions of the personal into the supposedly objective and analytical. In such a live performance inside a conference, I sensed that my audience felt disoriented, even panicked. As the tales unfolded from a cold academic start into ever more intense and personal testimony, were they wondering: 'Will she be able to say the words, and will we be able to listen?' I was asking myself, 'Will my body stand up to what I am touching through speaking thus or will it betray me with eruptions of its encrypted grief?' In this encounter, audience and speaker were alike challenged by soliciting affectivity in a place usually protected from personally-charged affects.

I structured my freighted and affecting memories into a symbolic, seven-part form in which the journey into and out from the central section (number four lying between two groups of three stories) was flanked by shifting degrees of public knowledge or historical reference. My experiment developed into art-based performance work by translation of the spoken paper into a video, shown on a television monitor atop a filing cabinet lined with photographic traces.[8] The voice-over was distanced from the 'speaking head' and its cabinet of memories by being played through headphones placed on chairs across the space. The voice was thus not televisual and spectacularised, but intimately played through the resonating chamber within the listener's own body. The voice spoke with the viewer as the viewer then contemplated the flow of images across the distant screen. In speaking the text as a live performance twice during the exhibition the fragility of my body as the hysterical site of traumatic affect introduced profound risk, charging the time of my speaking and their listening with what sometimes was felt as unbearable tension.

I started with a reading of a highly ritualised sixteenth-century painting of a dead mother mourned by husband and son in which the female body functions as vessel for the passage of a dynastic lineage, moving through a reflection on the suicide of cultural theorist Walter Benjamin and the meaning of premature ends to intellectual projects, to the sudden death of my father-in-law from an un-diagnosed cancer, a man who had to live with the knowledge of how his parents had died in Auschwitz. These tales intertwined stories of my mother's early death aged fifty-two and my first miscarriage before returning through a discussion of Roland Barthes's mourning for his mother at the heart of his text on photography, *Camera Lucida*, and Freud's failure to grasp the psychic significance of the mater-nal in his scheme of paternal/filial succession. I ended with Tom Stoppard from whom I draw the insight that 'death is not anything ... death is not ... It's the absence of presence, nothing more ... the endless time of never coming back ... a gap you can't see, and when the wind blows through it, it makes no sound'.[9]

In the central section, I sought to make sense of my own time-bending experi-ence during pregnancy, and its failure, of a restaging of maternal loss. The future hope of bearing a child, surely a daughter, was unconsciously a desire to recreate the vertical bond with my own mother, who would somehow be also in the child I was carrying. I would love this child better and thus death could be obliquely defeated. But this child did not come to term. I was plunged into a deep mourn-ing, a transferred depression that remained in possession of me until the date predicted for the birth had the child lived. Possessed by the transitivity of memory that invested the unborn child with my lost mother, I was also subject to the power of a psycho-corporeal clock that appeared to know the moment it might release me into life again. In serving out in grief the due period of anticipation of new life, I found myself ultimately able to begin to mourn my mother. Death, maternal bereavement, and bereavement in pregnancy could then become topics of research, writing and teaching. A new form of writing would be needed that would refuse the opposition which at once silences the affective dimension in public discourse and abstracts intellectual life from embodied, affective experiences.

I have been telling you, my reader, why, when faced with the announcement of Rosie's cancer, I felt panicked into a kind of denial of her mortal danger. That has led to a story about beginning to do a different kind of work within the con-text of being a professional academic, work that bridged aesthetic and intellectual operations, intimate encounters with death and loss and cultural explorations of representations of death and loss. I share these stories in order to situate the fol-lowing more historical testimony because I have come to recognise, in mourning Rosie, that she and her writing were the source of what enabled me to do both, then and now, and line all my work as an art historian with an intensity of feel-ing. She enabled my *feminist writing otherwise* to perform the feminist gesture of breaching the rigid separation of knowledge from experience, thought from affect. In the 1970s Rosie had created a form of art writing that would compel me for most of my working life. It was, however, only once she was missing, that the full realisation of her inspirational presence became excruciatingly clear to me. So writing of her is about the dying to which, in Felman's terms, survival can only bear its painful but constant witness.

Feminist beginnings: Rozsika Parker reading and writing

How heady were the days of the early women's movement! We were so unencumbered by the now wonderful but still heavy weight of feminist theory. It is hard to imagine what it was like when there was in effect nothing to read about women and art, about feminist psychoanalysis, literary theory, sociology, about poststructuralism, deconstruction and certainly no post-feminism. We had to invent every move. We did it in informal reading groups and constantly forming and morphing collectives. We worked together with the deluded ambition of youth, believing that we could, and we had to, change things. That aspiration and its energies came from unblocking the steel doors between officially sanctioned knowledge and that which we might draw out from sharing stories, experiences, questions and curiosity.[10]

When I met Rosie Parker in 1973, and we set out on our adventure to construct our own contribution of emerging feminist art history in Britain, she was already wonderfully equipped with what we would nowadays call a truly interdisciplinary mind. In fact, it was her gift to think across borders, elegantly to bring her passionate insights from psychoanalytical understanding – already fully formed before her formal training – and her compassionate reading of literature into relationship with visual art past and contemporary. She had studied art history at the Courtauld Institute, which was, in the later 1960s, one of only three or four places where this now highly popular subject was taught. But what would that Institute have given her but facts and figures about great men studied within the limited parameters of formalist (modern) or iconographic (premodern) analysis? I went to the same Institute a few years after she graduated to receive the same diet of dullness. So, where did Rozsika Parker's ability to create a new form of art writing emerge from when she became a feminist writer on art in the first British feminist magazine *Spare Rib* launched in June 1972?

Against a tide of esoterically abstract art and formalist art talk, Rosie made art matter. In her recent film, *!Women Artists in Revolution* (2011), Lynn Hershman Leeson reminds us of the paradox of the huge disjuncture between art and society in the later 1960s, notably in the United States. Minimalism, abstract, esoteric, and self-absorbed, ruled the artworld while American society was combusting with civil rights, black power, student movements and anti-war demonstrations in which students were shot, when the carnivalesque women's movement exploded onto the streets. American critic Lucy Lippard became a feminist when she refused this separation and championed art that bridged the social and the everyday.[11] Rosie's feminist vision was different from Lippard's social agenda. Rosie revealed the relation between pain and pleasure, or rather she acknowledged the power and depth of suffering, of conflicted feelings and ambivalence while also seeing in that very human dimension of susceptibility the counter-capacity for laughter and life. Long before formal trauma studies emerged, she was tracking the generic traumas of class- and race-inflected femininities, of bodies at odds with subjectivities, of subjectivities dislocated from their social and cultural worlds, their forms of desire, unanchored through obliterated histories and unknown forebears in art and literature.

During our first collaborative writing project, from 1975 to 1981, we wove together, hilariously, painfully and with the help of a certain amount of chocolate a text that challenged the central tenets of conventional art history: individuality, authorship, competition, formalism that abstracted art from lived experience, both socially and psychologically inflected.[12] We dedicated our collective abilities to exploring, through visual and cultural inscriptions, the questions that shaped our own lives as women: sexed, raced, classed, desiring and wounded. We found such questions resonating across time and space in what we read or saw in older art now rediscovered and reinterpreted by 'feminist desire' and re-visioned through the novel lens of later twentieth-century feminist attention to bodies and psyches.[13]

In 1980, Rosie wrote a review of *Women's Images of Men* at the ICA, London, a challenging exhibition of contemporary figurative works based on inverting the masculine gaze at women by showing how women artists represented masculinity. Rosie bypassed the clogged criticism that derided the value of merely inverting the terms of who looks at whom. She ignored the difficulties much of the work posed in some avant-gardist artistic circles by its figurative orientation. Her review opens with a quotation from a letter written by novelist Georges Sand to her lover, Frédéric Chopin, that already indicates a recurring trope in women's management of masculinity. Drawing later on novels by the Brontës and May Sinclair, Rosie showed how often women loved and cared for men who were in some way invalids – she referenced Jane Eyre and the blind Mr Rochester, for instance. Rosie tracked the unconscious repetitions of this trope of women's compassion for wounded masculinity across a diverse range of work, media and purposes in the 1980 exhibition. While men might cry out 'castration!' when seeing images of men seemingly disempowered by sleep, disability, or other forms of constriction, Rosie contested the one-sided reading by reminding the Western world of the most widely circulated image of masculinity: the crucified Christ which represents an archetypal wounded man. Yet as a symbol of profound pathos, the image of the invalided man resurfaces in secularised contemporary forms transcending individual artists' purposes. Using her knowledge of nineteenth-century women's literature, Rosie compassionately and imaginatively read contemporary artwork by women that dealt with mute anxiety about power relations and domination by creating scenarios in which masculinity can be approached with empathy and returned to the tender, or sometimes exhaustingly needy, relations with woman as mother.[14] Rozsika Parker was an eclectic reader often of forgotten women authors, soon to be rediscovered and republished by Virago and the Women's Press. She had discovered an underground spring, an earlier source of affective and intellectual nourishment in nineteenth century women's literature that could reorient the abstracted official art discourses that prevailed for the study of the visual arts in the later twentieth century.

Rosie favoured and pioneered the interview as conversation with the artist as a means of discovering the complex configurations of life and work. In 1974 she talked with Margaret Priest (b.1944).[15] The interview with the artist was a relatively new form in art history, indicative of the intense individualisation of the modern artist. In the United States, Cindy Nemser used this format in her feminist research that appeared first in *Feminist Art News* and then was collectively published as *Art Talk* in 1975.[16] Like Nemser, Rosie used the interview format to explore areas of experience that were usually not mentioned in artist interviews: gender, ethnic and class specific aspects of women's access to artmaking, experience of institutional discrimination, gender consciousness and the role of socio-personal formation in the art practice itself. Rosie starts by asking a simple question about Margaret Priest's background – not to draw out the usual legendary tropes that prevail in masculine narratives of the artist's childhood but to draw a feminist-attuned portrait of a physically fragile child and a sometimes insecure, yet self-directing, working-class woman, with intellectual ability to move into the professions via university, who, against the grain of both her parents' class expectations and those of her bourgeois peers, then chose to go to art school.[17]

> RP: I am surprised you had the courage and confidence to persist.
> MP: It's not courage, it's effrontery – there is terrific effrontery to becoming an artist…
> RP: Were you encouraged at school to go on to art college?
> MP: No, because the area in which I lived – Dagenham – was a cultural wilderness. I went to the only grammar school in the area. And once you prove yourself to be clever, everybody expected you to go onto art school. I just had this terrible thing that I had to escape, I didn't know what from, but just where I'd be valued, and I didn't feel valued there.[18]

Through this almost analytically prompted conversation, major themes emerge through the personal lens of Margaret Priest's experience. Priest reflects on the pressure women experienced to conform to currently desirable body types. Yet if they presented themselves fashionably, they are deemed to lack the intensity necessary to become an artist. Insight into anguished fantasies about one's body and the spectacularisation of femininity emerge from Priest's life story while also leading to wider theorisation of class and gendered bodies and minds. Directed to graphic design rather than 'serious' fine art reserved for male students, Priest rebelled and became a painter only to reject the obligatory female impersonation of the great male painter working in oil on a vast scale. She turned to delicate and precision drawings in pencil, risking a new range of stereotypes that turned her exquisite vision and precise craft skills into a frigid sign of feminine deficiency. Margaret Priest defines her own contradictory relation to mimicking the impersonal perfection of media reproduction while using a craft-based practice as a 'vehicle for emotion'.[19] Crucially the artist herself brings back the relation between craft and affect to the body. Priest suffers from asthma, and the drawing named in the article's title is about a dream of going where American asthmatics are sent for therapy – Arizona – but arriving even there, 'still out of breath'. The interview has been shaped to move through childhood formation, encounters with the art institution, negotiating social attitudes and gendered stereotypes to the intimacy between process and effect, all mediated by the sexed, classed and physically as well as psychically vulnerable body. Margaret Priest left Britain in 1976 and has since lived in Canada, now being Emerita Professor of Fine Art at the University of Guelph.[20]

In 1974 Rosie also wrote about astonishing American photographer Diane Arbus (1923–71), and British cartoonist Posy Simmons.[21] Both deal in totally different ways with a relation to the body. Rosie wrote:

> Diane Arbus' vision is infectious. Just as some authors write with such a powerful vision that you continue to see the world through their eyes, even after closing the book, so too with Diane Arbus. After looking away from her work, people seem alienated, exposed, bathed in a vaguely unhealthy sheen. To what extent are we sharing a personal nightmare, and to what extent is she opening our eyes to reality? [22]

In being able to pose such questions that avoid the art historical attempt to place the artist in a narrative of nation, period or movement, Rosie Parker grants the artist personal integrity of a vision and social effect in disclosing an aspect of the external world. The body would also be the focus of another major article of that year on the British artist Judy Clark (b.1949).

Judy Clark studied fine art at Portsmouth Polytechnic and the Slade School of Art, after which she emerged onto the London artscene with a series of exhibitions called *Issues*. In 2010, her work, which had finally been bought in the 1970s by the Tate, appeared in a show titled *Beneath the Radar in 1970s London* organised by the England & Co. Gallery, in London. Clark's show *Body Works* in 1974 led to an interview by Rosie Parker.

Judy Clark did not identify with nascent feminism. Her work was inspired by anthropologist Mary Douglas' work on taboos around dirt and purity, which function as symbolic forms of control over the threatening chaos of life and death.[23] Clark collected, and framed in minimalist grids and boxes, remnants and traces of the body from blood-stained plasters to dabs of menstrual blood, from semen-stained tissues to body hair accumulated over a week of sleep in a bed, from bodily fluids to weekly collections of dust from everyday living. Rosie's questions focus on the way that the artworks handle bodily materials intersects with the psycho-social imaginary that underpins taboo and enforced invisibility, the anxiety about things 'out of place' and the fear of structural disorder in the social and symbolic universe. Rosie identified the considerable intellectual charge of Clark's conceptual art project about time, rhythms, cycles and sexual as well as gendered embodiment. What is distinctive is how Rosie integrated these insights with respect for the artist's working process and 'curiosity' about how we function as bodies generating and living amongst waste. The article is a monument both to the artist and her work and to the subtlety and erudition of the interdisciplinary interviewer who recognised the theoretical foundations through which the artist's project acquired its significance for feminist thinking at the time.[24]

Affects

In 1975 Rosie Parker authored a benchmark article rediscovering for our generation the once notorious nineteenth-century Russian artist and diarist Marie Bashkirtseff who succumbed to tuberculosis aged only twenty-five in 1884 but was renowned in the following decades when censored selections of her daringly confessional diaries, which Bashkirtseff had written since the age of thirteen, were translated and published.[25] The original sixteen volumes have since become available in the Bibliothèque nationale de France in Paris. Rosie's article formed the basis for an initial discussion of Bashkirtseff in *Old Mistresses,* but also for the introduction to the 1987 Virago reprint of the diary.[26] By that time Rosie had trained as a psychoanalyst, bringing a wider range of theorisations of feminine narcissism and narcissistic injury to bear on the reading of Bashkirtseff's diary. The *Spare Rib* article had already established her model of compassionate interpretation of the psychological complexity of a privileged, aristocratic young woman who wanted to be an artist in order to be famous, and to be loved for what she had done, rather than for mere appearance. Such ambition was doubly contrary to the prescribed passivity and decorativeness of a woman of her class. Bashkirtseff used the pages of her diary to invent a virtual space through which both to imagine herself as a person in her own right and to play with being the object of another's desire, but more importantly, the object of their admiration as well. Conditioned by various childhood losses and dislocations, Bashkirtseff had been extensively cited by Simone de Beauvoir in *The Second Sex* (1949) as the castastrophic example of fatal feminine narcissism.[27] For Parker, the job was, however, to listen to the voice emerging across the diary, understanding its ambivalence and contradictions without de Beauvoir's dismissive judgement of one damaged woman who served as type for women's deformation under patriarchy. Rosie exposed narcissistic injury as neither individual pathology nor the generic condition of woman: it became a key to rethinking the psychosocial complexities that contemporary feminism was exposing through consciousness-raising and feminist attunement to the psychic formations of sexual difference. Bashkirtseff had indeed, under a necessary pseudonym, published political writings in leading French feminist papers. But careful feminist study of the diary also revealed the core of self-doubt that assailed this apparently arrogant, ambitious and petted aristocrat. It also revealed her courage in facing the imminence of premature death in her mid-twenties with dignity and acceptance. It highlighted the daring with which she breached class protocols in order to make herself into someone by making herself an artist, inspired by an earlier period of feminist activism.

Rosie Parker wrote many articles on the campaign for equality in exhibitions and museum collections as well as reviewing one of the major shows curated by Lucy Lippard that was brought to London in 1974 despite the refusal of the Royal College of Art to offer the space and of the Arts Council to fund the show.[28] With only transport paid for, the show, titled *Ca. 7,500,* was sustained solely by volunteers at The Warehouse, a small gallery in Earlham Street. It introduced many of us in London to the work of American artists such as Laurie Anderson, Eleanor Antin, Mierle Laderman Ukeles, Agnes Denes, Adrian Piper, Martha Wilson and other now recognised international conceptual artists. Lippard made the show all-women to challenge the prevailing idea that no women were making conceptual art, in which formal or material considerations give way to ideas and a critique of representational conventions. Lippard also wished to bring out the potential for a specifically feminist critique of cultural norms facilitated by the expanding possibilities of non-formalist performance art, photographic work, interviews, re-enactments and so forth. Having made her own selection of works to mention, Rosie then turned on the other critics for their astonishingly sexist and ignorant assault on this show. This was a new move that we had already used in *Old Mistresses:* subjecting the terms and assumptions of critical writing to feminist deconstruction by tracking metaphors and modes of judgement in art criticism as a sexist system, structural to how art history sustains masculine hegemony, rather than merely personal prejudices. The exhibition, only some of which engaged with issues of gender and sexuality, was tarred by mainstream critics like Caroline Tisdall as 'stinking of the ghetto', and being aesthetically second rate.[29] The crudity of the put-downs show how *feminist* conceptual art disturbed the critics, who consistently used a negatively coded *gendered* vocabulary to avoid any engagement with what women-artists were seeking to make visible in this new cultural form: the contradictions they experienced between identities as women and artists.

> 'Self-preoccupied', 'narcissistic', 'self-indulgent' were words constantly used in reference to the show, yet communication was the central theme – communication based on the recognition of shared experience, and an implied need for change. But then once the artist and the audience communicate the critic's role as a mediator becomes obsolete.
>
> Although critics attacked artists for being self-preoccupied, it didn't occur to them to ask why women artists should feel the need to question their identity as both artists and women, or whether there was a discrepancy between the stereotype of the artist and the female stereotype. Instead they viewed it in the light of established definitions – it wasn't conceptual art, it was second-rate.[30]

In her own voice

These snippets indicate something of the voice that emerged in Rosie's wide range of writings and the imagination that enabled her to lay out a field of new ways of writing art for others. Perhaps her most famous article is 'The word for embroidery was work'.[31] This would form the kernel for her most celebrated single-authored book, *The Subversive Stitch: Embroidery and the Making of the Feminine.*[32] Rosie's work not only challenged the dominant hierarchy of aesthetic value that elevates art over craft and aligns the latter with the feminine as mindless and repetitive, but it also developed subtle readings of the historically shifting psycho-social formations of femininity that were formed across social practices of enforced domesticity, passivity and silencing encoded in obligatory needlework. Furthermore, Rosie revealed the scope within the textile arts for negotiation and counter-self-inscription by rebellious women. To explain the notion of femininity as a formation, schooled, disciplined, performed, yet also contested, revised and historically as well as subjectively shifting, no other work of cultural analysis is as compelling. It defies classification while opening up an entire new field of approaches to cultural practices using cloth and needle that has since been elaborated across museums, fine-art schools and feminist studies.

One final article is significant in this context of writing as testimony to trauma and survival. In 1979, Rozsika Parker wrote her bravest article, which anticipated by over a decade the recognition that femininities come not only classed, and variously sexualised, but also marked by cultural ethnicities and hence deformed not only by racism but by a particular form of it that remained below the threshold of utterability.[33] In 'Being Jewish: anti-semitism and Jewish women', Rosie addressed feminism as well as the unimaginable resurgence of anti-semitism in contemporary Britain and Europe at the time.[34]

A montage of quotations from women she had interviewed, Rozsika Parker's article weaves a subtle analytical web around women's testimonies to the trauma of racist abuse and to their conflicted relations to both Jewish and non-Jewish worlds. At one point, voicing a more general point, the text reads:

> There can be no single explanation for anti-semitism: yet nor have there been satisfactory linkings of the economic and psychoanalytical factors which contribute to it. It's here, I think, that feminists could provide an understanding of anti-semitism, because feminism has a framework which enables us to see the connections between the wider oppression and the individual oppression, and that the individual psyche reflects the structure of society.[35]

Firstly, Rosie confronted the ambivalence felt by some contemporary Jewish feminists about their Jewishness, about their attachments to or dislocations from Jewish life and community, and above all about what to do about anti-semitism in general and specifically within the women's movement. Touching on a range of historical and contemporary political issues, the article opens up a field held together, however, by an implicit model that refuses to separate facts, statistics, histories, from the bodies and minds that 'live' out, negotiate and indeed suffer from internalising their effects. The often unspoken sense of 'difference' or enforced outsiderness, shaped through social encounters but also through the gaze and hence the sense of embodied otherness is traced into language. Rosie elegantly introduces economic, political and psychoanalytical explanations of anti-semitism that constitute the wretched stereotypes not only of the Jew (the emasculated masculine) but also of the Jewish woman in particular – *la belle juive* over-endowed with sexuality and perfidy – while filtering these 'structural' analyses through excerpts from conversations with a highly diverse group of Jewish feminists who offer testimony to contingent experiences in family, education, work and political activity. While writing an article that was ground-breaking and remains a crucial resource, Rosie also performed her own bond of reading with those who shared their experiences of this difference with her.

I am seeking to show how Rozsika Parker's work was a form of *feminist writing otherwise* that cannot be classified simply as as art journalism, art history, or literature. Looking back as a result of her untimely death, it is ever clearer to me that she had created a space at that initiating moment in the pages of a collectively published feminist magazine, and that she was doing more than writing about art. Writing met art to write back to life those lives that had hitherto been without either art or writing, hence unknown, uninscribed, unvoiced. What Rozsika Parker evolved was itself an artform exploring traumatised feminine existences whose autobiographies were missing – insofar as the traumatic is the unsaid, the unsayable, the burden of experience that has yet no form to mediate its affects and no terms to allow it to become a form of self-understanding.

Rozsika Parker's art- and life-writing with art and artists exploded the oppressive structure of assumed authority to speak about others, in order to weave and plait texts made from working with her peers. Her writing caught up a chorus of voices building out from conversational encounters what can only be named a theoretical framework for registering the networks of forces and resulting lived ambivalences that constituted some of the traumas of contemporary femininities – classed, raced, ethnicised, desiring, embodied, sensate, material, psychically vivid, thinking, speaking, writing and making. Ancient Hebrew and hence Jewish thought locates both mind and passion in the heart, 'Lev', refusing to isolate intellect and emotion. Rozsika Parker's was indeed a *writing from the heart*, a gift of a subtle intelligence that defied so many of the tortured theoretical divisions that have since fractured feminist theory. I was privileged to have worked with Rozsika Parker over fourteen years when feminism was a constant process of opening possibilities. In mourning the loss of her continuing contributions, literary, analytical and by personal example, I have written now, I hope, from my own heart, not only a small personal tribute but a work of necessary reinscription of Rozsika Parker into a feminist genealogy of *writing otherwise*.

Notes

1   Shoshana Felman, 'The question of autobiography and the bond of reading', p. 16.
2   *Ibid.*, p. 14
3   Rozsika Parker, her full name, was used for monographs. As an art critic she wrote as Rosie Parker and was generally known to friends as Rosie.
4   Rozsika Parker and Griselda Pollock, *Old Mistresses: Women, Art and Ideology*.
5   Parker and Pollock, *Old Mistresses*; *Framing Feminism: Art and the Women's Movement 1970–1985*; *The Journal of Marie Bashkirtseff*.
6   Elisabeth Bronfen, *Over Her Dead Body: Femininity and the Aesthetic*.
7   Pollock, 'Deadly tales'.
8   It has been shown in exhibitions at Leeds Metropolitan University Art Gallery in 1996 and in London at the Institute of Contemporary Art in 2011.
9   Tom Stoppard, *Rosenkrantz and Guildenstern Are Dead*, pp. 90–1.
10 The earliest and still significant critique of a man-centred canon of knowledge and academic institutions is Adrienne Rich, 'Towards a woman-centred university'.
11 Lucy Lippard, in *From the Center*, recounts her becoming a feminist critic and ambivalent relations to the central trope of the body in women's new art forms. See also her 'Sweeping exchanges: the contribution of feminism to the art of the 1970s', which values feminist turns to narrative, autobiography and public engagement art.

12 See also Jackie Dea, 'Old Mistresses: Women, Art and Ideology': Rozsika Parker and Griselda Pollock describe the book's genesis'.

13 I formulated this theoretical impossibility in 1999. 'Feminist desire' signals a desire for difference, for other stories and for the discovery of the otherness of feminine subjectivities in all their complexities. See Pollock, Differencing the Canon: Feminist Desire and the Writing of Art's Histories.

14 Parker, 'Images of men'.

15 Parker, '"Still Out of Breath in Arizona" and other pictures: an interview with Margaret Priest'. See also Parker, "Dedicated to the unknown artists": interview with Susan Hiller.'

16 Cindy Nemser, Art Talk: Conversations with Twelve Women Artists.

17 Ernest Kris and Otto Kurz, Legend, Myth and Magic in the Image of the Artist: A Historical Experiment.

18 Parker, 'Still Out of Breath in Arizona', p. 38

19 Ibid., p. 40.

20 I contacted Margaret Priest in Canada and she responded to my email enquiry: 'The interview with Rozsika – or Rosie as I then called her – was an important marker in my early career and I have remained enormously thankful to her, to Spare Rib and to you. At the time, her piece brought some serious attention to my work and I found it did so yet again many years later when the interview was included in Framing Feminism.' (3 May 2012; permission granted to cite, 14 July 2012)

21 Parker, '"Chocolates" by Posy Simmonds'.

22 Parker, 'Diane Arbus', p. 39.

23 Mary Douglas, Purity and Danger.

24 Parker, '"Body Works": Rosie Parker talks to Judy Clark about her recent exhibition'.

25 Parker, 'Portrait of the artist as a young woman: Marie Bashkirtseff'.

26 Parker and Pollock, 'New introduction'.

27 Simone de Beauvoir, The Second Sex.

28 See for instance, Parker '"A piece of the pie?": a preview of the Hayward Annual Exhibition'.

29 Caroline Tisdall, '26 conceptual artists in London'.

30 Parker, 'Art of course has no sex, but artists do' [Ca. 7,500: Exhibition of twenty-six American conceptual artists, curated by Lucy Lippard], p. 35.

31 Parker, 'The word for embroidery was work'.

32 Parker, The Subversive Stitch: Embroidery and the Making of the Feminine.

33 The exploration of feminism and Jewishness was taken by Lisa Bloom, Jewish Identities in American Feminist Art: Ghosts of Ethnicity.

34 Parker, 'Being Jewish: anti-semitism and Jewish women'.

35 Ibid., p. 28.

Bibliography

Beauvoir, Simone de, The Second Sex, trans. H. M. Pashley (New York: Vintage, 1997 [1949]).

Bloom, Lisa, Jewish Identities in American Feminist Art: Ghosts of Ethnicity (New York: Routledge, 2006).

Bronfen, Elisabeth, Over Her Dead Body: Femininity and the Aesthetic (Manchester: Manchester University Press, 1992).

Dea, Jackie, '*Old Mistresses: Women, Art and Ideology*: Rozsika Parker and Griselda Pollock describe the book's genesis', *Spare Rib*, 113 (December 1980), 52–8.

Douglas, Mary, *Purity and Danger* (Harmondsworth: Penguin Books, 1966).

Felman, Shoshana, 'The question of autobiography and the bond of reading', in W*hat Does a Woman Want? Reading and Sexual Difference* (Baltimore, MD: Johns Hopkins University Press, 1993).

Hershman Leeson, Lynn, *!Women Art Revolution* (!Women Art Revolution LLC, 2010).

Kris, Ernest, and Otto Kurz, *Legend, Myth and Magic in the Image of the Artist: A Historical Experiment* (New Haven, CT: Yale University Press, 1981).

Lippard, Lucy, *From the Center: Feminist Essays on Women's Art* (New York: Dutton and Co., 1976).

Lippard, Lucy, 'Sweeping exchanges: the contribution of feminism to the art of the 1970s', *Art Journal*, 40:1/2 (Autumn–Winter 1980), 362–5.

Nemser, Cindy, *Art Talk: Conversations with Twelve Women Artists* (New York: Charles Scribner and Sons, 1975).

Parker, Rosie, 'Diane Arbus', *Spare Rib*, 22 (April 1974), 38–41.

Parker, Rozsika, '"*Body Works*": Rosie Parker talks to Judy Clark about her recent exhibition', *Spare Rib*, 23 (May 1974), 37–8.

Parker, Rosie, '"Chocolates" by Posy Simmonds', *Spare Rib*, 23 (May 1974), 43.

Parker, Rosie, '"Still Out of Breath in Arizona" and other pictures: an interview with Margaret Priest', *Spare Rib*, 24 (June 1974), 38–40.

Parker, Rosie, 'Art, of course, has no sex, but artists do', *Spare Rib*, 25 (July 1974), 34–5.

Parker, Rosie, 'Portrait of the artist as a young woman: Marie Bashkirtseff', *Spare Rib*, 34 (April 1975), 32–5.

Parker, Rosie, 'The word for embroidery was work', *Spare Rib*, 37 (July 1975), 41–5.

Parker, Rosie, '"Dedicated to the unknown artists": interview with Susan Hiller', *Spare Rib*, 72 (July 1978), 28–30.

Parker, Rosie, '"A piece of the pie?": a preview of the Hayward Annual Exhibition', *Spare Rib*, 74 (September 1978), 20–2.

Parker, Rosie, 'Being Jewish: anti-semitism and Jewish women', *Spare Rib*, 79 (February 1979), 27–31.

Parker, Rosie, 'Images of men', *Spare Rib*, 99 (November 1980), 5–8.

Parker, Rozsika, *The Subversive Stitch: Embroidery and the Making of the Feminine* (London: I. B. Tauris, 2010 [London: The Women's Press, 1984]).

Parker, Rozsika, and Griselda Pollock, *Old Mistresses: Women, Art and Ideology* (London: Routledge, 1981; new edition London: I. B. Tauris, 2012).

Parker, Rozsika, and Griselda Pollock, *Framing Feminism: Art and the Women's Movement 1970–1985* (Ontario: Pandora, 1987).

Parker, Rozsika, and Griselda Pollock, 'New introduction', in *The Journal of Marie Bashkirtseff*, trans. Mathilde Blind (London: Virago Press, 1987).

Pollock, Griselda, *Differencing the Canon: Feminist Desire and the Writing of Art's Histories* (London: Routledge, 1999).

Pollock, Griselda, 'Deadly tales', reprinted in *Looking Back to the Future: Essays on Art, Life and Death* (London: Routledge, 2000 [1992]).

Rich, Adrienne, 'Towards a woman-centred university' in *Lies, Secrets and Silence: Selected Prose 1966–1978* (London: Virago, 1980 [1973–4]), pp. 125–55.

Stoppard, Tom, *Rosenkrantz and Guildenstern Are Dead* (London: Faber, 1967).

Tisdall, Caroline, '26 conceptual artists in London', *Guardian* (27 April 1974), p. 10.

Contact

Mary Cappello

Language, both everyday and scientific, is particularly prolix where the skin is concerned … Every living being, organ and cell has a skin or covering, husk, carapace, membrane, meninx, armour, pellicle, tunica, septum or pleura. And the word 'membrane' has a great number of synonyms, including amnios, aponeurosis, blastoderm, corium, calyptra, caul, diaphragm, endocardium, endocarp, ependyma, fascia, fraenum, hymen, mantle, mesentery, operculum, pericardium, perichondrium, periosteum, and peritoneum … The entry for 'touch' is the longest in the Oxford English Dictionary.

(Didier Anzieu[1])

In my late thirties, I awoke one weekend morning not only suddenly sure of needing but absolutely ready to let a stranger touch me. Therapeutically. I had become an 'owner', not in the sense by which the term figures at the racetrack, but in real estate. I certainly wasn't an investor in any high stakes way – I didn't have enough capital for that. But a time had arrived and the accumulation of enough pocket money to encourage me to follow my lover's suggestion to 'buy'. A house. And so she and I sat in leather chairs that seemed stuffed with something hard, suited to make you feel your investment wasn't an indulgence but a trial, not a source of comfort but a sign that you had what it took now to protect your property. Home ownership must not signify relaxation, the furnishing in the lawyer's office seemed to say, but wariness, vigilance, an ability to spring out of that hide-bound tightly strung seat and into defensive action at any moment. It was never enough to own; you would have to polish what you owned to the high shine of a deflective surface (financiers used that locution, to 'protect' your investment, like your own second skin).

I don't think it was middle-class angst that took me to the massage therapist – the burden of ownership followed by requisite release only more of your money can buy. It was, owing to my origins, a working-class identification with one of the men, one of three movers, who lugged the file cabinets bearing my papers up three flights of curving stairs to the room I had designated as my study.

I pointed, and he heaved. 'Just one more flight', I would say, and his ankle would nearly buckle, his arm muscles shaking under the weight; he would pause to gasp, but never long enough to rest.

What kind of human contact was this? Where one person's body bore the weight of another person's 'things', and what did it mean that the heaviest things were pounds and pounds of papers, a life in letters, bodies of thought, inscriptions?

It was a hot and humid summer day; added to this, the man who laboured under the strain of my pages was suffering from a palpably painful case of what I recognised to be, medically speaking, 'conjunctivitis', aka, 'pink eye'. The upper lid of his right eye swelled and bulged, causing his bottom lid to sag open so that the red pulsing vessels that were usually hidden from view blazed scarlet. 'It looks worse than it feels', doctors are wont to say; still, I was simultaneously horrified for him, and, knowing that 'pink eye' was contagious, afraid for myself that I might catch the infection.

Certainly I couldn't hold him accountable for the smudges, smears, plaster gouges and dents left by his having to cantilever the non-pliable cabinets around the winding stairs. Later I was told that houses like the one I had purchased, built in the Victorian age, might feature indentations called 'coffin niches', designed to protect the walls that braced a curving staircase when a person in her coffin was carried down the staircase and out of the house. A corner of the coffin could be inserted into the niche, allowing the pallbearers efficiently to manoeuvre by turning their otherwise awkward load at a landing.

You should never own more than you yourself can carry, otherwise you'll be doomed to awkwardness, heavy and dependent.

In light of the move, and remembering the sight of the body of the person who carried my things up stairs, I perceived my papers as sacks of flour that had been deposited into the wrong room. Heavy and monochromatic, bags and bags of it. My study was populated by dummies whom I didn't know how to animate, blocking the door. During the night I felt sharp pains in my rib cage – the stuffing of a dummy ripping at the seams, the flour mixed with water and plumping into vast amounts of dough – pains beneath my heart extending into my left arm. In the morning, Jean suggested we clean the basement. I proposed, in place of an industrial vacuum cleaner, a massage.

In my first session with Tom, I tried to sink into silence while his fingers worked to release me from myself, but I laughed a lot. My ticklishness, he explained, was a sign of tenseness. Could the sound a person made when touched a certain way be considered tactful or tactless, a sign of receipt of the touch or a flight from it? Unexpected laughter in a therapy situation reminded me of a visit from my childhood doctor, Dr Kelly, who, on a house call, feeling under my arms for my lymph nodes, made me laugh. I'd expected the pain of a hypodermic needle in Kelly's visit, so was relieved by this tickling encounter, but in later years this same doctor would attempt to molest my mother during a gynaecological exam, by which time, I, anyway, had already learned to fear rather than invite a doctor's touch. So many visits to the doctor were characterised by trauma rather than care, so much of my early family life consisted of violated borders, so many visits to the doctor were marked as well by the unusual touch of an especially caring specialist – those moments when you felt a nurse handle your arm as if it were the wounded hoof of a doe, so many of my relatives touched to show their love – but there was desperate holding too – that allowing for a massage was bound to require the crossing of some bridge of trust in terms of not only harm or pain but also the very exposition of some part of yourself, the unveiling of your ticklishness, the announcement of your body's network of defences, your own fragility.

Some people are ticklish around the edges; others, at a core. There are ticklish subjects, and subjectivities; touchy topics and touchy individuals. Both require the greatest exertion of tact, which doesn't mean they can't be touched at all, but touched considerately, deftly, and with care. They might need to be pressed and skirted all at the same time. On the coasts of Newfoundland and Labrador, a narrow, difficult strait or passage is called a 'tickle'. A fancy can be tickled, as also the ivories; when we're deeply, surprisingly pleased, we say we're tickled pink (which must also suggest a degree of embarrassment in the flush of flesh tones). Though the etymology of the word 'tickle' is uncertain, the idea of a dangerous passage inheres in ticklishness where feeling treads a fine line between vexation and excitement, pleasure and pain.

Adam Phillips' famous essay on the subject puts it best and most succinctly: when tickled, we can be made 'helpless with pleasure'.[2] Tickling, he theorises, resists the mapping of predetermined erotogenic zones. Where we can feed ourselves, and masturbate ourselves, we cannot tickle ourselves: tickling, he concludes, 'is the pleasure [a person] cannot reproduce in the absence of the other'.[3] By way of tickling, we learn our earliest lessons in reciprocity, yes, but also in manipulation and restraint, in keying our bodies to meet another's demands.

'Tickly, tickly on the knee, if you laugh, you don't love me'. This was a game exacted by the Neapolitan members of my family upon my childhood kneecaps. The adult tickles and sings the rhyme, and the child laughs while trying not to. The Sicilian side of the family played a game that was more complexly menacing. 'Round ball, round ball, pully little hair', the adult would sing, while first drawing a circle in my child palm and then tugging on a curly forelock. Once in the grip of the hypnotic chant and its unexpectedly changing focus from hand to hair, I'd feel the person draw a line with the side of his (sometimes hairy) hand up my forearm as he continued, 'one slice, two slice', as though cutting into a piece of bread but it was my arm he was pretending to cut, until finally arriving at my underarm, at which point he'd scream with triumph, 'tickle under there!'

Every tickling encounter has an earlier one inscribed within it, just as every conversation is a conversation we've already had, orchestrated by an absent interlocutor of yore. This doesn't mean that our pasts are bluntly deterministic, but only that we are haunted beings, and that those encounters we consider to be 'new' are probably balefully repetitious. 'The tickling narrative unlike the sexual narrative has no climax', Adam Phillips speculates. 'It has to stop or the real humiliation begins'.[4] Could the same be said of massage? I find myself wanting to ask a different kind of question; like, what kinds of narratives does a massage therapy produce?

Contact

I've described my papers, lugged and unloaded, as dead matter, and plumped up dummies, as sacks of flour, dis-barged and awaiting a use. Inert on their own. I can't deny that this is what they seem to me – like so much baggage – and I'd venture to guess that you, too, have experienced your share of existential lifelessness around your accumulated piles and scripts. Still, I take seriously the fact of paper as writing surface (I still compose by hand) – writing as an occasion of texture, and the creation of voice; as barely perceptible movement of skin on (onion) skin; as a form of scratching even though the ballpoint has displaced the quill: writing as a means to quell one's ticklishness, or to reach toward a metaphysical itch?

Though in real life I'm a skill-less seamstress, I like to inhabit the workshop in which I write as though I were a weaver. Here, my pen moves the way light shifts, putting down a pattern, blocking out others, letting still others bleed through, projecting a screen, and the sound of writing, like the whir of a loom, tells me how to move next. Sound answers touch answers sound in this process, making the whole body reverberate much in the way that the whole body thrums if you run a finger along the rungs of a stair or draw a stick across the rhythmically positioned posts of a fence. Today I'm at this loom, but yesterday I was getting ready for this day by looking at the passing whir of a landscape in a rare drive in the country with my father. My father was a phobic driver; my father was a violent man. But if at a certain distance we got sailing, I found myself able to get lost in the mesmeric flickering of the landscape, looking through the window from the floor of the car, and imagining I could traverse whatever passed us on a sled.

Such a writing requires two hands – one to make an impression on the cloth, and one to move the paper along. It's antithetical to pointing, which is the i-age's communicating gesture *du jour:* our way of making contact. As a child, I used to have a nightmare whose main character was a figure I called 'The Finger'. The finger had no body, but only finger, and in the dream it would appear sticking out from behind a picket fence. Classic phallic imagery, you might presume – and indeed it was a large and scary finger, overgrown, much like The Carrot I sometimes imagined growing like a fetid protuberance from the side of my neck, out of bounds and oddly placed, like Pinocchio's nose. What frightened me about The Finger was how it pointed, as if to embarrass, expose or accuse. In writing, I don't like pointing, not least because it's rude. It reminds me of poking as the worst kind of touching, especially in the stomach. There's nothing worse as a form of taking liberties, as parlaying power plays, or making the other recoil or retract, than a poke to the stomach. On two ends of my experiential spectrum, I could cite as evidence the time my university's President poke-tickled my stomach during a public faculty protest, thus reducing me to a Pillsbury Doughboy, and the day my lesbian cleaning woman poke-touched my stomach in an attempt at flirtation. Both times, I experienced a sickening ticklishness at the pit of my being and no recourse to reply in defence.

If an essay digresses, we can be hopeful or fearful of missing its point or indexical charge.[5] Everything it does is beside the point. 'Improvisatory' might be a better descriptor than 'digressive', whose assumption is an invisible line we've tacitly agreed to toe.

Affects

Psychoanalyst Didier Anzieu describes a nightmare common to children 'of a surface full of humps and troughs which folds, buckles and tears'.[6] The surface of the writing I wish to do needn't be smooth, only resonant.

Tom never used his index finger when he massaged me. He used all of his fingers, each part of each finger, his thumb, and the palm of his hand. He used his wrist and his forearm, and that was just about all.

Eventually meeting with Tom once a month, I came to experience various forms of exquisite pain and release with him, from the pulling of toes apart (you feel as if the skin would break but suddenly something like water breaks instead and you realise at base you are a web-footed creature, reptilian), to the pulling of hair, the gentle lifting of the scalp away from the skull (making you realise what it would take to pull the hair out from the root, how beautifully bounded you are, and the conviction too that silt had gathered in the space between the scalp and the skull, hardened deposits of erstwhile energy that could be made to evaporate if properly loosened and coaxed). Tom touched to rid me of my knots, and there was nothing more sweet than feeling my sinuses open when he pressed into the muscles of my upper back.

Talking had always been essential to the touching relationship I had with Tom. Not the anatomising talk of a visit to the doctor where they use talk to distract me from my body, where words are designed to absent the presence of a finger in an orifice, or to deny the discomfort that wells when that same cold finger palpates in search of disease. This is the worst form of tactless talking and tactless touching – where words serve merely as vehicles of de-realisation, words directed in such a way to encourage me to leave my body, or leave the room while they examine it, to leave it up to them, to leave my body in their hands, while I dither in the zone of vacant chatter. These situations assume a mind/body split: language occurs only in the mind and has nothing to do with the body. Does the doctor engage me in irrelevant conversation when he touches me to take my mind 'off' my body, or does he affiliate talking with mentation, pure and simple and detached. He assumes, I think, what most of us do: that talk is of the mind and touch is corporeal, and never the twain shall meet.

Clearly, people also used talking in massage to avoid experiencing whatever sensation might emerge in silent touching. Maybe talk was a tactic for maintaining familiarity, whereas silence would make room for the introduction of the strange, or for whatever language had more regularly barred. Talk could quell the otherwise awkward silence. I'm sure that I used talk this way – as a form of reassurance and a defence – but that was only one small part of talk's role in navigating the intimacy of shared sentience.

Each person can answer for herself where talk resides or how it figures with regard to 'tact' – at the hairdresser; in the forced proximity of bodies pressed together inside a subway car; in gynaecology's stirrups or dentistry's chair; in the sexual encounter. In such situations, are you compelled toward speech or silence? Why and how? 'Some lovers chat like old friends when they are making love, keep each other informed, as if they were engaged upon a common house purchase,' reflects the narrator of Patricia Duncker's *Hallucinating Foucault*. 'For others making love is their language; their bodies articulate themselves into adjectives and verbs'.[7]

In my relationship with Tom, talk was a form of touch, aimless and wandering in contrast to his deliberate kneading of the body from head to toe, which was mapped, timed, apportioned. Wending and free associative as it was, talk didn't function here as in a psychoanalytic situation, therapeutically, where talk is read for hidden patterns, and subtexts and where analysts screen the speaker's body for signs of the word's truer meanings, where the body betrays the id, the body as a sign of one sector of consciousness, the talk, another. Nor did touch assume the role of release from repression; it had nothing of the requisite disburdening of confession as in 'we have ways of making you talk!', or in the notion of memories like scripts buried in the body which, if touched, tactfully, would find their way back into language and consciousness.

At first my talking with Tom had an instructional Q and A feel: my gnarls are loosening, there are pops and the feeling of an emptying of pockets, and I'm curious to know if Tom can feel it in his fingers as I'm feeling it in my back. He needs to ask me if his touch is too hard or too soft. He asks me what I want him to work on, and I ask him questions out of curiosity about the physiology of muscle groups and nerve endings, posture and gait. Eventually, something else begins to happen in our talk. Short stories. Nothing on an epic scale, no grandeur here, but narrative, reciprocal and companionate, parts of tales born of touch and speech, like unexpected poetry in the examining room. It's never clear what takes us to the things we tell, but only that talking and listening now are integral to the massage for me, that touching is a ground for telling, and telling is a form of touch.

Our shared interest in tending gardens leads to exchanges on foliage, descriptions of our favourite flowers, leaf textures, or kinds of shade-loving plants. Tom has knowledge that I lack, and I leave his office with tips the books won't tell you on cultivating holly or preserving wintergreen, digging up bulbs or putting down peat. During one session, he describes to me a grove of fern and variegated moss that a friend of his has found in a nearby woods and the friend's account of going there alone of an afternoon to meditate. The man has claimed the grove as a place to be alone in. He refuses to tell Tom exactly where it is. He's kneading my fingers as he tells me this. My eyes are closed, but I feel that I can see the place vividly, enter it and wonder about my own retreats. Do I have the guts to wander into a wood alone and sit among the tips of fern curling into the quiet?

The absurd phenomenon of plastic plants comes into our conversation one day, and Tom tells me about a plastic philodendron, complete with faux gravel and post for the plant to climb on that was a centrepiece in his family for decades. One day, he convinced his father, now a widower living with Tom and Tom's lover, Bill, to discard the plant. Not only was it covered with dust, but the sun had faded some of the green leaves pink. The plant couldn't serve the memory of his mother to whom it had belonged, and Tom reminded his father that the house he would be moving to was full of living plants. His father agreed to let Tom put the plant out on the kerb with that day's trash, but it hadn't been moved in so many years that it was stuck to the varnish. He pried it loose and left it on the kerb as if releasing himself from a paltry legacy. Within minutes, a car pulled up in front of his house. A woman got out, and began to inspect the plant, then got back in her car and drove away. An hour later, another car arrived. The same woman got out along with another woman who appeared to be her daughter. Now they inspected and appeared to share words about the plant with each other, nodded, and together shimmied the plant into the backseat of the daughter's car.

My friend Jenn made a huge bucket of fudge around the Christmas holidays, I was telling Tom as he pressed into the muscles that attach the head to the neck. I'd been eating so much of it on winter afternoons, as though it were lighting a fire in my belly, that it had begun to feel like a fourth meal: breakfast, lunch, dinner, fudge. On his route as a paperboy, Tom replies, there had been a woman, who, instead of a dollar tip for the holidays, would give him and other paperboys homemade fudge. He tells me about how much he loved 'Mrs. Beauregard's fudge' and how he could hardly get through his route thinking about his arrival at her door.

I'm a keyboard on which Tom is playing a form of Gregorian chant; he's boring deep into an occipital lobe when he tells me the sadly harrowing tale of the death of his dog, a Great Dane, and the behaviour of the surviving dog around his missing companion – how he searched for him and wept and behaved erratically and restlessly until they were forced to bring the body of the dead dog home from the vet for him to see. The dog smelled him, lay down beside him, and mourned. Then he returned to being himself, but not before claiming all of the deceased dog's toys.

I imagine that a person could find it awkward to talk or be talked to during a massage. Concentration on 'the body', it is assumed, would be broken. Having to attend to another's consciousness, or memory, or talk would hold one rather than release one into forgetfulness, oblivion, bliss. Topics would have to be generated, when, a friend of mine argued, there was no reason to converse with a person rendering you a service. To pretend to be interested in them would be even more condescending than simply letting them do their job. Or talking to them would be demanding something of them for which they weren't getting paid.

Facing down, hovering above ground, needy, one day I asked Tom how he'd been, and he proceeded to tell me gruesome details of the suicide by hanging that a friend of his had recently carried out, his attempt to cope with it, his lover and he driving to Provincetown – that gay American mecca – to get away only to learn of an even more gruesome act: an acquaintance had killed another man in a sexcapade gone awry. Dismemberment was involved, and worse: the murderer went to work for several days thereafter as though nothing had happened. The man who had killed himself was also gay, and Tom didn't spare me the details of the belt and heft and the shock of the friend who found him, falling with a thud onto the bathroom floor.

Here I was paying Tom to release me and he was burdening me with the story of this month's chaos and pain, an indescribable violence. I was lying on the table in hope of returning to the body, or at least an ability to feel, and he was feeding me senselessness in the form of words. I felt temporarily bludgeoned, used. I felt uncomfortably disembodied. 'Hey! Hey!' I thought, 'you should be paying *me* for this!' But I didn't finally protest.

Sometimes each of us enunciated things we'd never say in public. We allowed each other a certain crassness bordering on stupidity. One day, we discussed the question of whether gay men would rise to the occasion of breast cancer as activist-caretakers in the way that lesbians responded to AIDS. Another day, Tom is massaging my skinny calf when he says, 'So, I think I can ask you this and you won't be offended. I really want to know, and I think you'd be okay with my asking this, or at least tell me what you think'. Long pause. 'Why are so many lesbians fat?' I should be sitting up for this; I should put my glasses back on, get dressed, and make a bee-line for the door. Gay men, I knew, could be just as sexist as Everyman reared in a sexist world. Instead, I rolled my eyes inside their closed sockets, and explained, 'Lesbians aren't, as a people, any differently shaped than other women on the planet'. And then I offered a platitude from Feminism 101: 'What you read as 'fat', is a form of self-fashioning that doesn't have heteronormative notions of the female body in mind'. 'See, I learned something', Tom said, and continued the work of his intelligent hands.

Tom wants to talk and so do I. Not endlessly, and not all the time. Not to pass the time or fill the awkward gaping gap of intimacy between strangers. Punctuatedly. Unpredictably. Talking in this touching context happens on a threshold of sensation. At a limen. Tom's stories, literally, impress me; they keep our intimacy from being dumb. I don't carry our talk home in my heart, or stow his words in my ankle. I think of our talking as a locale that we've made together, a tactful space.

Tom's words are places I can return to, but our talking is also entirely of the moment – requisite to the situation of his touching me touching him. A muscle recoils, retracts, it tickles, or gives back, lets the hand enter, into a yawn. A voice locates: I know where Tom is standing in relation to me even though when he talks I usually cannot see him. A voice reverberates larynx, belly, breath and lip. Eyes closed, my palm turns upward on the bed beside me as I talk. Facing down, today politics are on the tip of my tongue on the verge of a tear. Nothing intricate – just the raw fact of the death in war and the culture's demand to ignore it, to live, live your daily life in all its stupidly doggy dailiness. If we remain stupid long enough, there will be no need to talk. Certainly not to go so far as feeling talking's stroke or sting, tongue's touch.

<hr />

'As if skin can hold you!' I remembered this line from a poetry reading I once heard by the New York performance artist, Annie Lanzillotto. No, skin cannot hold you, but a voice can. The sound of our earliest caretakers' voices creates our sense of skin, that significantly foundational projection of a membrane that Didier Anzieu psychoanalytically dubs the 'sonorous envelope'.[8] Listening's nearest sense is touch; early sonorous envelopes create a holding environment that is protective but also precarious. Out from within the sonorous envelope, the child produces its own cries, what Steven Connor citing Guy Rosolato calls an 'excitation which is life itself', a response to hunger and an attempt to defeat it.[9] The material of life itself – this meshing and piercing of the sonorous envelope by the infantile cry is the matter we compose ourselves out of, the interfacing fabric of the voice we come to call our own, the voice we will use to arrest or command, seduce or invite, to sing or write or speak to others with.

Mothers talk to their babies when they touch them, or not, and thus establish future relations to talk as embodied or abstract, talk as dangerous or secure.

Massage was a gift I gave myself at a juncture in my life when I was ready for it. Many years later, in the aftermath of an illness, and in spite of its being a bourgeois cliché, I gave myself yoga. I experience Yin positions of self-holding as especially surprising for the way they quiet one part of my mind and activate another; for the way, in de-familiarising my relationship to my body, they remind me that I *am* a body. My teacher, a life-long dancer named Suzie who re-named herself Divya, introduced a simple gesture to the class to hold for five minutes. I was surprised by how disarming it felt to follow her instructions:

> Sit up straight and in a comfortable position; bend your head to one side and rest the cheek of your face in one of your hands; place the other hand cross-wise atop your heart. Close your eyes. Breathe.

Neither the taboo of self-pleasuring nor the impossibility of self-tickling, the posture pointed up the challenge and uncommonness of self-comforting. Here was something I'd never ever done before, I thought, and it felt marvellous, until I remembered the unconscious assumption of a similar pose several years previously as uncanny prototype. On that occasion, I'd been sitting up in bed reading, but instead of gracing or grazing my cheek with my hand, I rested it inside the pages of a book I was reading. I didn't point to the words on the page, following each phoneme with my finger; I felt the pages the way I always do when I read, like a skin upon which words are sometimes embossed and other times concave, depending on the voice of the prose I am hearing. With my other hand, I did something I never do: I blithely laid my hand across my chest, but as I did so, I felt a lump, a tumour that turned out to be cancerous and that no mammogram had ever discerned.

Since then, I've been the fortunate recipient of unexpectedly tangible gifts: in another yoga class, this one taught by a gay man named Terry, I'm lying in the end-of-class death pose called 'Shavasana'; my eyes are closed and I'm on my back, when I suddenly become aware of a pair of hands gently pulling my massively sweaty head out of its scrunched position and toward the palms of these hands. The same hands part my forehead, making my eyes relax more fully into my head, before drawing a line in the space above my nose as if deepening the crevice that is the spine of a book. It's an impartial touch that imparts the utmost love.

I don't know what kind of mould such people as Tom and Divya and Terry are made from; I only know I have no desire to touch, or hold, comfort or massage another person's sweaty head even though the gesture filled me with a sense of supreme gratitude. In an extreme circumstance, I'm sure I would be okay with it. All protocols of skin-to-skin contact would lapse if, say, I found myself in a situation in which another human being were wounded or harmed or for some reason suddenly needed help. The difference was that these acts didn't require extraordinary contexts in order for them to be carried out. Which isn't to say they were all in a day's work. Such acts exceed a (social) contract without effacing a (professional) border.

Because Shavasana requires silence, I was kept from verbally thanking Terry. Better than an audibly articulated 'thanks', I suspect he felt my thankfulness in my surprise, the more I tried to listen to his hands.

Years before my diagnosis, Tom announced one day that he and his lover had decided to make a big move. They'd be re-locating to California and selling his father's house. They were getting rid of everything, he told me, and starting fresh, and he invited me over to see if I might want anything. I remember feeling hurt that he had no parting gift for me – that everything in the house had an over-blown price tag, including the plants. Still, I bought a number of plants; a rug for my study; and a filing cabinet. It was the type of cabinet that was less like the office ware I already owned and more like furniture. Like the genre of refrigerator that blends with the kitchen cabinets so that you can't find the food and can deny that kitchens are for eating in, this file cabinet was crafted from sleekly tanned wood, lighter than the voluminous heft it was capable of holding.

In the ensuing years, I got rid of the rug (it was never really 'me'); all of the plants died (I was surprised to see that, for the most part, Tom, who knew so much about plants, had neglected to pot them in containers that were porous). Only the filing cabinet remains, though it's been on its way out for a very long time. Jean and I have decided it's way too cumbersome for the small rooms of our nineteenth-century house, so it sits on a landing now awaiting a body capable of getting it to turn at all the right angles down the stairs.

I stopped getting regular massages after Tom left Rhode Island. A few times, in extreme circumstances, I ventured the chance of new practitioners, but the technique of the people whom I saw ranged from what I call the 'feather duster' approach (massage as a bodily dusting) to a violent form of kneading that left me bruised. In all the talking I was capable of, I had never learned to ask a massage therapist to adjust his touch to suit my needs. With Tom I didn't have to do this. He simply 'knew'.

Tom once told me that his route to this profession came in caring for men, beginning with his own brother, who had died of AIDS. Realising how far the small relief of a massage well-done could go in easing the profound discomforts of the disease, Tom decided to become a licensed practitioner and make muscular therapy a meaningful career. Tom must apply his touch to suit the body tactfully, like the person skilled at finding the right words, pressure, tone and weight to suit the situation; or like the person intent on setting words inside a page to make a voice.

I loved to learn of more than one gay person in a nuclear family – it flew in the face of the image of a family's queer progeny as singular and aberrant and weird.

Affects

Imagine the mother's burden, or release. Imagine her philodendron. I wonder if, when she held her sons as babies, she spoke to them. Did she talk to them as she touched them, or, in perfect silence, stroke their heads?

The author would like to thank Rhode Island-based architectural designer, Aaron Brode, for discussions of 'coffin niches'.

Notes

1 Didier Anzieu, *The Skin Ego*, p. 13.
2 Adam Phillips, *On Kissing, Tickling, and Being Bored*, p. 9.
3 *Ibid.*, p. 9.
4 *Ibid.*, p. 10.
5 In *Awkward*, I composed in a genre I called a 'detour'. Rather than theorise awkwardness as a concept, I followed it like a language and thereby happened upon unanticipated realms in its name. This distinction is elaborated in French psychoanalyst J. B. Pontalis' *Windows*, where he suggests that if you enter something as a language, you find it wants and needs to travel, and it won't allow you to come to the point, but to wander toward multiple points, arrived at from multiple directions. Pontalis' context is the psychotherapeutic encounter: the circuitous non-narrative routes a person must take in order to achieve psychological insight and change in the talk therapy that defines the psychoanalytic relation. As a literary mode, a detour can make possible a kind of truth-telling otherwise barred by writing that fails to allow for wandering, accident, estuarial swerve, or straying from a purported centre.
6 Anzieu, *The Skin Ego*, p. 100.
7 Patricia Duncker, *Hallucinating Foucault*, p. 37.
8 Anzieu, *The Skin Ego*, p. 158.
9 Steven Connor, 'What I say goes', p. 29.

Bibliography

Anzieu, Didier, *The Skin Ego*, Chris Turner trans. (New Haven, CT: Yale University Press, 1989).
Cappello, Mary, *Awkward: A Detour* (New York: Bellevue Literary Press, 2007).
Connor, Steven, 'What I say goes', in *Dumbstruck: A Cultural History of Ventriloquism* (New York: Oxford University Press, 2000).
Duncker, Patricia, *Hallucinating Foucault* (New Jersey: The Ecco Press, 1996).
Phillips, Adam:, 'On tickling', in *On Kissing, Tickling and Being Bored: Psychoanalytic Essays on the Unexamined Life* (Cambridge, MA: Harvard University Press, 1994)
Pontalis. J. B., *Windows*, Anne Quinney, trans. (Lincoln, NE: University of Nebraska Press, 2003).

On being open to difference: cosmopolitanism and the psychoanalysis of groups

Jackie Stacey

What might it mean to be open to difference? The touchstone of the current cosmopolitan vision, the concept of openness to difference, has been widely welcomed in debates across the humanities and social sciences.[1] But how do we know when others are open to the differences we represent and vice versa? What is the register of such openness: is it cognition, intention, affect, viscera? And difference in relation to whom or what exactly? What kind of openness is at the centre of such claims: celebration, neutrality, tolerance, indifference, recognition? And what is the register of the success and failure of such an aspiration? Is it simply the absence of aversion, or is it the presence of something quite tangible?

My exploration of the concept of openness to difference in this essay reflects upon two concurrent experiences in contrasting contexts: one academic, the other therapeutic. Placing academic discourse in dialogue with therapeutic practice, this piece is something of an experiment in writing otherwise, not so much stylistically, like some of the other essays in this collection, but more as a consideration of my own ontologies of knowledge production. To put it more simply and more personally, this essay traces how my own thinking has been generated by my experiences of these two rather different contexts, one inside and the other outside the academy. In this particular story, the political aspirations of an intellectual project are repeatedly thrown into doubt by my encounters with the limits of some of their foundational claims in a therapeutic context.

There are two immediate caveats to this framing: first, psychotherapeutic practices of course have their own research cultures and publications, many of which deal with questions of difference;[2] so, in some senses, there is nothing new about bringing social concepts into a psychoanalytic domain. But my project pushes in a rather different direction. My writing otherwise here is an account of how an encounter with therapeutic practices might transform contemporary academic approaches to cultural criticism. This essay is a reflection upon how intellectual work might be unsettled by experiences in quite different contexts. A second caveat is that psychotherapeutic practices operate through important rules of confidentiality, so my account uses pseudonyms where necessary and relies on typifications and amalgamations of events to protect those people involved.

My starting-point for the following account is that it is a highly invested narration. My selections and partialities are inevitably subject to my own psychic as well as intellectual investments. Other people from each of the two contexts in question might tell very different stories. The account that follows is thus informed by my own personal and intellectual responses to these academic and therapeutic encounters. And that, indeed, is part of the point, as we shall see.

I

In September 2007 I started a new job at the University of Manchester at the Research Institute for Cosmopolitan Cultures (RICC). It was an interesting interpellation for those of us appointed to this new endeavour, all of whom were concerned with the general issues suggested by its title (justice, equality, openness, diversity) but none of whom had been involved in its inception or naming. A number of questions swiftly presented themselves. Were we expected to be the advocates or representatives of cosmopolitanism in some way – its champions perhaps? Was the University articulating its own cosmopolitan aspirations in establishing such a research institute? Should our research perform the kind of cosmopolitanism it sought to address through its own methodological procedures and cultural practices? How did the two terms (cosmopolitan and culture) of the institute's title inform each other and were they separable? Should we attempt to produce some shared definition of cosmopolitan cultures in order to position ourselves, theoretically and politically in relation to these concepts and to each other?

The title of the institute signalled to me something highly specific with a very particular history[3] but with an interdisciplinary breadth and inclusivity that promised to speak to contemporary questions of great political urgency. To the extent that the agenda of this new initiative seemed genuinely open-ended, we spent the next few years in reading groups, workshops and seminars debating the history of the term cosmopolitanism and its significance to understandings of contemporary culture. Wrestling with an ambivalence towards a certain imperative to generate a definitive account of the cosmopolitan culture that named our endeavour, we rehearsed our competing and highly divergent responses to the multitude of publications on the subject.[4]

The idea of openness to difference is a central one within debates about cosmopolitanism. Inextricable from a certain sense of worldliness that expands beyond geographical locality, openness to difference runs across much of the literature as a touchstone of a better way of living. Cosmopolitanism has been theorised as a disposition, a mode of consciousness, an engendered sentiment, a political aspiration, a system of affiliations, a form of citizenship, a structure of feeling, a cultural and/or critical practice and a habit of sociality. For many academics seeking to respond to the ideological conservatism that consolidated so swiftly post-9/11, cosmopolitanism has presented an alternative way of imagining a more 'convivial' culture,[5] where difference is welcomed and might even thrive, partly by virtue of becoming unremarkable: what Paul Gilroy has called 'living with difference', and Mica Nava refers to as 'the normalisation of difference' in the context of a 'visceral cosmopolitanism'.[6] Combining the cosmos and the polis, the 'consciousness of being a citizen of the world'[7] is enabled through an ontological receptivity to the differences others represent.

On being open to difference

Across the disciplines, academics have embraced cosmopolitan cultures as a place of political optimism and potentiality. Berthold Schoene, for example, states in his eponymous book, that 'the cosmopolitan novel' should be welcomed as 'an open-ended *tour du monde*'.[8] For Schoene, 'There is nothing that ought to prevent us imagining the world as one community or capturing it inside the vision of a single narrative ... Nothing less, in fact, than the world as a whole will do as the reference point, catchment area, and addressee of what I designate as the cosmopolitan novel'.[9] Literary criticism is seen by Robert Spencer as a process which might 'demonstrate how reading postcolonial literature can ... engender the critical consciousness and the global solidarities ... [that] uphold cosmopolitan political arrangements'.[10] Exploring art's particular ability to convey 'the intimate relation between the material and the conceptual' that is required to invoke 'the contingency of home' so central to 'generosity, intimacy and care',[11] Marsha Meskimmon asks: how does contemporary art practice materialise a cosmopolitan imagination that engenders 'a global sense of ethical and political responsibility at the level of the subject'?[12] This call for an imaginative relation to the world as community, or what some call 'worldliness', is indicative of the cosmopolitan project more generally. A vision of what we might call imaginative mobility, such a community would be defined by and achieved through an encounter with difference characterised by openness to the other, an encounter which is unthreatened, curious, even welcoming and hospitable. As the editors of *Cosmopolitan Urbanism* suggest, cosmopolitanism blends 'a philosophy of world citizenship [with] a particular set of skills and attitudes towards diversity and difference'.[13] Or, as I have defined cosmopolitan culture elsewhere, it is premised upon an *ease of proximity to the unfamiliar*.[14]

Across such conceptualisations, the desirability of cosmopolitanism has been invoked through the persistent claim that it represents a more open relationship to difference – more ethical, democratic, understanding and tolerant. This openness to other worlds and other ways of inhabiting them is seen to facilitate cosmopolitanism's breadth of identifications and rescaled consciousness of world citizenship. In this version, affiliations and loyalties beyond the national, the local and the located are generated through a sense of common values – typically justice, freedom and equality. The openness to difference in question here is named in the literatures on cosmopolitan cultures in a number of intersecting ways. It has been variously identified as: the product of a new cultural diversity and multiculturalism; a characteristic of the everyday practices of urban and migrant communities; a strategic disposition produced by economic necessity; the consciousness generated by global media networks and virtual connectivities; the potentially radical aesthetic of 'world-making' literature, art or cinema; the moral or ethical basis for universal human rights; a kindness to strangers based on common human values; a philosophical mode of being in the world; a conviviality towards a common humanity.

The question of openness to difference has been a key concept in research projects on cosmopolitan cultures. For example, anthropologist Daniel Hiebert discusses transnational neighbourhoods in Vancouver thus: 'I think of cosmopolitanism as a way of living based on "openness to all forms of otherness", associated with an appreciation of, and interaction with, people from other cultural backgrounds'.[15] Sociologist Craig Calhoun borrows Richard Sennett's language of comfort to signal something similar: 'a cosmopolite ... is a man [*sic*] who moves comfortably in diversity; he is comfortable in situations which have no particular links or parallels to what is familiar to him'.[16] In our reading groups and seminars in RICC, the notion of openness to difference somehow became the benchmark of a more desirable mode of sociality. It became a kind of shorthand which signalled a consciousness sufficiently orientated towards a collective good, such that otherness could become unthreatening even where it brings with it the unfamiliar. To put it succinctly, cosmopolitan cultures are imagined as spaces 'in which people could be different without fear'.[17]

Who could not see the appeal of such admirable ideals in a world where violent rejection and exclusion of undesirable others continue to govern national and religious conflicts, ethnic cleansing programmes, homophobic attacks and hate crimes, misogynist contempt and sexual violence, class abjections, immigration and asylum policies and a whole host of justifications for the current so-called war on terror? In this context, the notion of openness to difference, especially the welcoming of foreigners, hospitality to strangers and ease of proximity to the unfamiliar, has an immediate appeal. Which liberal-minded person would not want to be associated with such a vision, a politics based not on what we are against – discrimination, injustice, exploitation, prejudice, violence, terror, fear – but on what we are in favour of – inclusiveness, diversity and mutual acceptance and respect? But each time this concept of openness to difference was used in our discussions, as a cosmopolitan aspiration even if a not fully realisable one, I found myself hesitating. Whilst there was something appealing about such a vision, its premise also troubled me (perhaps because of my own shameful intolerances). Is openness to difference a transparent and self-evident phenomenon? If we were to aspire to such a disposition, how would we know if we had achieved it?

Claiming cosmopolitan culture as a place where difference might be unthreatening, whether inspirational or aspirational, academic theories have often attributed a sense of individuated autonomy and lack of perceptual ambiguity to people's encounters with each other. My concerns with the limits of these cosmopolitan models of subjectivity led me towards more psychoanalytic ones, which assume that, despite our desire for self-knowledge, subjects always remain somewhat opaque to each other and to themselves. Jacqueline Rose has argued that the term cosmopolitan 'hovers somewhere between an assertion ... and a desire', and, in expressing certain political aspirations, may be in danger of 'idealising the psyche'.[18] Rose's statement expresses something akin to my own discomfort with the ways in which advocates of cosmopolitanism almost seem to want to purify the psyche in the name of social harmony. How might we theorise the threat posed by the unfamiliar as the starting-point for a better political vision?

If the cosmopolitan project rests, as Jacques Derrida has argued, on the notion of an 'ethic of hospitality to strangers',[19] then, according to psychoanalysis, the stranger for whom cosmopolitan culture demands hospitality may also reside within. In *Strangers to Ourselves,* Julia Kristeva argues that with Freud's notion of the unconscious, 'the involution of the strange in the psyche loses its pathological aspect and integrates within the assumed unity of human beings an *otherness* that is both biological *and* symbolic and becomes an integral part of the *same*'; henceforth, she claims, 'the foreigner is neither a race nor a nation … Uncanny, foreignness is within us: we are our own foreigners, we are divided'.[20] According to Kristeva, Freud suggested how and why it was important 'to face the other's discontent as ill-ease in the continuous presence of the "other scene" within us'.[21] And she continues: 'My discontent in living with the other – my strangeness, his strangeness – rests on the perturbed logic that governs the strange bundle of drive and language, of nature and symbol constituted by the unconscious, always already shaped by the other'.[22] Transference, she argues, is the major dynamic of otherness, of 'love/hatred for the other, of the foreign component of our psyche' and it is only in unravelling transference that 'on the basis of the other, [she] become[s] reconciled with [her] own otherness-foreignness'.[23] In this way, Kristeva suggests, 'psychoanalysis is then experienced as a journey into the strangeness of the other and of oneself, *toward an ethics of respect for the irreconcilable*'.[24] 'How', she asks, 'could one tolerate a foreigner if one did not know one was a stranger to oneself?'[25] This argument, that we are strangers to ourselves and that our projection of this uncanny 'other scene' within onto people whose strangeness we then love/hate, offers a different starting-point for theorising cosmopolitan culture.

What might a cosmopolitan politics look like if it were not based upon a notion of openness to difference but instead upon an 'ethics of respect for the irreconcilable'? If our discomfort with the unfamiliar may in part draw its affective force from our own internal unknowability, then perhaps this might provide a starting-point for thinking through the importance of psychoanalysis for cosmopolitanism. This leaves us with the task of how to theorise an 'ethics of respect for the irreconcilable' in ways that might have wider political and cultural significance. Following Rose, we might ask if the cosmopolitan vision offers the 'flexibility of the individual psychic processes … as the answer to the rigid identifications of political life?' If she is right and it does, then perhaps, as Rose suggests, 'strangely, the individual – in a strikingly pre-Freudian incarnation – is being mobilised as a corrective to the perils of the group'.[26] It is to this relationship between individual psychic processes and the 'perils of the group' that I now turn in my discussion of negotiating differences in a therapeutic context.

II

Shortly before starting this job in RICC at Manchester, I completed the part-time, one-year 'Introductory Course in Group Psychotherapy'. One weekend each month we attended a lecture by a group psychoanalyst, a seminar discussion of assigned readings and a series of large and small group meetings with no agendas or leaders.[27] Combining psychoanalytic theory with experiential approaches to working with groups, this course disturbed some of my most deep-seated habits of 'being with others' and challenged my thinking about a number of subjects I had previously written about in feminist, queer and cultural studies. Concepts such as identification and recognition, difference and otherness, subjectivity, affect and emotion, trauma and recovery, and, across all of these, the question of personal and political (psychic and cultural) transformation – all these and more took on a different inflection through the lens of analytic group work.

Contrary to expectation, of the two experiences – the academic and the therapeutic – it was the group work sessions that offered me the most nuanced ways of thinking about the problem of being open to difference. My sense of this emerged from a central component to the course – what was called the 'experiential group' or 'small group'. The small group, as I shall refer to it here, comprised six to eight members who met together for ninety-minute unstructured sessions three times across each weekend of the course. Not a therapy group as such, because too infrequent and short-term, this was as much about generating the experience of being in a group without a structure as it was about giving an account of oneself to others, though this obviously occurred too, if unevenly. It was completely up to each group member how much they spoke about themselves, and in what ways. In the micro-dynamics of these encounters, I found condensed many of the social relations addressed by the cosmopolitan agenda. Why is difference so threatening, and how can we find ways of being more open to the uncomfortable differences we imagine others to represent and vice versa?

In this small group, I found myself reflecting upon how difficult it was to be in such close proximity to others who expressed or represented something I did not like, something I felt opposed to, or negated and threatened by. In these sessions, propinquity to both personal and structural differences was unavoidable and an unwelcome intimacy with aversion was sometimes required, as women listened to men expressing their misogyny, people from 'ethnic minorities' heard others grappling with their fear of being touched by 'foreign' doctors, lesbians and gay men navigated heterosexist assumptions about sexuality, reproduction, the family and parenting. Interactions between people in the group blended the personal with the cultural in complex ways which often produced unexpected outcomes and surprising loyalties. These small groups worked as microcosms of wider cultural formations, functioning to bring together a random collection of people who didn't know each other previously into a series of encounters in which they worked through (amongst other things) an evolving and shifting sense of recognition and differentiation or isolation. In much the way that contemporary life brings strangers into proximity with each other, this course required people to relate to whomever happened to be in their group. Of course, some self-selection occurs in terms of who might be likely to do such a course; however, some of the more predictable homogeneities (the predominance of white professionals) pushed against a sense of emergent diversity in other respects, some of which were more immediately visible than others.

Although a trained group analyst was present in every meeting of the small group, this person rarely intervened, except to time-keep and ensure the group remained 'open' (as it was called). This signified almost the opposite of a cosmopolitan 'openness' through which difference might ideally be unthreatening and even welcomed. Instead, openness here meant enabling the group to continue its process, in which people often heard antagonisms and aversions to difference being expressed quite directly. Within a group analytic approach, the expression of perceived differences as threatening can generate productive group dynamics. It was deemed pedagogically important to enable some kind of reflection upon group processes, based on sharing the ongoing experience of shifting responses to others in our small group. This approach was marked not by a cosmopolitan sense of openness to difference, but, on the contrary, by an interest in the *obstacles* to such openness (their histories and their affects). And for me, this became precisely the point of these group meetings: as a small group, we had to figure out how to respond to the perceived differences of relative strangers who, across the year, gradually became more and more familiar.

The ontology of these unstructured groups produced a context for the difference present to be negotiated. How to be present and stay connected in the group, especially to those most different from oneself, was never off the agenda. The small group seemed to enact the precariousness of our sense of affective presence in ways that influenced my thinking about the idea of openness to difference which is at the heart of the cosmopolitan project. If the unconscious is a sign of never being fully present to oneself (or to others) then perhaps these group exchanges prove both disturbing *and* therapeutic precisely because of the ways in which they condense and make more tangible the collaborative, and yet always enigmatic, production of a sense of self. As Judith Butler has famously argued, the intelligibility of subjects to one another is necessarily incomplete and our desire for recognition is always in tension with our inevitable partial opacity to ourselves and to others.[28] In these small-group exchanges, the intelligibility in question did not merely concern understanding of each other's accounts of ourselves, or even readings of each other's emotional states. What was at stake was the intelligibility of the group process. As we all repeatedly failed to grasp the purpose of this process, I witnessed the fracturing of the line between intention and outcome, and between political or ethical ethos and interpersonal group dynamics. Good intentions sometimes masked hostility or envy; recognition offered in solidarity was sometimes felt to be reassuring but just as often seemed unexpectedly to negate someone else rather than confirm or affirm them.

Far from the transparent subjects upon which cosmopolitan aspirations of openness to difference so often seem to be premised, these intense small-group meetings seemed to demonstrate precisely the slipperiness of intelligibility. To be *open to* difference assumes a self-evident boundary marking out someone as recognisably dissimilar. The unfamiliar or the strange here is placed *in the other person* and is seen as something we recognise and respond to accordingly. But what if one's own sense of openness to difference might appear to others as closure, assimilation or even appropriation or incorporation?

Time and time again the small group generated just such instances of misapprehension. On one occasion, for example, Bethan described a series of relationships with men which had never lasted long, explaining how she envied the other people in the group with more sustained ones. Jane asked her directly why she thought she hadn't really ever had a long-term relationship with a man – perhaps it was something she herself was doing that meant they did not last. Caroline intervened, objecting to the prescriptive direction of the conversation, trying to rescue Bethan from the pain of envy and reassure her that long-term heterosexual monogamy was only one model of how to do sexual relationships. Intended as a moment of solidarity and offered in the spirit of opening up space for difference to exist, this intervention shifted the mood in the group. Bethan then seemed really upset. Different members of the group began to draw their own conclusions from this. Caroline thought she had been shamed into feeling a 'failure'. Bethan became frustrated and angry, saying she had wanted to respond directly to the question about her lack of romantic success with men but that she had been robbed of that chance as she felt the moment had now passed.

On another occasion, Tim had not been able to pay the final instalment of the course fee because of lack of funds. The question of access to money was introduced and the group discussed the ways in which they were all in very different financial circumstances. David introduced a discussion about class inequality and poverty and tried to urge the group to find ways of thinking how they could help Tim, suggesting delayed payments or a sliding scale based on income. Tim started to talk about the shame tied to being poor in his family history. David responded by saying it made him furious that any sense of embarrassment should get tied to this social injustice and the discussion moved to a more general exchange about economic inequalities. Tim became very quiet. After some time, he spoke about how he had wanted to explore feeling of shame around money but that he no longer felt able to take that risk as the discussion had moved to a different register.

In both cases, an attempt to keep the group open to difference by one member intervening on behalf of another produced the opposite effect. In the first example, the intended openness of the feminist intervention (refusing the prescriptions of heterosexual norms) produced another kind of closure (it no longer felt safe to explore a difficult sexual history); in the second, the desire to keep the group open to someone who could not afford the final fee payment had instead generated an affective closure around the discussion of the shame of poverty. It is not simply that one register is structural and the other emotional; rather, the dynamic processes of interaction condensed here are indicative of the unpredictable ways affect is mutually constitutive. Being open to the difference of others is not a self-contained state of mind, nor is it predictably a continuous one; it is a constant negotiation of shared uncertain affective terrain.

Integral to the small-group process was the negotiation not just of how others in the group represented particular combinations of socially differentiated categories, refracted through personal histories, but also of the struggles that emerged over narrating the group's own accumulating history. The question of being open to difference quickly included the challenge of how to respond to other people's accounts of what had happened in previous groups. What emerged over time was a sense of the irreconcilability of different members' accounts of themselves, of each other, of the broader categories they represented and, especially, of the group process itself. Given that there was never consensus – only highly invested and contested narrations – the challenge became how to live with other people's accounts of the group's previous interactions and communications with which you did not agree. At particular moments a different account of our previous sessions together became intolerable.

The differences that had to be constantly negotiated here thus blended into a threefold configuration of personal, cultural and group-historical. Over the course of the year, the group produced its own contested history of itself. This presented a familiar problem which lies at the heart of group dynamics generally: whose version of the group gets to count as a shared history and what happens when your version does not get recognised or endorsed? How could we live with these irreconcilable accounts? The small group repeatedly enacted the problem of how, in an intimate space, to respond to relative strangers whose stories were sometimes deeply moving, and, at other times, intensely frustrating and irritating, or even just plain boring. Shifting between compassion and intolerance or empathetic connection and alienation or violent hatred in unexpected ways meant submitting to the affective power of the group and confronting the limits of one's own liberal aspirations.

This was often a question of the power of affect. If affect moved the group in particular directions, it did so with unpredictable consequences for its members who might read the mood in opposing ways. By *affect* here I am referring to a sense of the potential of others to impact on us and vice versa: *being subject to others*. The mood in the room seemed to expose our susceptibility to the impressions of other people that reminded us that we were social subjects. The impossibility of considering oneself an autonomous individual, somehow beyond the affects of others, was reiterated through the processes of constant negotiation of our relational subjectivities.

But understanding this process was only half the story. The transformative force of such encounters lay in the affective dynamics of the small group over the duration of the many months of the course. These moments had their most profound impact through the event of the group exchange. As one group analyst writes: it might not be the interpretation as such that creates change but rather the event or what she calls the *'mutative moment'* of an encounter with someone else in the group.[29] There is always more at stake in these group exchanges than any one of its members can grasp. Complex and condensed interactions demonstrate the overdetermination of intersubjectivity and relationality, and the unpredictable unconscious dynamics at play in such interactions. In this context, good intentions often produced their opposites, affective connections mutated unexpectedly, alliances based on shared values shifted regularly, and surprising moments of compassion repeatedly surfaced.

What characterised this group process for me was an overwhelming sense of the mutable line between recognition and misrecognition, comfort and discomfort, compassion and contempt, and pleasure and anxiety (and of course, openness and closure). If in one meeting two people bonded, for example, over their shared understanding or values (what the group analytic theory calls 'pairing'), at the next they might feel utterly opposed to each other in relation to an unexpected turn in the conversation. If one person seemed endlessly defensive about a particular version of him/herself repeatedly fed back by the group, another person found witnessing these moments the most instructive and beneficial dynamic of the whole small-group process. And, if our readings of how we were all placed in relation to institutionalised inequalities seemed at certain moments to confirm our previous understandings of such histories of social privilege and power relations, at others, unexpected loyalties and shared emotional landscapes emerged which undid any preconceptions about how such categories might play out in the group. Sibling placement sometimes undercut class privilege. Education sometimes undid religious solidarity. Workplace bullying sometimes destabilised gender affiliations. At other times, experiences of illness, parenthood, bereavement and relationship failure superseded the injustices of a more structural character. All of these fluctuations were overlaid by the affective histories of the group's own internal processes and the repeated narrations of these by different members of the group.

In other words, there was no steady or predictably enduring form of my sense of the openness (or closure) to the differences the others in the group represented. Rather, the impact of other people's affect upon the changing processes of inclusion and exclusion was in constant flux, and our accounts of this process to each other were always highly invested ones. If my feminism enabled me to bond with some members of the group at certain moments, it also led to misunderstandings, poor judgement and clumsy interventions on my part at others. If particular assumptions about anti-racism seemed to produce a safe space between particular people at certain moments, at others the same group members got caught up in ignorance and prejudice. I became acutely aware of the temporary and shifting nature of my own sense of openness to others in these group meetings. Conscious affiliations and loyalties were tripped up by the stubborn repetitions of personal and familial histories. Inevitably tied up with the ambivalence and the contradictions of intersubjectivity and its unconscious manifestations, I found my affiliations to be always partial, temporary, contingent and fragile in ways that were often well beyond my control. Any desire to be open to and accepting of difference could quickly transform into a complex interpersonal exchange where envy, anxiety, anger and resentment muddied the clear waters of good intention.

The power of the small group was its capacity to be both unexpectedly generative and inhibiting. The place of difference within these dynamics was central and yet elusive: difference understood as a cultural category competed with difference understood through personal history which in turn competed with difference understood through accounts of the group process. Difference was central to the extent to which the group might have been described as open or closed, and yet openness did not necessarily map onto acceptance or ease, as in the cosmopolitan vision of the term. Openness in the small group might better be defined through the notion of generative affect, even if, or often because, this might *include* aversion. The group worked best when connections between people flowed in new directions driven by energetic exchange. In short, difference was always contingent; openness was always provisional. Irreconcilable accounts of the group process became an inevitable aspect of being present within it.

On being open to difference

In giving this account of the course, I am struck by the obvious ways in which it is shaped by my own investments as an academic preoccupied with questions of difference, equality and justice. Others on the course would probably have given a different sense of the processes of the small group, depending on their concerns. Caroline might have said that its challenge lay in how to remain emotionally present to oneself and to others in the face of the anxiety generated by being in a group with no structure, plan or agenda. Bethan might have told of how she had found it hard to take up space and demand attention even when she longed for it. Jane might have focused on how hard it had been not to fill silences with nervous chatter, controlling gestures or symptomatic diagnoses of everyone else in the group. Tim might have reflected on the burning humiliation of exclusion or shameful confessions in the group context. David may have told of how he had learnt how to hear with compassion the stories of suffering narrated by those he most disliked in the group. Kiran may have reflected on how he had found new ways to articulate discomfort, frustration and anger without criticising and judging. Ingrid may have written about how she had trusted the group processes sufficiently to take the risk of transformation, while Bill may or may not have disclosed that he had not.

III

Juxtaposing an intellectual project (RICC) with a short course on the psycho-analytic approaches to group work is likely to invite a number of protests about the limits of their comparability: the first is an academic engagement with cultural issues, the second is an account of the dynamics of face-to-face encounters of a small group of people working on a course together. Comparing visions of a more cosmopolitan culture with the vicissitudes of small-group processes may seem to some like an indefensible refusal of the glaringly obvious macro–micro distinction. How can an account of the meetings between a group of six to eight people be the basis for any kind of critique of a political aspiration for cultural transformation? Surely this reduces the cultural to the 'merely' interpersonal in such a way as to lose any sense of the determining forces of wider structural and institutional histories? My counterarguments to such scepticism are less concerned with justifying the micro as a methodology for understanding the macro, and more with my interests in how the small-group experiences influenced my own practice of cultural criticism.[30] My conceptualisation of the 'culture' that is to be 'cosmopolitanised' has been transformed by my encounters in these small groups. This particular convergence of experiences sharpened my sense of how the *cultural* might work as a modifier to the cosmopolitan in the RICC project. In the final section of this essay, I try and elaborate.

The point that cuts across these brief descriptions is that just as there are no neutral accounts of the group's history – only necessarily invested ones – so there are no autonomous subjects within them. Participation necessarily requires engagement with the multiple relationalities and affiliations that constitute the group. There is by definition no neutrality in which to hide. This is crucial in explaining my discomfort with the models of openness to difference discussed in RICC. All accounts of oneself in the group were relational ones, mediated through the imagined others that had been psychically internalised through previous histories, as well as through the fantasies of self and other generated by the group in the room at one time. Rather than the individuated subject of so much cosmopolitan theory, who is imagined to encounter the stranger as external to him or herself, members of these small groups negotiated differences through multiple mediations – intrapsychic and interpsychic – that were in constant flux and were assumed to already exist within themselves.

At its best, the group produced what we might tentatively call a kind of 'emotional democracy', whereby participation was premised upon an ethical relation of the necessary emotional investments of all its members and of the interdependence in their relational accounts of each other. There was a levelling effect to the ways in which there was no participation in the group process without risking unpredictable and unknown consequences for others. Taking responsibility for the particular history we each brought into the room, without feeling responsible for the always unexpected affects generated by it in the group, pushed us to learn to tolerate the discomfort of an uncosmopolitan openness to each other. Since each member's account is necessarily an invested one, an acceptance of the affective investments of all group members generated a kind of democratic sense of mutual vulnerability – in Kristeva's terms, 'an ethics of respect for the irreconcilable'.

In this context, both openness and difference become contested terms generated by shifting affective attachment and never possessions or permanent dispositions. As such, neither could be conceptualised as self-evident or observably transparent. Instead, the accounts we produced of ourselves in relation to difference in the small group shifted ground and changed form, depending on our negotiation of unconscious, as well as conscious, responses. At any one time in the group, someone's account of themselves was necessarily generated partly through their own and other people's unconscious projections.

Projections (and introjections) were seen not as signs of neurosis but rather as necessary ways in which we constitute ourselves through our imaginary relations with others. I found myself wondering how to rethink the idea of cosmopolitan cultures through this group analytic model of subjectivity. Projection (literally, throwing in front of oneself) refers to the process by which 'specific impulses, wishes, aspects of the self, or internal objects are imagined to be located in some object external to oneself'.[31] Introjection involves the opposite: 'the process by which the functions of an external object are taken over by its mental representation, by which the relationship with an object "out there" is replaced by one with an imagined object "inside"'.[32] On the course, we spent much time discussing the concept of projective identification which combines both these processes and refers to the ways in which unconscious projections can generate a change in the behaviour and emotions of other people in the group. Projective identification explains the ways in which group members may begin to feel (even though they had previously not done) that which is being projected onto them by someone else and may thus respond in a way that confirms the original projection. We might call this an example of what Teresa Brennan refers to as 'the transmission of affect'.[33]

In the small group, conflicts and disagreements about projections and projective identifications became a key dimension of our discussions, partly because of the dynamics between us and partly informed by our course reading. The point was not to catch people out or to prove that someone's response was a projection by some objective or neutral standard, or to suggest that some interactions were somehow free from such emotional relays. Rather, it was to ascertain how it might be productive to *work with* these aspects of group interaction. The aim was to transform these unconscious processes into conscious verbal communications that we might work with productively. In this context, 'openness to difference' was only ever partial, always temporary and often ambivalent because of the unconscious fears and desires which governed our interactions with each other.

If we think of subjectivity as constituted through a constant flow of mutual projections, then difference becomes not the property of the other person but a shifting dynamic of mutual phantasmatic ground. And, if intersubjectivity is re-framed as a relational process consequent upon irreconcilable group associations, then the unfinished business of producing an account of oneself and of others defies the securing of closures of ontological evaluations which deem a person 'cosmopolitan' because they are 'open to difference'.

A number of concerns about a so-called openness to difference emerge. First, there may not be a shared sense of perception between oneself and others of these moments of so-called openness. Secondly, and this was frequently borne out in these group dynamics, what if those moments or gestures of intended openness were precisely the ones the recipient experienced as the opposite? What if my expression of identification, recognition or empathy had the inverse effect and delivered instead unintended alienation, misapprehension or exclusion? And, finally, what if declarations of openness produce new occlusions, even as they seem to reveal the limits of old ones?

Such dynamics only make sense through a psychoanalytic framework of self and other in which the unconscious continues to play a constitutive part, in ways we might find highly inconvenient or just simply unpredictable. The affective force of the small group was generated by our lack of transparency to ourselves and to each other, and our frustrations with the irreconcilability of conflicted versions of the group's history. The work of the small group I have described here narrates repeated encounters with the stranger in ourselves and in others, as animated by other people's own invested histories. A theory of intersubjectivity which assumes that culture reproduces itself through our own dynamic emotional relays might enable us to reconceptualise cosmopolitanism. For me, this remains the challenge of writing cosmopolitan cultures otherwise.

⚬

I would like to express my thanks to colleagues both in RICC and on the Group Analysis North Course 2006–7. I am also grateful to Janet Wolff, Hilary Hinds, Monica Pearl and Erica Burman for feedback on earlier drafts of this essay, and to Clara Bradbury-Rance and Rose Deller for assistance with its final preparation.

Notes

1   Debates about cosmopolitanism include work by scholars in diverse fields. For discussions in sociology, see Ulrich Beck, *The Cosmopolitan Vision*; and Craig Calhoun, 'The class consciousness of frequent travellers: towards a critique of actually existing cosmopolitanism'. For scholarship in philosophy, see Jacques Derrida, *On Cosmopolitanism and Forgiveness*; Kwame Anthony Appiah, *Cosmopolitanism: Ethics in a World of Strangers*; Pheng Cheah and Bruce Robbins, *Cosmopolitics: Thinking and Feeling Beyond the Nation*; and Pheng Cheah, *Inhuman Conditions: On Cosmopolitanism and Human Rights* and 'Cosmopolitanism'. For political theory, see Daniele Archibugi, *Debating Cosmopolitics*; and Seyla Benhabib, *Another Cosmopolitanism*. For publications in cultural studies, see Homi Bhabha in Carol Breckenridge *et al.*, *Cosmopolitanism*; Paul Gilroy, *After Empire: Melancholia or Convivial Culture?* and Mica Nava, *Visceral Cosmopolitanism: Gender, Culture and the Normalisation of Difference*. For work in literary studies, see Bertholt Schoene, *The Cosmopolitan Novel*; Timothy Brennan, *At Home in the World: Cosmopolitanism Now*; and Robert Spencer, *Cosmopolitan Criticism and Postcolonial Literature*; For debates in art history, see Marsha Meskimmon, *Contemporary Art and the Cosmopolitan Imagination*. For geography, see David Harvey, *Cosmopolitanism and the Geographies of Freedom*. For recent analysis within European film studies, see Stephan Schindler and Lutz Koepnick, *The Cosmopolitan Screen: German Cinema and the Global Imaginary, 1945 to the Present*; and Tim Bergfelder, 'Love beyond the nation: cosmopolitanism and transnational desire in cinema'.
2   See, for example, Farhad Dalal, 'A transcultural perspective in psychodynamic psychotherapy.'
3   Cosmopolitanism used to refer to a worldly and sophisticated European intellectual ethos, and its recent return in a more globalised form in academic, political and corporate discourse arguably still carries traces of this association. For a history of the term, see Cheah, 'Cosmopolitanism'.
4   There has been an explosion of publications on cosmopolitanism in the last ten years; in August 2012, Google Scholar registered 60,000 articles related to this category.
5   Gilroy, *After Empire: Melancholia or Convivial Culture?*
6   Nava, *Visceral Cosmopolitanism: Gender, Culture and the Normalisation of Difference.*
7   Robert Fine, 'Cosmopolitanism: a social science research agenda', p. 242.
8   Schoene, *The Cosmopolitan Novel*, p. 30.
9   *Ibid.*, p. 30.
10   Spencer, *Cosmopolitan Criticism and Postcolonial Literature*, p. 40.
11   Meskimmon, *Contemporary Art and the Cosmopolitan Imagination*, p. 8.
12   *Ibid.*, p. 7.
13   Jon Binnie, *et al.*, *Cosmopolitan Urbanism.*
14   Jackie Stacey, 'The uneasy cosmopolitans of *Code Unknown*'.
15   Daniel Hiebert, 'Cosmopolitanism at the local level: the development of transnational neighbourhoods', p. 212.
16   Richard Sennett quoted in Calhoun, 'The class consciousness of frequent travellers: towards a critique of actually existing cosmopolitanism' p. 106.
17   Theodor Adorno quoted in *Ibid.*, p. 102.
18   Jacqueline Rose has argued for a more psychoanalytically grounded notion of a 'non-redemptive … cosmopolitanism'; see Rose, 'Provocation'.
19   Derrida, *On Cosmopolitanism and Forgiveness*, p. 16. On strangers, see also, Sara Ahmed, *Strange Encounters: Embodied Others in Post-Coloniality* and Appiah, *Cosmopolitanism:*

Ethics in a World of Strangers.

20 Julia Kristeva, *Strangers to Ourselves*, p. 181.

21 *Ibid.*, p. 181.

22 *Ibid.*, p. 181-2.

23 *Ibid.*, p. 182.

24 *Ibid.*, p. 182 (my emphasis).

25 *Ibid.*, p. 182.

26 Rose, 'Provocation'.

27 This course was organised in Manchester by Group Analysis North (GAN).

28 Judith Butler, *Giving an Account of Oneself*; see also Adriana Cavarero, *Relating Narratives: Storytelling and Selfhood*, who distinguishes between *what* someone is (the universal philosophical question) and *who* someone is (the biographical knowledge of narration to another).

29 Claire S. Bacha, 'The courage to stay in the moment', p. 285.

30 See the introduction to this volume for examples of practices of cultural criticism that have previously reflected upon personal investments in the production of knowledge.

31 Charles Rycroft, *Critical Dictionary of Psychoanalysis* p. 139

32 *Ibid.*, p. 87

33 Teresa Brennan, *The Transmission of Affect*.

Bibliography

Ahmed, Sara, *Strange Encounters: Embodied Others in Post-Coloniality* (London: Routledge, 2000).

Appiah, Kwame Anthony, *Cosmopolitanism: Ethics in a World of Strangers* (London: Penguin, 2006).

Archibugi, Daniele (ed.), *Debating Cosmopolitics* (London: Verso, 2003).

Bacha, Claire S., 'The courage to stay in the moment', *Psychodynamic Counselling*, 7:3 (2001), 279–95.

Beck, Ulrich, *The Cosmopolitan Vision*, trans. Ciaran Cronin (Cambridge: Polity, 2006 [2004]).

Benhabib, Seyla, *Another Cosmopolitanism* (Oxford: Oxford University Press, 2006).

Bergfelder, Tim, 'Love beyond the nation: cosmopolitanism and transnational desire in cinema', in Jo Labanyi, Luisa Passerini and Karen Diehl (eds), *Europe and Love in Cinema* (Bristol and Chicago, IL: Intellect and University of Chicago Press, 2012).

Binnie, Jon, Julian Holloway, Steve Millington and Craig Young (eds), *Cosmopolitan Urbanism* (London: Routledge, 2006).

Breckenridge, Carol, A. Sheldon Pollock, Homi Bhabha and Dipesh Chackrabaty (eds), *Cosmopolitanism* (A Public Culture Book) (Durham, NC: Duke University Press, 2002).

Brennan, Teresa, *The Transmission of Affect* (New York: Cornell University Press, 2005).

Brennan, Timothy, *At Home in the World: Cosmopolitanism Now* (Cambridge, MA: Harvard University Press, 1997).

Butler, Judith, *Giving an Account of Oneself* (New York: Fordham University Press, 2005).

Calhoun, Craig, 'The Class consciousness of frequent travellers: towards a critique of actually existing cosmopolitanism', in Daniele Archibugi (ed), *Debating Cosmopolitics* (London: Verso, 2003).

Cavarero, Adriana, *Relating Narratives: Storytelling and Selfhood* (London: Routledge, 1997).

Cheah, Pheng, and Bruce Robbins (eds), *Cosmopolitics: Thinking and Feeling Beyond the Na-*

tion (Minneapolis, MN: University of Minnesota Press, 1998).

Cheah, Pheng, *Inhuman Conditions: On Cosmopolitanism and Human Rights* (Cambridge, MA: Harvard University Press, 2006).

Cheah, Pheng, 'Cosmopolitanism', in *Theory Culture, Society*, 23 (2006), 486–96.

Dalal, Farhad, 'A transcultural perspective in psychodynamic psychotherapy', *Group Analysis*, 30:2 (1997), 203–15.

Delanty, Gerard (ed.), *The Handbook of Contemporary European Social Theory* (London: Routledge, 2006).

Derrida, Jacques, *On Cosmopolitanism and Forgiveness,* trans. Mark Dooley and Michael Hughes (London and New York: Routledge, (2001 [1997]).

Fine, Robert, 'Cosmopolitanism: a social science research agenda', in Gerard Delanty (ed.), *The Handbook of Contemporary European Social Theory* (London: Routledge, 2006).

Gilroy, Paul, *After Empire: Melancholia or Convivial Culture?* (London: Routledge, 2004).

Harvey, David, *Cosmopolitanism and the Geographies of Freedom* (New York: Columbia University Press, 2009).

Hiebert, Daniel, 'Cosmopolitanism at the local level: the development of transnational neighbourhoods', in Steven Vertovec and Robin Cohen (eds), *Conceiving Cosmopolitanism: Theory, Context, and Practice* (Oxford: Oxford University Press, 2002).

Kristeva, Julia, *Strangers to Ourselves* (New York: Columbia University Press, 1991).

Meskimmon, Marsha, *Contemporary Art and the Cosmopolitan Imagination* (London and New York: Routledge, 2011).

Nava, Mica, *Visceral Cosmopolitanism: Gender, Culture and the Normalisation of Difference* (Oxford: Berg, 2007).

Rose, Jacqueline, 'Provocation', in Nina Glick-Schiller and Andrew Irving (eds), *Whose Cosmopolitanism?* (New York: Berghahn, 2014 forthcoming).

Rycroft, Charles, *Critical Dictionary of Psychoanalysis* (London: Penguin, 1995 [1968]).

Schindler, Stephan, and Lutz Koepnick (eds), *The Cosmopolitan Screen: German Cinema and the Global Imaginary, 1945 to the Present,* (Ann Arbor, MI: University of Michigan Press, 2007).

Schoene, Bertholt, *The Cosmopolitan Novel* (Edinburgh: Edinburgh University Press, 2009).

Spencer, Robert, *Cosmopolitan Criticism and Postcolonial Literature* (Basingstoke and New York: Palgrave Macmillan, 2011).

Stacey, Jackie, 'The uneasy cosmopolitans of *Code Unknown*', in Nina Glick-Schiller and Andrew Irving (eds), *Whose Cosmopolitanism?* (New York: Berghahn, 2014 forthcoming).

Vertovec, Steven, and Robin Cohen (eds), *Conceiving Cosmopolitanism: Theory, Context, and Practice* (Oxford: Oxford University Press, 2002).

Touching lives: writing the sociological and the personal

Carol Smart

This essay is about how, in the process of engaging in empirical research and field-work, lives touch often in startling and disturbing ways. It is also about the difficulties entailed in subsequently writing about the qualities of these lives and also about the effects of being touched in certain, sometimes intangible, ways. The constraints of certain academic disciplinary conventions – and here I am specifically thinking of sociological writing – are such that I often feel that the richness of lives is omitted from written accounts. In addressing these two related matters, my field of concern is necessarily sociology because it is within this particular disciplinary embrace that I have forged a career in researching and writing. It is the field best known to me, to the extent that over several decades I confess that I have *become* a sociologist. Yet at the same time, while being saturated in and shaped by the rigours and requirements of this discipline, I find it sometimes irksome and constraining. Of course what I experience as the imperfections of this field of endeavour may well be found in sister disciplines, so I do not claim some kind of exclusivity of irritation or limitation. Indeed there will be strong overlaps with other fields where empirical and ethnographic methodologies are an integral part of the research process. But my criticisms I reserve for the discipline I know (and love) best because this chapter is also in part personal and it is about my own commitment to expanding the ways in which the discipline represents the lived world.

In this project I have been much influenced by Avery Gordon's critique of sociological analysis and writings.[1] In the second edition of Gordon's book *Ghostly Matters* Janice Radway wrote in the Foreword:

> It is the particular density, delicacy and propulsive force of the imagination that Avery Gordon wishes to see figured in sociological analysis, which she believes is limited by its restrictive commitment to an empiricist epistemology and its supporting ontology of the visible and the concrete.[2]

Gordon's desire that sociology should not simply present flat, descriptive accounts of what can be seen or said is widely compelling. It also addresses itself explicitly to empirical work which is, arguably, the hardest methodological problematic to transform. I shall explore this point more fully below, but before returning to Gordon's thesis I propose to build my argument in stages. First, I will explore how the researcher might respond to 'being touched' by the lives of others met in the process of sociological research. Second, I will examine how touching and connecting with other people's lives through the research process influences understandings of the social world and subsequent modes of analysis. Finally, I will look at how some of these ideas might be carried through into writing sociologically and the dangers and pitfalls of trying to write otherwise.

Disciplinary frameworks and touching lives

Ken Plummer (following Wright Mills) insists that sociology's heritage is a triple focus on biography, history and structure, but of course, as he acknowledges, the real task is to weave these strands together while also being attentive to the real lives we study.[3,4] Often these three dimensions can pull in different directions, particularly the biographical element which can sit uneasily alongside analyses which focus on social structure. Notwithstanding the growth in the sociological appreciation of biographical approaches, the discipline still cleaves to its grand narratives, its 'big' visions.[5,6] Even on the smaller canvas provided by qualitative empirical work, the incorporation of the biographical and/or the personal can be problematic. Case studies are the traditional way of providing depth to an account which might otherwise seem rather general or as needing a concrete example in order to anchor the explanation. But case studies stand in a specific relationship to all the other instances captured in the sociological research process, which is to say they exemplify a particular *pattern* of experiences or they are established as *typical*. There are therefore rules governing the use of case studies, and this prevents them from becoming disruptive of conventional methods or merely fanciful and (perhaps worst of all) unsystematic. But these approved and legitimated ways of selecting the sociological case study in the research process can mean that the lives of people who have touched one most are never spoken of. These lives may never feature because they do not 'fit' even if they are, for some reason, unforgettable and meaningful.

There is a view that electing to write about a story or person who has affected one (or haunts one) is illegitimate because personal feelings may override what are perceived to be the legitimately informed processes of sociological analysis. This is of course the point that Gordon addresses so forcefully. It is her argument that to smother these possible hints and clues about something intangible or less than concrete is to do a disservice to the lives of our interviewees or informants. This does not mean that there are no reasons to be wary of 'simply' following our strong emotional attachment to particular stories. They may, for example, be an unreflexive grasping at something that evokes untheorised feelings in the author (for example a shared trauma or experience). At worst, such a lack of reflexivity could mean that the story that is told is more about the writer than those written about. However, it is also possible that being touched personally is not necessarily such a naive reflex, since the person being touched in this instance is already a sociologist (or anthropologist or other methodologically astute researcher). This may seem a preposterous assertion in a way, as if I am arguing that researchers are special or unlike other ordinary mortals. This is not what I mean; rather, I am arguing that a discipline like sociology has the capacity to provide reflexive tools and a wide social vision such that research encounters are not simply 'ordinary' or casual meetings. Reflexive methodological thinking becomes gradually embedded or sedimented in the scholar, which means that in any encounter several levels of comprehension are available at one time. The analyst can move back and forth across these levels, bringing to bear insights from theory, other empirical studies, experience of interviewing a wide range of people and, of course, a particular kind of attentiveness that is essential in the research context. I shall elaborate further on this point below, but here I suggest that ignoring the potential of being touched by the lives of others may mean ignoring potentially important insights. This attentiveness is not a mere personal indulgence, because analytical work is always required in order to understand the experience and the feelings associated with being touched.

In order to elaborate on this point I shall revisit a study I carried out with Amanda Wade some years ago into the lives of primary school children.[7] The children in this study were all around ten years old when we interviewed them. The study was based on volunteer samples from four very different kinds of schools in and around Leeds. One school was in a very deprived area of Leeds, another was a faith school (Jewish), a third was a middle-class, predominantly white school, and the last was a more heterogeneous school (in terms of social class and urban/rural mix) in a nearby market town. We were interested in how the children managed family change, and for the majority this change entailed their parents separating and/or divorcing, although there could be other reasons, such as a father being sent to prison.

One child's narrative has stayed with me ever since we carried out the research. We called her Miriam, and all the names in her story have been changed to protect anonymity. There are a number of fascinating elements to Miriam's narrative, but the essence which has remained with me has been the way in which she appears joyfully to dramatise some quite harrowing events. She is plainly angry with her parents (and grandparents) but seems not to lose a sense of herself and she clearly blames the adults in her life for their various misfortunes without appearing to feel diminished. Indeed she is an active agent throughout – within the limits of the scope she is structurally allowed.

Miriam and her younger brother used to live in a house built by her maternal grandfather on a twin plot where her grandparents had also built a house for themselves. Her parents' relationship deteriorated and her mother found herself a boyfriend and moved out. This meant that Miriam had to move too and change schools. She spent two weekends out of three back in her original home with her father. Her maternal grandparents moved away because they no longer wished to live so close to their son-in-law. Much of Miriam's story is taken up with living through the process of splitting up.

> When it first began, when they first started being horrible you know, um, they used to have fights all the time and they were ones where they used to be screaming at each other. So I once arranged for us to go to our grandma's. […] we used to live opposite each other. […] So you could just nip over in the middle of the

night. And I, I once arranged for me and Danny to go to my grandma's and stay over because I couldn't stand it. It was horrible.

I once left in the middle of the night. I just, um, I just took all my shoes. I had this Barbie swimming bag [...] so I just stuffed all my shoes in it. I didn't realise that it had a hole in the bottom; I just stuffed all my shoes in it. And I grabbed an overnight bag and everything. And I just ran across the garden because we used to have a step and then it was my garden and then on the other side it was my grandma's garden. And I used to just jump over the step and um, just run to Grandma's. And my dad came up to check on me apparently. [...] And they found like a shoe on the step. And then I was, and then he opened the door and he saw me because we have got a big lounge, a really, really big lounge and you can see out of the windows. And he saw me walking across with this trail of shoes behind me.

I used to stuff myself with chocolate as soon as I got to my grandma's, to forget about it and watch TV 'til about three o'clock in the morning.

(*Did you? So did that help you? Eating chocolate, did that help you to forget?*)

Yeah (*laughing*). I used to, and my grandma used to, say that was my ice cream and I had this big tub and she used to put 'Miriam's Ice Cream' on it. And [...] I just got my stool and grabbed the ice cream and I was just eating out of the ice cream [tub]. It was really good.

Miriam was a very vivid story teller who was able to turn most of her stories into vignettes in which she was the heroine. She was able to offer the most vivid descriptions of other people too. The two examples below will always stay with me:

And [Mum] sometimes slags off my dad because he has got a green Jaguar and she says it's an old man's car and stuff.

But it is major stress because my grandma is here and she is like completely into cleaning – she's like Mrs Muscle. She is there with her rubber gloves; she's in heaven with her cleaner and scrubbing brush. Strange thing is that Oliver's [the new boyfriend] mum is as well, so they are alike. [...] It was like a match made in heaven.

Miriam seems to have the ability to turn the key people in her life into characters who positively dance off the page. She turns the emotions of the events in her life into dramas which are enriched by the telling.

In the study, Miriam (but not Miriam alone) could depict an emotional roller-coaster where people and kin in her life were both liked and not liked, where events were dreadful yet also incredibly interesting – even funny (for example, she is desperate to hear the gossip on her dad's new girlfriend). She is angry about adults' bad behaviour (mum's boyfriend had the cheek to visit her at the former matrimonial home), yet she is defensive (her parents did not row *that* much). She would run to her maternal grandmother for comfort, but then run away from her when she 'slagged off' her father. She thinks that her parents separated because her father's business went 'broke', yet she also knows her mother started an affair with Oliver and she knows who introduced him to her. This is not a particularly happy story. Miriam may have developed an eating disorder (as did some other children we interviewed) and her brother was showing signs of having problems, particularly to do with controlling his anger. It is of course pointless to speculate – except that it is hard not to get involved with these lives and to start to have hopes and aspirations on behalf of Miriam precisely because she manages to touch one so forcefully.

For all these reasons Miriam's narrative has haunted me. I think it is because she comes across as a fighter, and her way of dealing with her situation is to call upon dramatic storylines almost akin to a style of soap opera. She allows one almost to live her experiences with her because she can speak of distress without becoming distressed. I do not cry when I read her tale as I have done over the accounts from other children; although her experiences are distressing, she does not break my heart because she does not assume the role of a victim or hapless legatee of her parents' and grandparents' behavioural bequests. Miriam, more than most children, was actively turning her life into a story, and this struck me as potentially empowering. In this case the research process seemed to offer her an opportunity of agency by allowing her to become the serious narrator of her own chronicle.

There is more to be found here than just a personal, emotional connection with this child. Her narrative speaks of power and powerlessness, of a specific class position, and of a close-knit, quite suffocating matrilocal family. She can be seen to be occupying different worlds, one with the adults in her life where she can almost be another adult or younger sister to her mother; and another with her grandmother and at school where she is still a child. Miriam's narrated life is a fragment of children's lives in England at the turn of the millennium. Her experiences are not uncommon, but they are also unique because of the specific combination of factors that surround her. Miriam's stories transport one to a place of complex relationships; she conjures up a childhood which is far from a popular idealised one but which evokes powerful insights into her life as it is lived. It does not matter that a year or a decade later she may see things very differently, or even that she might have forgotten much of her story. What matters is the immediacy of her narrative which carries the reader along to the extent that one can almost feel what she felt and can almost step into her shoes.

The issue for the sociologist becomes one of how to write with such a rich life narrative in a way which does not just describe it but which uses it insightfully and evocatively. In the next section I shall begin the process of laying down some tentative ideas about this process, and in so doing I return to what I regard as some important feminist/sociological roots.

Other people's lives

Sociology as a discipline has been much shaped by feminist thinking. This may seem an obvious point, but I am not referring so much to the theoretical or even political influence of feminism(s) but its more subtle ethico-methodological insights. At its very beginnings in British sociology, feminist work was strongly empirical. Undoubtedly this was driven by the desire to bring women into sociological view;

hence the numbers of books and articles written on subjects like women and work, women and crime, women and mental illness, or even just women in society. Even feminist theorising was grounded in the 'real' – most notably Dorothy Smith's thought-provoking piece on the relationship between theorising and women's domestic work, where she situated feminist thought in the daily activities (often caring activities) that women carry out.[8] In that paper she argued that feminist theory emerged from the position of women in the family, in the workplace, as mothers and so on. The idea of a free-floating intellectual was unthinkable in her schema because she argued that ideas were always anchored (initially at least) to a cultural and political place and space. Women, she argued, produced a different understanding of the world because of their position in it. She therefore began a tradition of standpoint feminism or simply grounded theorising and, even if few would totally agree with her argument now, it was immensely important because it gave a place to the everyday, the routine and interpersonal relationships in the development of sociological thinking. It also gave women a privileged position in sociological theorising because of their connection with mundane, everyday life. This was an important reversal of the status quo in terms of gender power in the academy, but it also provided a genuine bridge between the everyday world (which could be investigated empirically) and ways of seeing and comprehending.

For a while, in the United Kingdom at least, the pursuit of empirical research was a really important feature of feminist work. It was as if women were quite unknown and there was a real enthusiasm for simply discovering their lives and, from that baseline, developing new theories of power, exploitation, inequality and so on.[9] Ann Oakley pioneered a new kind of research strategy which gave feminist researchers permission to be affected by, or touched by, the women they met and interviewed.[10] This experience of being touched gave impetus to linking research with action to the extent that feminist researchers also became campaigners on behalf of women, using their research to fight for changes in law and policy.

However this enthusiasm began to wane in the 1990s: such work began to be experienced as theoretically limited precisely because it was perceived to be too rooted in what women did with all the restrictions that went with specificity of place, class, ethnicity and so on. There was a cultural turn in feminist work in which new forms of theorising became detached from empirical work.[11] Not all these newer ways of theorising could simply be harnessed to what was essentially traditional fieldwork. Cultural analysis in particular seemed to be more suited to analysis of media, images and texts than the everyday lives of women. A gap opened up between what seemed to be increasingly exciting theoretical work and more empirical and/or applied work.[12] Moreover, the more theoretical work seemed to have global appeal because it was not so embedded in the local or specific (even if one could claim that it was predominantly rooted in Western intellectual traditions). This more theoretically oriented work was also able to be much more poetic, metaphorical and evocative of the imagination than empirical work, which could at times seem so much more plodding, descriptive, repetitive and lacking in flair.

Here we come to a kind of paradox. As both a theoretical and an empirical sociologist I have been hugely influenced by theoretical arguments, particularly those that challenge one to think otherwise. At times the strong imaginary to be found in this writing frees one from rigid routines of thinking and requirements for apparently solid evidence. Zygmunt Bauman, working in a traditional social theoretical register, provides an example of such work:

> As long as it lives, love hovers on the brink of defeat. It dissolves its past as it goes; it leaves no fortified trenches behind to which it could retreat, running for shelter in case of trouble. And it knows not what lies ahead and what the future may bring. It will never gain confidence strong enough to disperse the clouds and stifle anxiety. Love is a mortgage loan drawn on an uncertain, and inscrutable, future.[13]

Bauman may not be a typical social theorist of course, but still the scope and impressiveness of the writing of thinkers like Michel Foucault, Karl Marx or Stuart Hall surely change how we think while also engaging the reader powerfully. Nisbet[14] has made a similar point in relation to the work of nineteenth-century sociologists who drew sketches of vast social landscapes, and immense panoramas of social change. They wrote of utopias and dystopias and created sociological portraits and characters (for example the lumpenproletariat, the Protestant Ethic, the bureaucrat). Such conceptualisations helped to frame understandings of the modern world and grabbed the imagination of generations of readers. But, notwithstanding the value of these experiences of intellectual elation, what has affected me most and has kept me committed to the enterprise of sociology has been the way in which empirical work has connected me to the lives of people I would never have encountered had I not engaged in fieldwork. To put it even more starkly, without all those lives peopling my intellectual universe, it would have felt rather pointless, esoteric and abstract. No matter how brief or faltering this connection with other lives might be, it too sets in motion a form of transformation. I would argue that encountering lives which are lived differently, and enquiring of people about their world views, transforms understanding just as much as theoretical thinking can. Connecting with people through research is not the same as meeting neighbours or colleagues, because one is put into a specific kind of relationship and this brings with it a responsibility to that person to try to understand their world and to listen questioningly but without judgement. This is emphatically not to say that doing this kind of empirical research (based, for example, on talking with people) puts you in touch with a simple and readily accessible reality; none of us can be so naive as to argue that. But I do want to suggest that it transports one *somewhere*.

The research encounter is fascinating because, if you are sufficiently open, it is possible to step through into another world. As it does for the hero William Parry in Philip Pullman's *The Subtle Knife*, it can feel like finding a parallel universe:

> It looked as if someone had cut a patch out of the air [...] If you were level with the patch so that it was edge-on, it was nearly invisible, and it was completely invisible from behind. You could only see it from the side nearest the road, and

you couldn't see it easily even from there, because all you could see through it was exactly the same kind of thing that lay in front of it on this side; a patch of grass lit by a street light. But Will knew without the slightest doubt that that patch of grass on the other side was in a different world. [...] And for that reason alone, it enticed him to stop and look further. What he saw made his head swim and his heart thump harder, but he didn't hesitate: he pushed his shopping bag through, and then scrambled through himself, through the hole in the fabric of this world and into another.[15]

One is constantly crossing through into this other place, which is entirely familiar at first glance but is sufficiently different to be disconcerting and unsettling because, in this other world, people's lives are profoundly different. These unsettling experiences mean that one never quite knows what to expect in doing research; some things or people who appear to be resolutely ordinary are indeed just so, but others are not. And, ordinariness itself is challenged since it too has its uniqueness and fascination. This 'stepping through' brings about a general degree of attentiveness to others, and of course within that heightened attentiveness some lives will impress themselves upon one more than others. Thus in the course of many empirical projects, some of these lives have left me with accumulations of attentiveness or perhaps what Eva Hoffman would call the 'cargo of knowledge'.[16] Thus empirical research may carry a cargo of people's lives which can pop into consciousness unbidden and which become part of the sedimentation of memory.

This cargo of knowledge is part of making the sociological imagination.[17] It is the inevitable result of following the invitation offered by Les Back, and others, of truly listening to people and taking trouble to imagine as fully as possible their multi-dimensional lives.

> The art of listening to the world, where we take the people we listen to as seriously as we take ourselves, is perhaps the most important quality that sociology can offer today'.[18]

Thus listening produces a capacity for sensitivity and attentiveness.

The repeated hearing of accounts of these ordinary lives produces layers of voices which deposit themselves in uneven ways to create a particular kind of methodological orientation. This is in part theoretical, but it also derives from accessing the experiences of others. So there is an interplay between stepping through into these other worlds of other people's lives and having these lives trigger theoretical understandings which may be based on existing sociological theories but which, I would argue, always need to be pushed further. As Beverley Skeggs has discussed in relation to her encounter with women's experiences during her PhD research, she made the mistake of trying to interpret their lives through her pre-existing frameworks:

> This led me at times to map my frameworks directly onto their [women's] experiences without listening to or hearing what they were saying ... It was a production of my desperateness to understand the infinite number of things that were happening around me that led to this lapse in reflexivity.[19]

Touching lives is therefore potentially transformatory but the issue is how to make this transformation more than simply personal and into something of wider significance.

This, of course, can be construed as familiar territory. The researcher goes out and collects 'data', then has to transform them into a narrative. But the point about Skeggs' remark is that there is an easy way to do this, and a harder way. The harder way entails working with the knowledge gleaned from getting close to other people's lives; not fitting their lives into a pre-existing understanding. This may sound relatively straightforward, but there is inevitably a disjuncture between how people tell their lives from within the cultural, chronological, economic and social context in which they live, and the sociological imperative to be meta-attentive to these contexts. This is part, I think, of what Les Back is getting at when he asks us to listen attentively to people's accounts. However, the process of transforming a sociological understanding through listening still remains something of a mysterious 'black box'. We could just say it is the enigmatic workings of the sociological imagination where we know the component parts but where the outcome is always more than the sum of these parts. Wherein resides that extra element?

I have looked to answering part of this question of transformation and knowledge production, in the process of writing, and this is where Avery Gordon reappears. Gordon's argument that sociology is a mode of 'conjuring up' social life and that sociologists are in fact storytellers seems to me to give a clue to how one can bridge the often wide gap between the engaging metaphors and compelling accounts to be found in some social theory and the often more earth-bound or descriptive accounts found in more empirically based work. In the final section I shall consider some of issues of storytelling for sociologists.

Writing otherwise?

To conclude, I hope to show how it is that sociology needs to engage with the project of *Writing Otherwise*. The point is to find ways to make the personal lives of the people one encounters in doing research much more multi-dimensional and layered, but equally vivid and evocative. It is also to encourage the theorisation of their lives to be more enigmatic, more absorbing and more able to engage the reader in the kinds of understandings one is trying to create. At the same time it is important to imagine the people one writes about reading these accounts, not because they actually will do so, but as a kind of theoretical and ethical check on too much allegorical exuberance. In other words one must stay grounded. It is important to think of layers of meaning in one's writing which fold into one another, as this can allow one to express different things in different moments in the text. Hence it becomes possible to mix different aspects of a created understanding, not quite as a collage but as a series of interlinking ideas. The point is not to become too avant-garde and impenetrable, since the aim is to involve the reader not to alienate him or her, and to create a readable, accessible story.

I only thought of sociologists as storytellers when I read Avery Gordon's book. As I note above, she was critical of sociology for failing to capture the complexities of life and for writing in a way that eliminated issues that were hard to express. Her argument is that sociology is impoverished if it is unable to represent the unseen and unsayable as well as the seen and spoken of. Further, she suggests that sociology needs to be much more reflexive about its role as storyteller. No matter what kind of social account we are presenting to the world, nor in what form (written or spoken), we are still storytellers. The stories we tell may be evidence-based but, Gordon argues, they are still stories about the social world. Collectively we tell stories about social class, about how gender inequality works, about patterns of migration, about the influence of the media and much more. We are constantly telling stories about how societies work.

> Sociology, in particular, has an extraordinary mandate as far as academic disciplines go: to conjure up social life. [...] As a mode of apprehension and reformation, conjuring merges the analytical, the procedural, the imaginative, and the effervescent. But we have more to learn about how to conjure in an evocative and compelling way.[20]

Once we think of ourselves as storytellers (though not as fiction writers), it is possible to begin to think about the form and structure of the stories that are told. Hence it becomes important to think about the quality, style, energy and fluency of such writing. This might entail questions about whether to deploy some of the sorts of literary and stylistic devices used by novelists and other writers. It raises issues too of whether empirical research deliberates enough about the use of metaphor, imagery, language and style in general. If sociology is charged with 'conjuring up social life' it does seem important to consider how this might be done while remaining in some senses true to the discipline and the constraints of writing with data.

Gordon is, of course, arguing that sociologists have been engaged in acts of conjuring up social life in perpetuity. The problem is that this conjuring has occurred either without a sufficient sensibility as to the impact of such writing or with a kind of assumption that writing according to disciplinary guidelines absolves one of responsibilities for any discursive consequences. She is critical of this lack of reflexivity and a kind of naivety in sociological writing. In a way this writing presents itself as if it simply represents what has been 'found'. It is as if writing needs only to meet the demands of quasi-scientific templates laid down by generations of social science journal editors and not the requirements of literary merit. This may be because writing within the discipline insists that at the stage of publication a specific kind of coherence and order is required. In particular, there is an assumption that a linear story should be constructed and that the conclusion should be a concise summation of what has gone before. It is rarely assumed (in the mainstream) that the literary journey en route to the conclusion is the most important part of a piece of writing. Moreover, there are strong assumptions that sociological writing should take as it primary audience the discipline itself. Thus peer reviewers are guardians of the standards of the discipline, not guardians of the quality of writing. Forms of writing which may adopt several stances (which reflect the multiple realities of the lived world) may be seen either as confused or as failing the task of engaging with the data in a *proper* way.

Finally I return to the issue of taking writing otherwise forward. It seems unlikely that empirical sociologists can abandon all of the traditions of academic writing that have become established. I am not even sure that it would be a good idea, as it is important to be able to write differently for different audiences and for different purposes. But the over-determination of sociological writing squeezes out other ways of conjuring social life and certainly can be said to crush the effervescence and evocativeness of which Gordon speaks. By effervescence she means that writing should be vivacious and enthusiastic, while evocative entails conjuring up strong images, memories or feelings. Nisbet also argued that sociological writing requires elegance and illumination rather than endless, dulling literalness. Finally, Wright Mills argued that there is a need to be aware of different reading publics and hence the requirement to craft writing differently for different audiences. Given the closeness to other people's lives and lived experiences that sociology affords, it seems positively irresponsible of the discipline to continue to ignore or shun the potential residing there.

Notes

1 Avery Gordon, *Ghostly Matters: Haunting and the Sociological Imagination.*
2 Janice Radway in *Ibid.*, p. viii.
3 Ken Plummer, *Documents of Life 2: An Invitation to a Critical Humanism.*
4 C. Wright Mills, *The Sociological Imagination.*
5 Michael Rustin, 'Reflections on the biographical turn in social science'.
6 For example, concepts such as Capitalism, Globalisation, or Cosmopolitanism; see *Critical Sociology*, 38:3 (May 2012), in particular David Fasenfest, 'Globalization and its discontents', pp. 343–6.
7 Amanda Wade and Carol Smart, *Facing Family Change: Children's Circumstances, Strategies and Resources.*
8 Dorothy Smith, *The Everyday as Problematic: A Feminist Sociology.*
9 For example Christine Delphy and Diana Leonard, *Familiar Exploitation.*
10 Ann Oakley, *The Sociology of Housework.*
11 Michèle Barrett, 'Words and things: materialism and method in contemporary feminist analysis'.
12 For example, Judith Butler, *Gender Trouble: Feminism and the Subversion of Identity*; Judith Halberstam, *Female Masculinity*; Iris Marion Young, *Intersecting Voices.*
13 Zygmunt Bauman, *Liquid Love*, p. 8.
14 Robert Nisbet, *Sociology as an Art Form.*
15 Philip Pullman, *The Subtle Knife*, pp. 15–16.
16 Eva Hoffman, *After Such Knowledge*, p. 33.
17 Mills, *The Sociological Imagination.*
18 Les Back, *The Art of Listening*, p. 176.
19 Beverley Skeggs, *Formations of Class and Gender*, p. 31.
20 Gordon, *Ghostly Matters*, p. 22.

Bibliography

Back, Les, *The Art of Listening* (Oxford: Berg, 2007).

Barrett, Michèle, 'Words and things: materialism and method in contemporary feminist analysis', in Michèle Barrett and Anne Phillips (eds), *Destabilizing Theory* (Cambridge: Polity, 1992).

Bauman, Zygmunt, *Liquid Love* (Cambridge: Polity, 2003).

Butler, Judith, *Gender Trouble: Feminism and the Subversion of Identity* (London: Routledge, 1990).

Delphy, Christine, and Diana Leonard, *Familiar Exploitation* (Cambridge: Polity, 1992).

Fasenfest, David, 'Globalization and its discontents', *Critical Sociology*, 38:3 (May 2012), 343-46.

Fasenfest, David (ed.), *Critical Sociology*, 38:3 (May 2012), 343–457.

Gordon, Avery, *Ghostly Matters: Haunting and the Sociological Imagination* (second edition) (Minneapolis, MN, and London: University of Minnesota Press, 2008).

Halberstam, Judith, *Female Masculinity* (London: Duke University Press, 1998).

Hoffman, Eva, *After Such Knowledge* (London: Vintage, 2005).

Mills, C. Wright, *The Sociological Imagination* (London: Oxford University Press, 1967 [1959]).

Nisbet, Robert, *Sociology as an Art Form* (London: Heineman, 1976).

Oakley, Ann, *The Sociology of Housework* (Oxford: Martin Robertson, 1974).

Plummer, Ken, *Documents of Life 2: An Invitation to a Critical Humanism* (London: Sage, 2001).

Pullman, Philip, *The Subtle Knife* (London: Scholastic Children's Books, 1997).

Rustin, Michael, 'Reflections on the biographical turn in social science', in Prue Chamberlayne, Joanna Bornat and Tom Wengraf (eds), *The Turn to Biographical Methods in Social Science* (London: Routledge, 2000).

Skeggs, Beverley, *Formations of Class and Gender* (London: Sage, 2001).

Smith, Dorothy, *The Everyday as Problematic: A Feminist Sociology* (Chicago, IL: Northeastern University Press, 1988).

Wade, Amanda, and Carol Smart, *Facing Family Change: Children's Circumstances, Strategies and Resources* (York: York Publishing Services for the Joseph Rowntree Foundation, 2002).

Young, Iris Marion, *Intersecting Voices* (Princeton, NJ: Princeton University Press, 1997).

II
Displacements

Atlantic moves

Janet Wolff

We have traveled quite a distance, but we never had so poor a day of it as to-day. It was the only day of our trip that we didn't enjoy the traveling. We got on a train at 4 p.m. and were supposed to reach Manchester at 8. Twice we had to change trains and each time you got to go and look up your train and see that it's taken out. It's a nuisance. To make matters worse, we had nothing to eat all day but a couple of ham sandwiches and some cold chicken which though historic (for it was brought up probably in the time of Shakespeare), was not very digestible. Of course the train was late and we got into Manchester at 9.15. Luckily, Maurice, knowing how punctual English trains are, did not get discouraged, and waited for us. It was a relief to get settled down at last, and an indescribable pleasure to come amongst friends after six weeks of hotel life. And here we saw friends I hadn't seen for nineteen years and most of whom I couldn't even recall. It was a reunion indeed and everyone was happy that we were able to meet. We remained at the home of our cousin, Israel, and he and his wife were very nice to us and went out of the way to accom[m]odate us. It was a relief to feel among your own, with your own flesh and blood and to know that people were nice to you not because they hoped or worked for a tip, but because they loved you and were a part of you. We staid up late to-night till 1 a.m. and some of the other cousins came over, Ely and his wife and Dora and we talked of old times and present times and future times and when we retired, a sleep of rest and contentment enveloped us.

(Travel diary of Henry Norr, 1909)

Henry Norr, born in St Petersburg in 1880, moved to the United States with his family (parents and two sisters) in about 1891. His father, Jacob Norr, was a tailor, who also established himself in the real estate business in New York. His mother, Dina, was a wig-maker for orthodox Jewish women. Henry went to City College, became a secondary-school teacher and, in 1926, took the post of principal of Evander Childs High School in the Bronx. His obituary in *The New York Times* in 1934, on his early death of a heart attack at the age of 53, quotes the new City Superintendent of Schools, Harold G. Campbell, as saying that 'Mr. Norr was one of the best high school principals in the City of New York. In spite of an innate modesty and a retiring disposition, he was one of the most forceful characters in secondary education... His going leaves a great void in our secondary schools which it will be difficult to fill'. (Mr Campbell also offers another compliment, which would today perhaps have been worded a little differently: 'He had a genius for handling boys and girls'.)

In 1909, Henry married Minnie Gold. The travel diary is the detailed hand-written account of their honeymoon trip in Europe, in the course of which the couple visited the English branch of the Norr family (whose spelling of the name was 'Noar'). Jacob's oldest brother, Joseph, had emigrated to England in 1886, and worked as a tailor in Manchester. Israel, Eli, Dora and Maurice – mentioned in Henry's diary – were four of Joseph's seven children. Maurice Noar was my maternal grandfather. He came to England as an infant, and would have been about twenty-four when he met his American cousin at the railway station in 1909.

It was Henry's son, David Norr, who showed me the diary in December 2003, at his house in Scarsdale, New York. I took the train from New York on a very snowy day, and he met me at the station to take me for lunch at home with his wife, Carol. It snowed all afternoon, so much that we weren't sure if I would be able to get a taxi back to the station that day. I had never met David Norr before. In fact, I had never heard of him until a couple of months earlier, when a cousin of my mother's in Manchester, who had kept in touch with the American relatives, urged me to see him while I was still living in New York. He was eighty years old at the time of my visit – still active as a financial analyst, and keen to discuss family history with me. Later he sent me photocopies of the 'Manchester' pages of his father's diary.

Our Honeymoon Trip.

to

Europe.

July 3rd, 1909 ———— September

Foreword.

The following pages are intended to give a brief account of the daily events in the course of the trip to and from Europe. Being written in the course of a rather hurried journey when time was very precious, no attempt at style was made; nor was there any attempt to give detailed descriptions of places of interest or detailed accounts of the impressions these places made upon the writer. The former may easily be found in various Guide-Books; the latter, unfortunately, must be left incomplete at present. All that was attempted to convey in the following pages was a narrative in brief form of the principal events that transpired and the chief impressions made, so as to serve as an everlasting memorial of this most memorable trip.

August 17th

The day is a dull and threatening one and the atmosphere is murky. But here in Manchester it is considered a fair day indeed, for rain and fog is the average lot of Manchestrians.

The city's main industry is cotton goods manufacturing and there are a great many mills here. The smoke of the chimneys together with the usual foggy atmosphere, casts a sort of mist about the city that blackens all the buildings, and the black and gray stone of London here become almost coal-black.

We are barely into the Manchester visit, and I am already getting defensive, and a bit irritated with the tone. Of course he is right, both about the weather and about the colour of Manchester buildings (though not about the inhabitants, who are of course Mancunians). Before the Clean Air Act of 1956, and the decline of industry, the pale stone was usually black with soot, and the air was often filthy. We sometimes had to walk home from school wearing smog masks. Still, the tone seems, to me, a bit condescending. It continues:

August 18th

This is an ideal Manchester day – that is, pouring all day.

Then there are the English eating – and drinking – habits to comment on, only partly affectionately:

Living with folks who have become Anglicized, we can get a pretty good idea of the English workman's home life. We were surprised to find how many times a day the people eat here. Breakfast, Lunch at 12, Tea (a meal with it) at 6, Supper at 9 and a light meal before retiring. They tell us this is the regular custom here

August 18th.

This is an ideal Manchester day – that is, pouring all day. There is no fog, but a light mist envelops the city all the time – rain or shine. We were unable to do very much because of the bad weather, but in the afternoon it cleared up and Maurice and Rajer who came to see us this afternoon, took us for a walk in the outlying sections of the city, Salford, as it is called. Here you can see some fairly good homes and quiet streets. We also saw the Cricket Grounds and the Race track. The English, following the example of their illustrious Ruler, are lovers of horses in general and of betting in particular and the race-track is an institution of the town.

Living with folks who have become Anglicized, we can get a pretty good idea of the English workman's home life. We were surprised to find how many times a day the people eat here. Breakfast, Lunch at 12, Tea (a meal with it) at 6, Supper at 9 and a light meal before retiring. They tell us this is the regular custom here but perhaps in their attempts to treat us well, they try to overfeed us. Another thing that surprised us is the way the English drink – whisky and beer. Everyonce in a while you take a drink. And the women and even the children drink too. It seems strange to us to hear one woman (the hostess) say to her guest, "Have a whisky." But then the English have a reputation that way.

To-night we went to Ely's house and we were again well received and again we were up till midnight. We are not keeping the early hours we did on the Continent but then we are getting up late and we have nothing to do all day.

but perhaps in their attempts to treat us well, they try to overfeed us. Another thing that surprised me is the way the English drink – whisky and beer. Every once in a while, you take a drink. And the women and even the children drink too. It seems strange to hear one woman (the hostess) say to her guest, 'Have a whisky?'. But then the English have a reputation that way.

There is a rather poignant counter to this expression of American puritanism. Here is the point of view of the English Noars, from a family history compiled in 1998, recalling Henry Norr's honeymoon trip:

He got the English cousins quite wrong as a bunch of drunkards, because wherever he visited, out came the Whisky bottle: little did he realize that it took a visit such as theirs before strong drink was taken.

> Supper at 9 and a light meal before retiring. They tell us
> this is the regular custom here but perhaps in their attempt
> to treat us well, they try to overfeed us. Another thing
> that surprised me is the way the English drink – whiskey and
> beer. Every once in a while you take a drink. And the
> women and even the children drink too. It seems strange
> to us to hear one woman (the hostess) say to her guest, "Have
> a whisky!" But then the English have a reputation that way.

Still, apart from a few more such asides, this is a wonderful document, with descriptions of family members, accounts of walks round the city, a trip to the Manchester Hippodrome, a visit to Bolton to see another cousin. The handwriting is beautiful, and the thoughts of a young visitor to Europe just over a hundred years ago never less than fascinating to read. In particular, it seemed important for once to be somehow in touch with my mother's family history. For a number of years it had been my father's life, in Germany in the 1930s and as a refugee in England, interned for a year in the Isle of Man, that had preoccupied me. On my mother's side, the dramas of persecution and flight were less immediate, a pre-history to her own life and experience. Even her parents were small children when anti-semitic pogroms in eastern Europe obliged the families to travel west. Now I began to see both how interesting these lives had been and how the memory of forced exile persists through the generations. Although I have some resistance to the notion of 'second generation' Holocaust survivors (that is their children, assumed to inherit their trauma at one remove), I am entirely persuaded by Marianne Hirsch's notion of 'postmemory'.

> Postmemory characterizes the experience of those who grow up dominated by narratives that preceded their birth, whose own belated stories are evacuated by the stories of the previous generation shaped by traumatic events that can be neither understood nor recreated.[1]

I have come to understand that this inheritance can have a longer trajectory, across more than one generation. Mary Cappello has written movingly about the 'ways that we inherit the pain or deformation caused by the material or laboring conditions of our forbears', linking her own chest pains to those of both her father and her grandfather.[2] In her case, the inherited injury – actual and psychic – related to the poverty and shame of earlier generations. As I read about Ashkenazi Jews in north Manchester in the twentieth century, and recalled visiting my own relatives as a child, I began to grasp the idea of the transmission of fear, caution and suspicion, even decades after the event. The children of those immigrants from eastern Europe retained, and in turn passed on to their own children, the unarticulated but painful recollection of persecution. What Anne Karpf has referred to as 'the war after' is one fought by Jews of east European origins as well as refugees from Nazism.[3] My mother as well as my father.

Left: Mark Gertler, photographed by Lady Ottoline Morrell
Right: Leland Bell: Standing self portrait

It was also from David Norr that I learned that one of the American cousins – Harris Norr, also known as Swifty Morgan – who made a living as a professional card player on transatlantic liners, may have been the model for Damon Runyon's character, the 'lemon drop kid'. Also cause for reflection was the fact that, while I had been developing my personal and academic interest in the English-Jewish artist Mark Gertler, largely on the grounds that he may have been a distant relative of my maternal grandmother – Rebecca Gertler, wife of Maurice Noar – I now discovered I had a bona fide, rather famous artist cousin in the United States. This was Leland Bell, nephew of Harris Norr and second cousin of Henry Norr. All of this has been especially interesting to me recently, since my return to England after eighteen years in the United States, and as I continue to rethink (and rewrite) my own stories about the two countries.

It seems to me now to be so transparent, the rewriting of narratives at different stages of life. Today, I seem inclined to take England's side against any criticism (especially, perhaps, by an American). But not so long ago I put quite a bit of energy into my own demonising of England – the other side of my idealising of 'America', perhaps. In 1976, my father wrote a short memoir of his own, reflecting on his experiences in Germany in the 1930s, recording the increasing processes of Aryanisation that he confronted in his work as a chemist, and the growing isolation in his everyday life. Towards the end, he expresses his gratitude to Britain:

'THANK-YOU BRITAIN' FUND

6, Fairfax Mansions, London, N.W.3

[letter reproduction, left column]

A. Wolff Esq.,
41, Pine Road,
Didsbury,
Manchester, 20.

20th August 1964.

Dear Friend,

    Some months ago you were good enough to promise support for an act of collective gratitude by all the refugees from Central Europe who have made their home in this country.

    This seems to be a good moment to count our blessings. Already a new generation is growing up among us to whom the word "Kristallnacht" is as unfamiliar as the terror it held.

    Now, therefore, is the time to act.

    The 'Thank-You Britain' Fund has been formed to give practical expression to the gratitude we own. The money collected – we hope to raise between £50,000 and £60,000 – will be invested to create a perpetual income for the benefit of British scholarship and research. The British Academy, which is to the Humanities what the Royal Society is to the Sciences, has agreed to administer this income as the 'Thank-You Britain' Research Award and periodically to choose suitable candidates for one or more research posts to be attached to a British university. The research will concern itself with the broad field of Human Studies, preferably having a bearing on the welfare of the people of this country. There will also be an annual public lecture on a related subject.

    Here is a permanent, direct and useful way in which we can respond to a genuine need in this country today, and do so in a way which befits the events we intend to commemorate.

THANK YOU BRITAIN.

[letter reproduction, right column]

By virtue of the power vested in me by the Secretary of State contained in Home Office letter dated 31st May, 1940, reference Gen. 200/110/5, I hereby authorise the arrest and internment of ____ Arthur ____ WOLFF ____ of ____ German ____ nationality, Police Registration Certificate No. 631582, at present residing at ____ No. 30, Snowdon Road, Eccles, Lancs., ____ and that he be handed over to the Military Authorities.

CHIEF CONSTABLE OF LANCASHIRE.

County Chief Constable's Office,
PRESTON, 11th June, 1940.

It is too often forgotten, how much we owe the British Government of the day, who, with the help of Jewish and other British organisations, in which people like Eleanor Rathbone played a leading part, saved tens of thousands of Nazi victims, when all the other countries refused to do anything.

I was glad, therefore, when a few years ago some of those who managed to start a new and successful life here launched a 'Thank-You-Britain Fund', which soon raised about fifty thousand pounds for a scholarship now administered by the British Academy. Its income is used to finance University scholarships in the field of Human Studies, particularly the welfare of people of this country.

Ten years later, though I don't think I ever discussed this with him, I was immersing myself in another point of view, reading the growing literature on England's own history of anti-semitism and following David Cesarani's account of Britain's rather more compromised activities in the mid-twentieth century (including the post-war acceptance of Nazi war criminals into the country).[4] I learned that the internment of aliens in 1940 (about which my father, who spent over a year in an internment camp, had nothing critical to say) was in fact an outrage.[5]

I read (and also wrote) about the earlier resistance to Jewish immigration to Britain, culminating in the 1905 Aliens Act.[6] In relation to my work on Mark Gertler and other Jewish artists in Britain, I read the work of historians, literary critics and art historians who exposed the ideologies of 'Englishness' (rural, southern, class-bound) across a wide range of texts and discourses. I even read John Osborne's *Damn You England*, before realising that there were probably limits to the allies I should be rounding up in the case I seemed to need to make.[7] Obviously there was a real personal, and psychic, investment here. It clearly wasn't as simple as a critique of Thatcherite Britain, or disappointment in the 1980s decline of higher education in England. Or even the weather.

The culmination of my narrative – the idea I had that, somehow, I needed to leave England to save my life – was an event that allowed me to conclude that this was literally true. England tried to kill me, and America saved me. In the spring of 1990, when I had been living in California for about eighteen months, a routine physical examination showed that I had thyroid cancer. Surgery (a thyroidectomy) further revealed that the cancer was already in one lymph node. There was, and is, no such thing as a routine physical exam in England, and since I had no symptoms, I could only conclude that it would likely have been too late by the time the cancer was discovered, had I still been living in England. Then I read Marilynne Robinson's 1989 book, *Mother Country*, and realised that England had *given* me the cancer in the first place. Robinson's book indicts the Sellafield nuclear processing plant, in the English Lake District, in the contamination of the environment and the British government for its criminal negligence with regard to safety laws and procedures. According to Robinson, 'Sellafield is the world's largest source of radioactive contamination'.[8] She offers this startling contrast:

> The release of radiation from Three Mile Island is usually estimated at between fifteen and twenty-five curies of radioactive iodine. Many hundreds of thousands of curies of radioactivity have entered the environment each year through Sellafield's pipeline and its stacks, in the course of the plant's routine functioning. In other words, Three Mile Island was a modest event by the standards of Sellafield.[9]

Robinson's well-documented study maintains that, through 'about three hundred accidents, including a core fire in 1957 which was, before Chernobyl, the most serious accident to occur in a nuclear reactor',[10] a large number of cancers were produced in populations within a certain range of the site. In 1957, when the accident and radiation leak occurred, I was fourteen years old and living in Manchester, less than a hundred miles from Sellafield. It is true that Robinson focuses more on leukaemia than on thyroid cancer, and that the most striking incidence of these cancers seems (despite the direction of prevailing winds and the jet stream) to have been in Ireland. Nevertheless, thyroid cancer (which she does also discuss) is known to be caused by exposure to radioactivity, especially in children. And Robinson makes this comment:

> The use of Cumbrian lakes as reservoirs for cities sheds an interesting light on the practice of expressing cancer rates as multiples of regional or national rates. The runoff from the mountains would surely concentrate contaminants in the drinking water of large populations. The nearness of Sellafield to Manchester and Liverpool is seldom alluded to, but there are hundreds of thousands of people living within the range of its effects.[11]

The origins of the Sellafield nuclear plant – originally, and at the time of the 1957 accident, called Windscale – lie in another British-American story. Indeed, the catastrophic failure of the reactor can fairly be described as a direct outcome of a critical trans-Atlantic event. The 1943 Quebec Agreement between Churchill and Roosevelt had promised British involvement in the Manhattan Project and the United States nuclear programme; many British scientists worked at the atomic bomb laboratory in Los Alamos.[12] The following year, another agreement confirmed Anglo-American co-operation after the war. But in 1946, by which time Churchill and Roosevelt had been replaced by Atlee and Truman, the U.S. Congress passed the Atomic Energy Act (known as the McMahon Act), which prohibited the passing of classified atomic energy to foreign countries.[13] As Lorna Arnold records: 'Britain felt entitled to post-war atomic status and was not prepared to leave the atomic monopoly in American hands. She was determined to create a successful national project both for its own sake and as a powerful lever to gain renewed Anglo-American collaboration'.[14] The consequence was an urgent, and incredibly fast, programme of building and implementation, by-passing any stage of pilot plants. The first weapon test, as a result, took place in 1952. Windscale was established in 1947 and operational two years later. Although Arnold acknowledges the two production piles which constituted Windscale as 'an extraordinary technological achievement for their time'[15], she itemises the causes of the disaster, apparent in retrospect:

> There were failures of knowledge and research … The piles were used for purposes not envisaged when they were designed and lacked adequate instrumentation. There were deficiencies in staffing, organization, management and communications. The whole project was overloaded with too many urgent and competing demands – to expand and extend military production, develop new reactor types, and support an arguably over-ambitious civil power programme.[16]

Reluctance to publish the full findings of the initial inquiry into the accident also had to do with Anglo-American relations: Harold Macmillan, then Prime Minister, did not want to give the Americans any reason to continue to block collaboration on military applications of atomic energy.[17] His diary note for 30 October 1957 records this concern:

The problem remains, how are we to deal with Sir W Penney's report? It has, of course, been prepared with scrupulous honesty and even ruthlessness ... But to publish to the world (especially the Americans) is another thing. The publication of the report, as it stands, might put in jeopardy our chance of getting Congress to agree to the President's proposal.[18]

Even in full that report, published only twenty days after the event, down-played the problems and actual effects of the radiation leak. It identified no danger from irradiation or inhalation, and considered the small risk of contamination by ingestion (mainly through milk) minimal, and satisfactorily dealt with. Marilynne Robinson's outrage was about what she saw as a gross understatement of risk and actual harm, and at the time of publication of her book she was challenged on this.[19] The fiftieth anniversary of the accident prompted further thought, with the benefit of new scientific and metereological research, including the recognition that there were likely to have been more cases of cancer attributable to the leak.[20] Even so, the numbers are small – perhaps 240 rather than 200 cancers (thyroid and breast cancer and leukaemia). And this news cannot help me pin down the blame for my own case:

'Several dozen more cancer cases may have to be added to our total', said epidemiologist Professor Richard Wakeford, of Manchester University. However, Wakeford said it was impossible to determine which individual cancer cases might be linked to the incident at Windscale, now called Sellafield. 'We can only say an excess in cancer cases was caused by the fire'.[21]

After all, some of those most closely involved in the event don't seem to need to create a drama of it, even with benefit of hindsight. Marjorie Higham, a chemist at Sellafield, recalls the event:

I remember the fire, of course. At the time I had a motorbike, this is before I was married. I was going in and out on this motorbike and of course I was wearing a crash hat. I went to Seascale and then along the railway, there's a track between the railway and the sea which we called the cinder track.

I knew something had gone wrong, but then things did go wrong, so you just don't take any notice. The less you know about it, the less you can tell somebody else. This day I'd got to the building where I worked and I was stopped at the door by the foreman of the industrials, who said, 'If you come in you can't go out.' By this time the plant was being shut down, but nobody had said anything, no notes put down. They'd been trying to keep it quiet for three days. It started on the Wednesday and this would be the Friday. Don't forget we'd been brought up during the war and you accepted things more.[22]

Neville Ramsden acted just as coolly, having been told 'Ey-up, lads, there's smoke coming out the pile chimney!' As he says, he realised then that the situation was 'obviously, not right'. He went home as usual, and went to the cinema, as Thursday was film night.[23]

⋯⋯

The point is, though, that this was a story I could tell myself, as both a metaphoric and a literal proof of the need to emigrate. The other side of it – the desire for 'America' as the playing-out of a teenage fantasy of 1950s rock music and American movies – I had always known; I wrote a bit about this in essays on Eddie Cochran, and on England in the 1950s, in my book *Resident Alien*.[24] It just took me thirty years to manage to follow up on it, finally moving to the States in 1988. It was on the point of returning in 2006 (not just to England, but specifically to Manchester) that I found I was willing to rewrite the story. What if the cancer only started in the States? If stress is a possible cause of cancer, then it seems quite likely. My first two years there, when I lived in northern California, contained a rather large quota of stressful events, including the following: the unexpected death of my mother three months after I left England (my father died almost exactly two years later); being in a 7.1 earthquake (Loma Prieta, October 1989, when I was teaching in Santa Cruz, only ten miles from the epicentre); a diagnosis of an ovarian tumour (a week later found to be a misdiagnosis); anxiety about money, since, for the first and only time in my life, I was freelancing and not getting a monthly salary (on leave from my job at the University of Leeds, and spending a couple of years as a peripatetic academic); travelling to too many visiting appointments; involvement in the custody battles of the person I was living with in California. And (not so trivial) living in the least beautiful apartment I've ever had. Is it time to blame everything on America instead?

⚬—⚬

At about the time of my revisionist thoughts, I reread Richard Hoggart's account of his time in the United States. By coincidence, he spent this year (1956–57) at the University of Rochester, where I taught for a decade, after I left California. Earlier, and just over ten years after his stay in the United States, I knew him for a while at the University of Birmingham, where I was a postgraduate student in sociology, spending most of my time at the Centre for Contemporary Cultural Studies, which he directed and had founded in 1964. It was during his year as a visiting professor in Rochester that his ground-breaking book *The Uses of Literacy* – the primary inspiration for the Centre's founding – was published in England.[25]

For Hoggart, it was a year off, with his wife and three young children, from his job teaching in the extra-mural department at the University of Hull. I am struck by a number of things in his appealing narrative. In some ways, the city he describes, looking back on the 1950s from the late 1980s, is very much like the one I lived in through the 1990s:

> Rochester – and I can speak only of the Rochester we saw just over thirty years ago – has the friendliness of a medium-sized city which cannot and does not wish to think of itself as an exciting metropolis; it believes it has more of a community spirit and is safer; it is sensitive to being looked down on by people from the great aggregations, and secretly knows it has better ideas about what makes for a good life: space for private and public gardens (it calls itself the Lilac City),

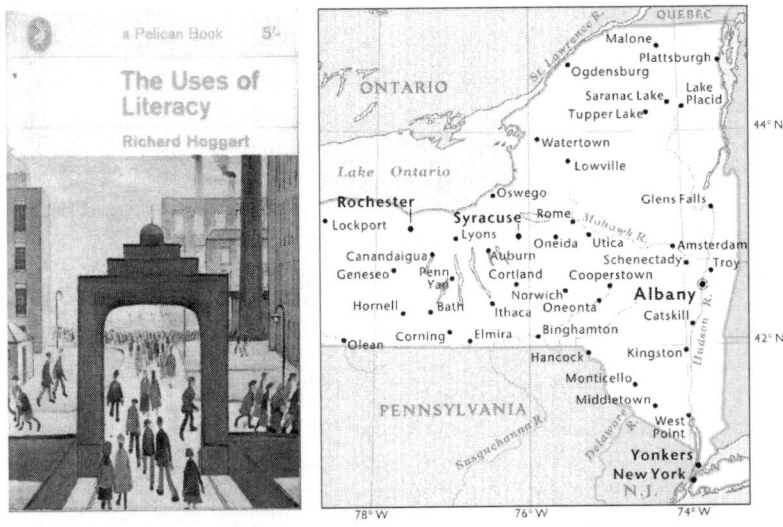

the air coming off Lake Ontario, the Finger Lakes nearby, sufficient good music, exceptionally good provision of films (the Eastman-Kodak museum being there), not much of a race problem or unemployment since its industries are mixed and many of them very much of the late twentieth-century (Eastman-Kodak, Bausch and Lomb, IBM); and those industries civic-minded … All in all and in general, Rochester is a decent, undramatic city much like Leicester, only much richer.[26]

His account of the University of Rochester is perceptive and sympathetic.

> The University of Rochester was a true child of the city in that it was of medium-size by American standards but quite large by British, privately funded and proud of it, academically in some ways modest, in other ways – like Rochester's large industries – of national and international caliber. Its staff and their manners mirrored their institution. Some knew they would move on and many did, regular movement for promotion or for tenure being a feature of the academic life for even near-high-flyers; but during their time at Rochester they did not feel, as some at Hull did, that they were in a backwater and only waiting for a call … Almost all of them believed … that we had to be friendly one to another, and the more so because academic life in the States is regarded as more of an odd backwater even than it is in England.[27]

He tells stories about his encounters with colleagues, neighbours and students, always reflecting in interesting ways on the differences between English and American cultures. This is something he is confronted with the minute he sets foot in the country, after crossing the Atlantic on the *Queen Elizabeth*. Arriving to what seemed like a chaotic immigration process, with his young children tired and thirsty, he has this exchange with a customs official:

I asked, in a very polite manner: 'Can you help me, please? I have three children'.
He stared at me callously and answered, before looking down at his papers again,
'Don't blame me, bud. See a doctor'.[28]

Characteristically, Hoggart does not take offence at this – on the contrary, even
in speaking he is aware of his 'thin Limey voice', and of the annoying English
tendency to 'elliptical speech'. For him, it is an occasion for reflection on cultural
difference, with his sympathy aligned, if anything, with the American.

A second encounter, this time with a student, encapsulates cultural difference
in a way that seems timeless – as he himself says, 'Henry James again, forty years
after he died'. It is worth quoting him at length on this. A student comes to see
him some weeks into his class on modern English literature, to make, as he puts it,
'a statement about plenitude and about the threatened loss of innocence'.

She said something like this: 'I am enjoying your course very much. But it is
disturbing me. Let me tell you about my background. I come from [she named
a medium-sized town twenty or thirty miles south]. My father is a lawyer; my
mother stays home but does a great many good works in the community. So does
my father. They are good people and greatly respected. They are loving parents
to me and my brothers. We have a pleasant life. In summer we have barbeques
with the family, the neighbours, members of our church. In winter we skate on
the Lake. I have to say, and I've only realized it after auditing your course, that
I've been happy, it's been a happy sort of life. But now I'm shaken. I enjoy hearing
you talk about, for example, T. S. Eliot and Graham Greene. I enjoy reading them
after the lectures. But there's so much unhappiness, so much cruelty, so much
accepting that life is grim and black and sinful. But it hasn't felt like that to us,
not at all. And I don't know how to make head or tail of it.'[29]

I searched out a copy of Hoggart's book – one volume of his autobiography – from
an internet used-books site, because I had remembered these two stories so clearly,
fifteen years after first reading them, and wanted to read them again. When I first
came across them, I had just moved to the States, and I took some pleasure in the
customs officer's put-down. It was American directness that I wanted, English
circumlocution and caution that I felt I needed to abandon (in myself, of course,
as much as in how others spoke to me). If Eddie Cochran (an arbitrary example –
though I had been to hear him in the Manchester Hippodrome in March 1960)
stood for the excitement and freedom of American rock 'n' roll (pathetically imi-
tated by English rockers like Tommy Steele), ways of speech – ways of being
– were just as exciting, and just as liberating.[30] I loved the story, told to me quite
a few years later by an English friend of mine, living and teaching in the United
States, of her father, a famous British composer, being invited to receive an hon-
our at some American campus. When he arrived, she told me, he said something
to the effect of 'I don't know why you are giving me this award – I really don't
deserve it'. Normal British modesty, and not even, in the end, false modesty –

simply expected behaviour. Of course the response should have been 'Nonsense, of course you deserve it!'. But this wasn't England, and so one of the hosts looked confused and said, 'Oh, perhaps we have made a mistake.' Or so my friend told me. It makes the point, even if it's clear that the American host was only teasing his distinguished visitor.

And Hoggart's second anecdote, about the student, resonated so strongly with ideas of American openness and optimism and sunniness, a myth to yearn for and to aspire to. You can go for the image (to the radical extent of moving across the Atlantic) while at the same time knowing perfectly well (as any self-respecting sociologist would know) that it *is* a myth – or, perhaps worse, an ideological construction. You can sustain your investment in that myth while also knowing its own dark side, which is denial of actual harm, glossing of real pain, inability to understand – and even enjoy – nuance, complexity, perversity. The difference between Hoggart and me, I now see, is that he didn't feel called upon to take sides. His sensitivity as an observer allowed him to make fun of his own excessively self-effacing culture while seeing both the great strengths and the disconcerting weaknesses of his host society. It seems that it is only when the personal investment in these matters abates that it becomes clear that it isn't a matter of black and white. Sometimes it takes a while to get to that point.

<hr />

The eulogy for Henry Norr spoke of his 'innate modesty', and it occurs to me now, as I conclude with my anecdote about British modesty in an American context, that I may have accidentally exposed an underlying theme. Or perhaps not so accidentally. Is there a certain 'modesty' in writing memoir through other people's stories? I prefer to think of it, in fact, as obliquity. Of course this has been a story about my own Atlantic moves – both geographical and emotional. If others – Henry Norr, my father, the Sellafield workers, Richard Hoggart – take up more space than me in these pages, perhaps my marginality is a rather immodest device. The people I write about are mobilised by my narrative, and serve the purpose of telling my story.

And yet there isn't 'a story' as such, and perhaps that is the point. David Shields, in his passionate defence of new forms of writing for our contemporary age, says: 'I want books to be equal to the complexity of experience, memory, and thought, not flattening it out with either linear narrative (traditional novel) or smooth recount (standard memoir)'.[31] Ambitious writing, he suggests, 'doesn't resolve contradictions in a spurious harmony but instead embodies the contradictions, pure and uncompromised, in its innermost structure'.[32] His project accords well with the strong antipathy I have long had towards the chronological, coherent account of a life. I cannot particularly claim honourable poststructuralist motives here – refusing to uphold the mythical centred self. Rather, my own resistance has more to do with a kind of constitutional attachment to uncertainty. The openness produced in an interplay of stories, switches of point of view and of opinion, as these stories are navigated, allows the protagonist – glimpsed from time to time, and often at an angle – the liberty to remain unfixed. What Shields describes as the 'standard memoir' tends to proceed in linear fashion, with the chronological story of the life, in which photographs and letters, clearly captioned, may serve as illustration or proof. In another kind of writing, the protagonist only takes centre stage occasionally – perhaps quite rarely – while the play of other narratives and other memories, cross-cut with visual texts, constructs the life in a less tangible way. Somewhere uncertain – perhaps mid-Atlantic – this oblique memoir situates its subject.

Thanks to Margaret Beetham, Janet Berlo, Brenda Cooper, Judy Kendall, Tony Platt and Jackie Stacey for helpful comments on this essay at various stages.

Notes

1   Marianne Hirsch, 'Mourning and postmemory', p. 22.
2   Mary Cappello, *Night Bloom: A Memoir*, p. 42.
3   Anne Karpf, *The War After: Living with the Holocaust*.
4   David Cesarani, *Justice Delayed: How Britain Became a Refuge for Nazi War Criminals*.
5   François Lafitte, *The Internment of Aliens*; Connery Chappell, *Island of Barbed Wire: The Remarkable Story of World War Two Internment on the Isle of Man*; Peter and Leni Gillman, *'Collar the Lot!' How Britain Interned and Expelled its Wartime Refugees*; Ronald Stent, *A Bespattered Page? The Internment of 'His Majesty's Most Loyal Enemy Aliens'*; David Cesarani and Tony Kushner eds, *The Internment of Aliens in Twentieth Century Britain*.
6   David Feldman, 'The importance of being English: Jewish immigration and the decay of liberal England', pp. 57–8.
7   John Osborne, *Damn You England: Collected Prose*.
8   Marilynne Robinson, *Mother Country: Britain, the Welfare State and Nuclear Pollution*, p. 11.
9   *Ibid.*, p. 11.
10   *Ibid.*, p. 6.
11   *Ibid.*, p. 168.
12   Lorna Arnold, *Windscale 1957: Anatomy of a Nuclear Accident*, p. 3.
13   *Ibid.*, p. 5.
14   *Ibid.*, pp. 5–6.
15   *Ibid.*, p. 17.
16   *Ibid.*, p. 124.
17   *Ibid.*, p. 84.
18   Quoted in *Ibid.*, p. 83.
19   M. F. Perutz, 'Is Britain "befouled"?'.
20   Robin McKie, 'Windscale radiation "doubly dangerous"'; R. Wakeford, 'Editorial: The Windscale reactor accident – 50 years on'; J. A. Garland and R. Wakeford, 'Atmospheric emissions from the Windscale accident of October 1957'.
21   Robin McKie, n.p.
22   Hunter Davies (ed.), *Sellafield Stories: Life with Britain's First Nuclear Plant*, pp. 47–8.
23   *Ibid.*, pp. 139–40.
24   Janet Wolff, *Resident Alien: Feminist Cultural Criticism*.

25   Richard Hoggart, *The Uses of Literacy*.
26   Richard Hoggart, *A Sort of Clowning: Life and Times, 1940–59*, p. 153.
27   *Ibid.*, p. 154.
28   *Ibid.*, p. 148.
29   *Ibid.*, pp. 161–2.
30   Janet Wolff, 'Eddie Cochran, Donna Anna and the Dark Sister', in *Resident Alien*.
31   David Shields, *Reality Hunger: A Manifesto*, p. 54.
32   *Ibid.*, p. 136.

Bibliography

Arnold, Lorna, *Windscale 1957: Anatomy of a Nuclear Accident* (Basingstoke: Palgrave Macmillan, 2007 [1992]).

Cappello, Mary, *Night Bloom: A Memoir* (Boston, MA: Beacon Press, 1998).

Cesarani, David, *Justice Delayed: How Britain Became a Refuge for Nazi War Criminals* (London: Heinemann, 1992).

Cesarani, David, and Tony Kushner (eds), *The Internment of Aliens in Twentieth Century-Britain* (London: Frank Cass and Company Ltd., 1993).

Chappell, Connery, *Island of Barbed Wire: The Remarkable Story of World War Two Internment on the Isle of Man* (London: Robert Hale, 1984).

Davies, Hunter (ed.), *Sellafield Stories: Life with Britain's First Nuclear Plant* (London: Constable & Robinson, 2012).

Feldman, David, 'The importance of being English: Jewish immigration and the decay of liberal England', in David Feldman and Gareth S. Jones (eds), *Metropolis-London: Histories and Representations since 1800* (London: Routledge, 1989).

Garland, J. A., and R. Wakeford, 'Atmospheric emissions from the Windscale accident of October 1957', *Atmospheric Environment*, 41:18 (June 2007), 3904–20. Accessed online 9 October 2007.

Gillman, Peter, and Leni, *'Collar the Lot!' How Britain Interned and Expelled its Wartime Refugees* (London: Quartet Books, 1980).

Hirsch, Marianne, 'Mourning and postmemory', in *Family Frames. Photography Narrative and Postmemory* (Cambridge, MA: Harvard University Press, 1997).

Hoggart, Richard, *The Uses of Literacy* (London: Chatto & Windus, 1957).

Hoggart, Richard, *A Sort of Clowning: Life and Times, 1940-59* (London: Chatto & Windus, 1990).

Karpf, Anne, *The War After: Living with the Holocaust* (London: Heinemann, 1996).

Lafitte, François, *The Internment of Aliens* (London: Libris, 1988) [Penguin Books: 1940].

McKie, Robin, 'Windscale radiation "doubly dangerous"', *The Observer*, 7 October 2007. Accessed online 26 November 2009.

Osborne, John, *Damn You England: Collected Prose* (London: Faber and Faber, 1999).

Perutz, M. F., 'Is Britain "befouled"?', *The New York Review of Books*, 23 November 1989. See also exchange between Marilynne Robinson and M. F. Perutz, *The New York Review of Books*, 12 April 1990.

Robinson, Marilynne, *Mother Country: Britain, the Welfare State and Nuclear Pollution* (New York: Farrar, Straus & Giroux, 1980).

Runyon, Damon, 'The lemon drop kid' [1934], in *Guys and Dolls: The Stories of Damon Runyon* (London: Penguin, 1956).

Shields, David, *Reality Hunger: A Manifesto* (London: Hamish Hamilton, 2010).

Stent, Ronald, *A Bespattered Page? The Internment of 'His Majesty's Most Loyal Enemy Aliens'* (London: André Deutsch, 1980).

Wakeford, Richard, 'Editorial: The Windscale reactor accident – 50 years on', *Journal of Radiological Protection,* 27 (2007), 211–15.

Wolff, Janet, *Resident Alien: Feminist Cultural Criticism* (Cambridge: Polity Press, 1995).

Wolff, Janet, 'The failure of a hard sponge: class, ethnicity and the art of Mark Gertler', *New Formations,* 28 (May 1996), 46–64. Reprinted in *AngloModern: Painting and Modernity in Britain and the United States* (Ithaca, NY: Cornell University Press, 2003).

Wolff, Janet, *The Aesthetics of Uncertainty* (New York: Columbia University Press, 2008).

Autopia: in search of what we're thinking when we're driving

Lynne Pearce

There can be little doubt that, in the popular imagination, the road trip is paradigmatically defined as a search for something that ends, even if it does not begin, with the self. In this respect it is strikingly similar to a host of other twentieth-century practices that have the pleasure and/or improvement of the self as their key ultimate objective, even when this goal is realised by an obscure and meandering route. Operations as various as psychoanalysis, romantic relationships and religious or spiritual enlightenment abide by what are, in essence, the principles of the quest: a journey undertaken in order to test, discover and (im)prove the self through its encounter with things that are variously surprising, threatening, inspiring and – above all – *unknown* at the point of departure.

For H. V. Morton, setting off 'in search of Scotland' for a second time in 1933, the purpose of the road trip was summed up in two words: 'hunger and anticipation'.[1] Anticipation – a concept which combines notions of the known and the unknown, as well as pleasure and a variable degree of apprehension – is what has sent many millions of motorists off on their latter-day quests since the very beginning of the twentieth-century and spawned a literary genre of truly staggering proportions (there are currently over 19,000 books listed on Amazon under the category of 'road trip'). From the days of Morton to the present, however, the extent to which driving *per se* is a feature of the road-trip narrative is extremely variable. For some authors (for example, Iain Banks on his tour of the whisky distilleries of Scotland) it is integral to the experience; for many, however, the car is merely a means to an end and the text itself centres on the people and places encountered along the way.[2] A stand-out exception to this instrumentality is the ur-fictional road trip, Jack Kerouac's *On the Road*, in which the thrill of driving – large distances, often at high speed – is fundamental to the text's existential heart.[3] Nevertheless, even Kerouac's iconic text is short on details of the sort of road trip I am interested in: namely, a journey that seeks to capture what we think *while we're driving* – the twists, turns and ellipses of the driver's consciousness during the drive – rather than the places, people and events that we encounter along the way or, indeed, the person we have supposedly become at our journey's end.

This essay is one of a number of portals to a book-length project that I've provisionally entitled 'Driving: a journey through twentieth-century consciousness'. Unlike my more scholarly investigations, however, this piece moves my own 'driving-events' to the centre in a conscious effort to take stock of all that I have

92

pondered on the topic for the past twelve years.[4] My objective, then, is to capture, as best I can, an indicative sample of my own thought-processes while on the road and then to organise and reflect upon them in an attempt to refine the questions that I shall subsequently bring to bear upon the textual representations of others.

My further reason for undertaking this experiment is to evaluate to what extent my project and its methodology may properly be thought of as phenomenological. To this end, the essay concludes with a section which sets out some of the ways in which my engagements may, and may not, be thought of as 'authentically' phenomenological, before observing the ways in which Edmund Husserl's 1964 lecture on 'internal-time consciousness' – which takes account of the muddying waters of *memory* – outlines a model of consciousness that speaks to the vagaries of my own texts.[5]

Driving events: 2004/2012

5 January 2004

I am driving south, from my cottage in Argyll, Scotland, back to my place of work: Lancaster, England. Conditions are good to damp: light rain most of the way, with some fog on the high ground at Abingdon and Shap. For most of the journey my thoughts have veered from low-key to a wee bit gloomy: thoughts cut on the edge of having finally sent the manuscript to G and having no idea of how she will respond or if we will (ever) meet again […].

Today the world [as seen from my car] is too closed-in to inspire much euphoria or ecstasy; there is no particular inscape of views or objects. After Glasgow, work – and its challenges – begins to play on my mind increasingly with some speculation on how I might pursue the Chair appointments [for my Department] or not. I also briefly seize upon the possibility of going part-time and ending forever the tyranny of administration and university politics. It is always there for me if I want it – that option, I mean – and for a moment I feel brave enough to take it and surrender a life of financial security for ever and a day.

9 July 2012

I leave Taynuilt at 11am after an extended visit to the tea shop. B has brought in some of his own antique maps and is, I think, genuinely interested in my trip. As I pull out of Taynuilt, and for the first mile or so towards Fearnoch, I'm preoccupied by the gravity of my leave-taking: the everyday event that foreshadows the unspeakable event that lurks at the back of everyone's mind on these occasions, especially where driving is concerned. As I leave the 30 mph zone I notice the temperature: 14.5 degrees. Nice and cool (for which I'm glad).

The hedgerows between Taynuilt and Connel are what K calls 'summer green': a thick, dense mass of greenness that is especially flat today because of the white, cloudy sky … I glance at the islands once or twice, imagining I can see seals (as usual), but mostly thinking about *this*: how to monitor my flickering, wayward consciousness in such a way that I can capture enough to write it down. This is a hopelessly artificial exercise, of course – the 'remembering' disrupting the normal stream of consciousness – but I suppose it might provide a rough sketch of what is going on.

Displacements

9 July 2012

The detour around Kinlochleven takes up a huge amount of mental space as my mind struggles to disentangle a thick palimpsest of competing memories. So many visits over so many years [twenty], not to mention all the visits of my imagination ... and G's letter [1992].

As I weave down the high road on the south side of the loch I'm especially struck by the profile of Garbh Bheinn, a surprisingly pointy mountain from this side. K and I talked about climbing it during our drive up this road in the pouring rain in October 2005. Hanging over Mamore Lodge I can also see the sheer slopes of what I assume to be Na Gruagaichean. This looks very steep indeed, and I can still remember us bemoaning its calf-crunching lower slopes on our way up in 1997.

As I drive through the Kinlochleven itself, I am, as usual, on the lookout for change ... I notice that one single-storey shop on the road in – with red paint – is closed and boarded-up, but don't know if this is a new thing or not ... As I pass the café that was once 'The Pink Lady' I recall, as ever, G having an iced bun there in 1993, though I know for sure this is a fossil-memory: there simply because I fixed it in my mind all those years ago. There is now nothing of the rest of that visit that I can remember at all.

Once I'm through the village and heading up the other side of the loch ... the traffic behind me starts to pick up – presumably diverted from St John's. I speed up accordingly and quite enjoy it: accelerating out of the bends, holding firm to the road. This side of the loch is very beautiful – and as I see it again I remember that this is so: waving bracken and weeping birch, though less summer flowers (buttercups, especially) than on the north side of the loch. Indeed, the hedgerow flowers all the way from Taynuilt have been very beautiful: buttercups, foxgloves, ox-eye daisies, cow-parsley and all the summer grasses, long and waving.

25 March 2004

This is a drive that certainly deserves recording since it takes me, and the car, quite literally to the top of a mountain. The road from Strontian to Polloch reaches well over 1,000 feet ... and involves some breath-taking gradients and hair-pin bends: driving that requires a nerve and focus few roads demand today.

The journey begins with me mildly out of sorts after a pointless visit to the doctor ... and I feel chilled and depressed to quite a severe degree all the way to Ballachulish. G weighs on my chest as a terrible ache, defying the morning sunshine and spring warmth – not that spring is very visible in the highlands just yet: this is the land at its most spare and bleached before its new clothes arrive.

I nevertheless enjoy the speed of the new, improved stretches of the A82 from Castle Stalker onwards and notice even more of the old road, and old buildings, that shadow the present route [...]. I cross to Ardgour via the Corran Ferry – another unique feature of West Coast driving – and proceed down to Strontian through some of the most open, desolate and beautiful landscape in Scotland. I don't think I properly saw this beauty the last time I was here with K (2003), but I do today.

I stop and 'recce' some sections of the route that we're planning for July, and take some photos. However, the road from Strontian to Polloch is the big thrill: a real roller-coaster of a drive that suddenly precipitates you over the summit of the hill with almost the same effect as if you were walking it ... Once my mission is complete I walk part-way up Loch Shiel, through the pine forest ... [and then] turn tail and drive home fast: 60 mph for most of the way. Where else can you experience motoring like this anymore? However, the heaviness in my chest has not shifted.

10 July 2012

The second day of my trip and I'm headed for Ullapool, some fifty miles from Beauly. However, a new worry besets me as soon as I set off: the oil warning light [in my car] comes on and doesn't go out even after I've topped up the engine. I sit outside the Co-op in Beauly for a while contemplating what best to do, but soon make the decision to head for Ullapool anyway in the expectation that I shall pass a garage or call the RAC.

As I pull away from 'civilisation' and head towards the wild, moorland uplands that separate East from West on this northernmost collar of Scotland, I smile at the 'authenticity' of my motoring experience. Even today, the unpredictability of motoring persists – and with it the one resounding question: 'Will I get there?' Indeed, I don't think about much else at all until I get here (Corrieshalloch Gorge). So: no delving into the past today, no music playing; just the constant rolling around in my head of what I should do *now*, what I should do *next*. Turn back for home? Head for Fort William (where there's a VW garage)? Or press on to Ullapool ... as I finally determine upon.

I nevertheless notice one or two things about the road to Ullapool as I pass 'over the top': first, how the landscape remains remarkably 'East Coast' in character for quite a while. There is a change beyond Garve when the road begins its climb north towards the bleak, moorland plateau of Strathvaich Forest, right enough, but it's still not a 'highland' landscape ... I stop in a lay-by a few hundred yards short of Aultguish to take a photo: moorland greyness in steady rain, a wet and winding road, and all the cars with headlights on.

Displacements

3 June 2004

This is my first drive down to Lancaster for nearly six weeks. It begins in torrential rain (like my [last ever] visit to G on the 12th January), and like my journey to collect Star [my new dog] on the 13th April: the two most memorable drives of the year thus far. Once again, water is throwing itself off the mountains in big waterfalls and I am gripping the steering wheel tightly as I accelerate past lorries, blinded by spray, and am minded not to brake for fear of skidding [...].

The further motoring context to today's drive is the soaring cost of petrol at the pumps as more fuel protests are threatened. I pay 82.9p at Dumbarton today, but they're forecasting prices in excess of £1 anytime soon [...].

The heavy rain makes this a pretty slow drive south, and there also road works on the M74. I make an extra stop for Star and then, again, at Gretna.

11 July 2012

The relief of collecting my hire car is immense: a wee, Nissan Micra into which I pile Star (back seat) and all my gear. I then drive across to Hawco to see if there's any news about my car, but they haven't got to the diagnostic yet. So I decide to head home immediately, glad that I decided to get the hire car first instead of waiting on the garage.

It's a bit of a bumpy start: scratchy gears and a stall. It's a long time since I've driven as badly as this, but I see now (I am writing this the next day) that I was mildly traumatised after the events of yesterday and the uncertainty of when, and how, I would get home – especially since I had Star with me. There is also the challenge of navigating myself out of Inverness from the industrial estate, and I'm pretty tense until I'm safely back on the A82. This is also a very different mode of driving ... than the one that brought me 'up' the road yesterday. What do I see on my way out of Inverness? Nothing but the road, road signs, and the other traffic ... I remember a bridge, a level crossing and the Caledonian Canal, but mostly my mind is preoccupied with getting me out of the city safely.

Even once back on a familiar road, I 'see' very little: all the landmarks (material, memorial) that I remarked upon on the way up I am oblivious to now. It is also raining steadily, impeding visibility and, in particular, views across Loch Ness.
I check-out what I am thinking about several times, nevertheless, only to find nothing more than a restless flitting backwards and forwards between the immediate past (the stress of hiring the car, getting to the garage across town by taxi) and the present ... Irrationally, I feel an urgent need to get home when, in truth, there is no more pressure for me to get there quickly than when I sauntered up on Monday.

I keep driving until Ballachulish, where I stop for a belated lunch. From this point in the journey, I start to relax a fraction, comforted to be, once more, in the land of very familiar things. I am still driven by the desire to get home quickly and, unusually for me, the time behind the wheel begins to drag. I suspect it's like this for many other drivers most of the time, but for me it's the opposite: driving is a blessed time-out-of-time, time to think, time to be 'not doing'. But now I want to be home as urgently as any Friday night commuter.

13 July 2012

This is a journey [Inverness to Taynuilt] undertaken in great relief and mild euphoria. At the same time, I feel much safer and steadier being back in my old
car again.

Exiting the city is straightforward now that I've sussed the route: four round-
abouts, and the dog-leg turn right back onto the A82 along Loch Ness. I am soon
on my way and able to enjoy the fact that this is a bright, sunshiny day. I am also
dreaming of the future again: this time, my long-term part-time and/or retirement plans which, along with where I shall end up living, have become a constant
preoccupation recently [...].

My more immediate crisis resolved [there was actually nothing wrong with
the car apart from some corroded wires], I am alert to things of interest in the
world again. I notice an old AA box opposite the Clansman Hotel and, later, a
derelict, corrugated-iron garage just beyond Invermoriston. I also wonder, again,
about the rock-fall risks on all the new roads created by blasting in the 1970s and
1980s [...]. [Hereafter, I stop at Fort Augustus for lunch, and then Loch Oich
to give my dog a walk].

I am back in the car by 5pm, feeling tired, and anxious now to get home ...
Probably because I am tired, I let go of thinking about work, my life, and the
future and focus mainly on the increasingly familiar sights outside my window.
Especially striking are: the hulk of the Ben [Nevis] with its snow-filled, northern
gullies; the small, and slightly run-down SEPA [Scottish Environment Protection Agency] offices on the northern outskirts of Fortwilliam [...]; and, most
spectacularly, the (huge) profile of Bidean nam Bian spotlighted in the evening
sun ... I stop and take a photograph just before Nether Lochaber Village Hall
(which K and I photographed at Easter). The bulk of the mountain, which I first
mistake for the Aonach Eagach, and then Beinn a' Bheithir, is awesome and,
from here, gives the impression of being comparable with Ben Nevis. I am momentarily transfixed, especially since this is the hill that K and I have next on our
list to climb and keep failing to do so.

After this, I am mostly focused on home – too tired either to think or to 'see'.
Instead, I begin to fret about the time – now approaching 7pm – and the need to
phone [my elderly neighbour] W. As was the case on Wednesday, anxiety creeps
over me, an inner censor telling me I should be home by now. My conscious brain
registers this irrationality, and triggers its own warning light: I mind my speed,
am alert to hazards, keep my eyes on the road. I finally arrive home at 7.15pm.

What I think I'm thinking when I'm driving

In this section I offer a reflection on the four horizons of consciousness that I
have identified as the most powerfully recurrent in the extracts reproduced above,
namely: nostalgia, disappointment, anxiety and anticipation. Although ostensibly affective states, these categories also capture the temporal binary of our driv-
ing-consciousness: thoughts drawn to the past and thoughts projected towards
the future, with both compulsions mediated and/or prompted by the perceptual
present. The fact that these trajectories also feature a utopian (anticipation, nostal-

gia) and dystopian (anxiety, disappointment) dyad lends further symmetry to my matrix, though here it is important to remember that my sample is merely indicative and that other categories (and, indeed, nuances within categories) could be identified without too much difficulty.

Nostalgia

For anyone who drives a lot and covers the same stretches of road over a period of years, it is no exaggeration to say that the past lurks around every corner. Encompassing a wide spectrum of emotions, all circled with sadness on account of their belatedness, nostalgia is nevertheless a species of remembrance which we are happy to indulge on account of the fact that it preserves for us an image of the past in which we are invested.

My detour via Kinlochleven (9 July 2012) is a *tour de force* of driving-nostalgia. Unexpected and unprepared for (it is a crash, someone else's misfortune, that sends me that way), I am especially vulnerable to the rapid succession of perceptual prompts that sends my memory into free-fall and then urgently scrambles to sort, date and catalogue. The recollections are of the people with which the place is associated, the 'scenes' in which they appeared, the things they said.[6] Interestingly, some of the memories (for example, the descriptions included in G's letter) are events that I learnt about second-hand but which are now seared on my inner-eye as vividly as if I had been there myself, while others survive only by virtue of my efforts to memorialise them years ago. To what extent such reconstructed memories may usefully be compared and contrasted with more recent acts of retention is something to which I return below, but it is interesting to observe that my recent memories are the ones in which the nostalgic impulse is more obviously mixed with the other affective/temporal registers (anticipation, disappointment) as implied in my description of Garbh Bheinn (one of the mountains K and I have earmarked to climb, but never got round to yet). This is raw, still-twitching memory in contrast to the 'fossil-memories' of twenty years ago.

This extract also reveals the extent of our nostalgic attachments to places and scenes that are only loosely connected to people and events. Even on this quick drive through Kinlochleven I am wired for signs of change. In signal contrast to what Husserl and Maurice Merleau-Ponty would identify as the correct phenomenological reflex,[7] it is not my 'unprejudiced'[8] perception of the red-painted shop that prompts me to lament the demise of Kinlochleven, but rather my apperception[9] of the scene against an established schema (I don't like change, and want to reassure myself that this dereliction isn't new).

Yet the extracts also reveal that it is a mistake to think of nostalgia as exclusively retrospective. The practice of anticipatory retrospection, whereby a subject checks, and memorialises something in the present with a view to revisiting it in the future, is arguably where nostalgia often begins (not least because proactive retention is widely understood to be a requisite of all long-term memory). My attention to the summer hedgerows on both my departure from Taynuilt (9 July 2012) and my journey out of Kinlochleven (9 July 2012) may appear to constitute a simple engagement with the perceptual present but, if I know myself correctly, I am also capturing these images (like a photograph) to stack against the fog of fast-fleeting time.

Disappointment

There are, of course, many past events that we prefer to forget, disavow or bury. Given the amount of pain and sorrow that commonly attend nostalgia, it might at first seem odd that I position disappointment – frequently associated with minor upsets – as the more negative figure of consciousness in this analysis. However, as several commentators have observed, disappointment can be experienced as devastating when attached to an event whose failure or 'spoiling' undermines a subject's narrative of their own past or future, which is why it is also something we struggle to repress or otherwise avoid.[10]

As several of my extracts reveal, driving is an activity that can be proactively undertaken to evade the intellectual admission of disappointment. While the emotion may erupt here or there – and, in my journals, I do my best to record this honestly – it is also, sometimes, possible to commandeer the fast-changing perceptual present of the drive as a welcome distraction. This doesn't always work, and it isn't a complete antidote, but I would suggest that my entry for 5 January 2004 is a good example of how potentially devastating disappointment has been diverted into the preferable melancholy of nostalgia. By giving myself up to the comforting familiarity of a drive – made along the same route, past the same landmarks – in happier times, I am able to temporarily evade a more deeply distressing scenario.

This driving-anaesthesia is repeated, though to a lesser extent, in the two further extracts from 2004. Even though 'the worst' has now ostensibly happened (effectively a double bereavement), my drives still enable me to counter the retrograde motion of my depressed (as opposed to disappointed) state with the illusory sense that I am nevertheless moving forward, going *somewhere*: in the first extract this is, of course, literal inasmuch as the excursion is a 'recce' for a future holiday, and the text reveals a skilful blend of place-nostalgia and anticipation to distract me from the intermittent stabs of pain; in the second extract (3 June 2004), by contrast, I embrace anxiety in its most absolute forms – risk of death or global apocalypse – in order to accelerate out of the pain and, *in extremis*, 'choose life'.

A quieter, but equally significant, instance of driving-occasioned disappointment occurs in those extracts (already noted in the section on nostalgia) in which I spot places not visited, hills not climbed. I shall return to the most arresting of these – the sight of Bidean nam Bian in the sunset (13 July 2012) – below.

Anxiety

Vis-à-vis the extracts featured here, anxiety may be arranged into a spectrum of concerns ranging from the short-term and material ('Does this warning light mean that my car is about to break down?') to the long-term and speculative ('How can I escape from my job?'). To take the former first, it is, of course, not without irony that my long-awaited road trip around the far north of Scotland is aborted on Day Two owing to an electrical fault in my car. Travelling alone (though with my dog) on this occasion, I am plunged into a sequence of stressful, decision-making scenarios, most of which proved even more stressful in execution. As evident in the extract itself (10 July 2012), I can only wrench my mind away from these decision-making anxieties with effort: my mind still clocks the landscape against familiar schema ('the landscape remains remarkably "East Coast" in character for quite a while') but – to invoke Husserl's vocabulary – it 'intuits' nothing.[11]

Another order of material driver-anxiety features in the extract describing my journey out of Inverness in the hire-car (11 July 2012). Finding myself in a scenario that will be familiar to many of us (strange car, tricky navigation), the extract describes how my attention is focused only on the information (road, traffic, traffic controls, signposts) that will get me out of the city safely: all other irrelevant cognitive activity has been suspended. Research on driving by psychologists and neuroscientists has shown that the brain's ability to switch between different types of neural activity at the command of the brain's 'central executive' is crucial to our ability to deal with the risks and hazards of motoring.[12] What is especially striking about my own account of a challenging driving situation, however, is the length of time it takes for the 'central executive' to relax its control. Non-driving-related thoughts do not resume for many miles after the immediate navigational stress is over, and even then, my mind is restless ('flitting backwards and forwards between the immediate past … and the present'). I attend neither to the landscape outside the car windows (except in the loosest, schematic sense) nor to any matters stored in my long-term memory.

Turning this formulation on its head, it would also seem that, in easier driving conditions, anxious thoughts are admitted to consciousness precisely because the driving-event is a controlled and productive context in which to address difficult concerns. As noted above with respect to disappointment, both the somatic experience of driving (propulsion *forwards*) and the sense of empowerment can create a safe environment for problem solving.[13] A long, fast car journey can certainly induce euphoria in the driver, even in times of severe personal distress, and it is possible that the work and lifestyle issues that surface in my extracts (5 January 2004; 13 July 2012) do so precisely because, when driving, I feel better equipped to deal with them.[14]

There are other occasions, however, when the somatic specificities of driving – the experience of being carried forward too quickly or, more typically, too slowly – can promote anxiety, as exemplified here by my two drives back from Inverness (11 July 2012 and 13 July 2012). In the second of these, my anxiety finds a particular focus (the need to phone W), while the former is characterised by the more pervasive insecurity caused by my recent car-trouble: as I observe, 'time behind the wheel begins to drag' and 'I want to be home as urgently as any Friday night commuter'.

Anticipation

As noted above, for Morton driving was defined by anticipation: the value, excitement and purpose of motoring was to see, and encounter, places and people that, at that time (pre-television) would be known primarily through the written text or word of mouth. Hence Morton's frequent references to the literary tourists and novelists, such as Sir Walter Scott, who preceded him on his travels. In this respect, indeed, the anticipation inherent in the motor tour was not necessarily for things entirely new and/or unheard of, but rather the pleasure of experiencing in the flesh, and with the eyes, things known previously by description and in the imagination. As already observed, such mental preparation may be seen as being against the spirit of phenomenology which, in its earliest incarnations at least, insisted upon an 'unprejudiced' intuition of that which presents itself to consciousness.[15] For other philosophers such as Ernst Bloch, however, all anticipatory consciousness should be embraced for its utopian potential (both individual and social), and correlations can clearly be drawn between his promotion of daydreams and the state of euphoric hypnosis that the driving-event will, on occasion, induce.[16]

In terms of my own extracts, the entry that best captures this daydreaming potential is, ironically, the return journey that ends my abandoned road trip (13 July 2012). The relief of being back in my own car again, and the removal of all immediate anxiety, permits a welcome resurgence of euphoria that shapes itself into a daydream of how I could go part-time in my job and escape the worst excesses of institutional life. The core reverie around which these speculations swirl, meanwhile, is where I shall be living: the house and village where I stay now or an, as yet unknown, 'elsewhere'? Also significant is the fact that this is the journey in which I begin to *see* the world outwith the car again: the old AA box, the garage, the cliffs along the side of the A82 enclosed in wire-netting, the views across Loch Ness. Contrary to what phenomenology would have us expect, this alert intuition of my immediate, if transitory, surroundings sits comfortably alongside my daydream. I see and dream simultaneously. Freshly conscious of these things as serial visual prompts flash by, all things seem possible once more.

Towards the end of this journey, however, I grow tired and my mood changes. Euphoric anticipation gives way to nostalgia, nostalgia to anxiety, and just before I begin what I always think of as the last leg of this particular route, I am seized by an image – Bidean nam Bian, the highest mountain in Argyll, picked out from all its shadowed neighbours by the setting sun – that confounds clear distinction between the axes of consciousness I have been outlining in this essay. Like Garbh Bheinn, Bidean nam Bian is a mountain circumscribed by disappointment inasmuch as it is one K and I have (repeatedly) failed to climb; yet the possibility that we might do so, and soon, is the thought that triumphs here, arguably on account of the anticipatory consciousness that has captured this drive. Significantly, it is the only sight on the whole road trip that has caused me to spontaneously stop the car, get out of the car, and experience the landscape directly.

Driving, phenomenology and 'internal-time consciousness'

As noted in the introduction, part of my reason for writing this essay has been to explore the extent to which my methodology may be described as phenomenological. My verdict, as numerous asides in the commentary foreshadow, is that I am doubtful that my practice ever wholly meets the requirements of an intuitive, 'unprejudiced' engagement with whatever is presented to one's consciousness. This applies both to what has been written down in my journals – the first-hand driver's report on what has disclosed itself in the course of the driving event – and to a second-level reflection as practised here in the previous section. The problem with the latter is that although it follows Husserl's instruction (post-'transcendental reduction') that we work to reveal the essential structures that subtend that which presents itself to us, it does so through a mechanism that undoubtedly *is* reflection rather than intuition and, crucially, is as interested in illusory and delusory thought-processes as those which constitute the 'essential structures' of consciousness.[17]

One could, of course, argue that such delusions are part and parcel of what has been revealed in my second-level analysis, but all that I have read suggests that these aspects of mental activity fall more properly within the remit of psychology precisely because they tell us everything about 'the subject' but little about 'our relation to the things themselves in seeing', no matter how deep we dig.[18] If a driver notices roadside flowers not because they present themselves to her in their 'givenness' but on account of old associations, or, alternatively, because they are memorialised in the interests of anticipatory retrospection, then neither the thought itself, nor anything I may subsequently say about it, is in the *spirit* of phenomenology as commonly understood. Indeed, the crucial factor for both (early) Husserl and Merleau-Ponty is the *primacy* of perception in the act of consciousness, while thoughts engendered by schemata, ready-made ideas and, indeed, memories were deemed anathema.[19]

In his lecture on 'Internal-time consciousness' from 1964, however, Husserl's focus on the temporality of consciousness caused him to re-evaluate the complicating significance of memory, variously conceived. In the early sections, he still strives to defend the significance of the primacy of perception in the cognitive act by drawing a clear distinction between 'retention' (or 'primary remembrance') and 'recollection':

> For only in primary remembrance do we see what is past ... On the other hand, recollection, like phantasy, offers us mere presentification ... The phantasied now presents a now, but does not give us a now itself [italics in the original].[20]

By Section 24 of the essay, however, Husserl appears to undermine this distinction by recognising that even recollections may be actualised, or made anew, in a continually changing present: 'As the recollective process advances, the horizon is continually opened up anew and becomes richer and more vivid'.[21] Implicit here is surely the inescapable recognition that 'intentional acts' may themselves exist as a *duration* rather than a singular moment of intuition and, as such, bring together elements of primary perception, retention, recollection and phantasy in a complex yet meaningful way. Construed thus, it may indeed be possible to describe my second-level analysis of the driving-event as a phenomenology of sorts.

With reference back to my own journal extracts, it is clear that while many of the recollections that arise in the course of a driving-event are habitual, rehearsed or ready-made (the repetition of my nostalgic response to the derelict cottages at Nether Lochaber, for example), others, such as my close attention to the roadside flowers, would appear to be bringing 'schema' and 'given' (see note 11) together in an acute awareness of the present moment. Further, the fact that this is an intentional act 'no sooner here than gone' means that it must necessarily take its place alongside other 'symbolic presentifications' in which the object of consciousness is *not* immediately present. Thus, although for Husserl these two modes of consciousness ('intuited' and 'symbolic') are fundamentally distinguished from one another (until the complications entertained in the 1964 lecture, at least), a car journey (no matter how short or long) necessarily mixes the two in a blended duration of consciousness that defines what I have characterised here as the 'driving event'.

Conclusion

As anticipated in the introduction, this essay has taken us on a rather different kind of road-trip. Neither the reflections I wrote whilst on the road, nor the second-level analysis I have subjected it to here, are especially concerned with the people or places I encounter along the way, or with the transformative effect of the driving event on my subjectivity. Instead, I have used the essay as an opportunity to dive deep into the states of consciousness that attend each driving-event: to monitor and account for the vagaries of our thought-processes as we sit behind the wheel. This investigation has revealed, amongst other things, the extent to which the practice of driving facilitates the suppression, expression and 'switching' of states of consciousness. Examples included the way in which both nostalgic and anxious thought-chains deflect attention away from looming disappointment and, more positively, the way in which anticipatory consciousness has the capacity to turn our attention to an, as yet, unrealised but potentially utopian future. Crucially, such anticipation may be seen as intrinsic to the driving-event and the unique, somatic experience of driving itself: notably, the sense of moving ourselves forward, towards and away – no matter how mentally or materially trapped we might have been when we stepped into the car.[22] And while other forms of transport (rail, air) may have a similar liberating capacity for propulsion, only driving brings the act and the sensation – as our foot touches the accelerator – within our agency and control. From utopia, then, to *autopia*: or, at least, sometimes.[23]

Notes

1   Henry Vollam Morton, *In Scotland Again*, p. 1. Many of Morton's travelogues have the prefix 'in search of'.
2   Iain Banks, *Raw Spirit: In Search of the Perfect Dram*.
3   Jack Kerouac, *On the Road*.
4   See Lynne Pearce, 'Automobility in Manchester fiction'.
5   Edmund Husserl's lecture is reproduced in Dermot Moran and Tim Mooney eds., *The Phenomenology Reader*, pp. 109–23.

6 'Scene(s)': a term derived from Roland Barthes, *A Lover's Discourse: Fragments*, p. 192.

7 Given the evolution of their philosophy over many years, it is impossible to sum up the position of these leading phenomenologists *vis-à-vis* perception in a note, but both Husserl and Maurice Merleau-Ponty are advocates of the primacy that attaches to the image in the production of consciousness, even though the former famously shifted from his early focus on 'direct eidetic seeing' (Moran and Mooney, *Phenomenology Reader*, p. 14) to a preoccupation with the 'essential structures' subtending the images via the 'transcendental reduction' (see note 17).

8 'Unprejudiced': 'Phenomenology may be characterised initially in a broad sense as the *unprejudiced*, descriptive study of whatever appears to consciousness, precisely in the manner in which it appears [my italics]', Moran and Mooney, *Phenomenology Reader*, p. 1.

9 'Apperception': in psychological discourse, this is commonly understood as the process by which we perceive new experience in relation to past experience.

10 'Spoiling': see Barthes, *A Lover's Discourse*, p. 28. Recent commentators on disappointment include: Lauren Berlant, 'Cruel optimism'; Hilary Hinds, 'Ordinary disappointments: femininity, domesticity and the nation in British middlebrow fiction, 1920–44'; Lynne Pearce, 'Beyond redemption? Mobilizing affect in feminist reading'.

11 'Intuition' and 'givenness': 'Givenness and intuition are correlative terms; the character of the intuiting corresponds to the character of the givenness or manifestation ... Phenomenology does not speculate about essences or make inferences, it is supposed to grasp them directly in immediate "intuition"'. Moran and Mooney, *Phenomenology Reader*, p. 7.

12 See John A. Groeger, *Understanding Driving: Applying Cognitive Psychology to a Complex Everyday Task*, pp. 55-74.

13 Driving and empowerment: see Kingsley Dennis and John Urry, *After the Car*, pp. 40-1.

14 Driving and euphoria: see Pearce, 'Driving north, driving south: reflections on the spatio/temporal co-ordinates of home'; also, Pearce, 'Automobility'.

15 See note 11.

16 Ernst Bloch, *The Principle of Hope*.

17 'Transcendental reduction': the term commonly used to account for Husserl's move from an insistence on 'eidetic' perception to a focus on the 'essential structures' that intentional objects reveal. It is significant that this mode of perception requires more work on the part of the perceiving subject (typically, by the process of 'bracketing') and thus effectively renders phenomenology a markedly proactive practice. See Moran and Mooney, *Phenomenology Reader*, pp. 14–16.

18 Quotation from Martin Heidegger cited in *Ibid.*, p. 19.

19 See note 7.

20 Husserl, reproduced in Moran and Mooney, *Phenomenology Reader*, p. 116.

21 *Ibid.*, p. 121.

22 Entrapment/escape: see Pearce, 'Automobility', p. 107. On the embodiment of driving, see also Mimi Sheller, 'Automotive emotions: feeling the car', and Tim Dant, 'The driver-car'.

23 'Autopia': this concept ('auto' + 'utopia') first entered academic discourse with Peter Wollen and Joe Kerr's superb collection of essays, *Autopia: Cars and Culture*.

Bibliography

Banks, Iain, *Raw Spirit: In Search of the Perfect Dram* (London: Arrow Books, 2004).

Barthes, Roland, *A Lover's Discourse: Fragments,* trans. Richard Howard (Harmondsworth: Penguin, 1990 [1977]).

Berlant, Lauren, 'Cruel optimism', *Differences: A Journal of Feminist Cultural Studies*, 17:3 (2006), 20–36.

Bloch, Ernst, *The Principle of Hope* (3 vols), trans. Neville Plaice, Stephen Plaice and Paul Knight (Oxford: Blackwell, 1986 [1938–47]).

Dant, Tim, 'The driver-car', *Theory, Culture and Society*, 21:4/5 (2004), 61–79.

Dennis, Kingsley, and John Urry, *After the Car* (Cambridge: Polity, 2009).

Groeger, John A. *Understanding Driving: Applying Cognitive Psychology to a Complex Everyday Task* (Hove: Psychology Press, 2000).

Hinds, Hilary, 'Ordinary disappointments: femininity, domesticity and the nation in British middlebrow fiction, 1920–44', *Modern Fiction Studies*, 55:2 (2009), 293–320.

Kerouac, Jack, *On the Road* (London: Penguin Modern Classics, 2000 [1957]).

Merleau-Ponty, Maurice , *Phenomenology of Perception*, trans. Colin Smith (London: Routledge Classics, 2002 [1945]).

Moran, Dermot, and Tim Mooney, *The Phenomenology Reader* (Oxford and New York: Routledge, 2002).

Morton, Henry Vollam, *In Scotland Again* (London: Methuen, 1933).

Pearce, Lynne, 'Driving north, driving south: reflections on the spatio/temporal co-ordinates of home', in *Devolving Identities: Feminist Readings in Home and Belonging* (Aldershot: Ashgate Press, 2000).

Pearce, Lynne, 'Beyond redemption? Mobilizing affect in feminist reading', in Marianne Liljeström and Susanna Paasonen (eds), *Disturbing Differences: Working With Affect in Feminist Readings* (London and New York: Routledge, 2010).

Pearce, Lynne, 'Automobility in Manchester fiction', *Mobilities*, 7:1 (2012), 93–113.

Wollen, Peter, and Joe Kerr, *Autopia: Cars and Culture* (London: Reaktion Books, 2002).

Sheller, Mimi, 'Automotive emotions: feeling the car', *Theory, Culture & Society*, 21:4/5 (2004), 222–42.

Cheap chickens and ethical eggs: the place of an English village in the world

Vron Ware

> I found myself thinking of the countryside as a giant graveyard, haunted by the ghosts of a lost tribe that had once imagined that its lifestyle would last for ever. Where others saw desirable villages and charming scenery, I saw the ruins of a collapsed civilization.
>
> Richard Askwith[1]

This essay grew out of an empirical study of a village in southern England which, from its inception, was a fraught and emotionally entangled undertaking. I was born in this place and have retained a strong connection to it through my family. I soon found, however, that my attempts to think analytically were blocked by my own contradictory feelings: an umbilical pull to house and land tempered by alienation from what was becoming, in my lifetime, an increasingly homogenous and suburbanised enclave. Childhood memories of people, events and spaces provided a reservoir from which I could draw selectively, but having shaken the dust off my shoes so long ago I had lost any sense of belonging to a community.

The rationale of my research was not so much to create a portrait of this parti-cular place as to explore how daily life in a place *like that* had been transformed by the tentacles of globalisation in the second half of the twentieth century. My aim was to sketch the contours of memory and experience by engaging with several generations of residents who were living in or passing through this part of the world, including my own family. Mindful of all the well-trodden conventions and predictable emotional terrain associated with writing about the inexorable decline of rural English life, I tried to steer clear of an abstract notion of 'change', looking instead for continuity, coincidence and disjuncture.

A year into the research I moved with my family from London to the United States, making a new home in a small town in Connecticut over three thousand miles away. In the absolute turmoil of that temporary relocation, the geographical and emotional distance from places I knew well finally offered a vantage point from which to explore them. The break with the past entailed in moving from one country to another gave me a triangulation point that proved useful in steadying my creative compass, at least as far as this project was concerned.

As I handled the disparate material I had gathered, comprising taped inter-views, assorted documents and hand-drawn maps, my own notebooks and countless photographs, I found that by being remote I was protected from the debilitating effects either of remembering too much or being overwhelmed by memory. There are dangers inherent in revisiting one's childhood environment, especially in unguarded moments. My sense of distance, both temporal and geographical, also offered me a sharper and more detached view of the ways in which demography and economics had contributed to a shift in social composition over the decades. And yet there was a value in being able to relate viscerally to the memories evoked by my interviewees and informants because I had my own interpretation of how the place had changed. My way of knowing it was marked by a temporality that insisted that an older 'way of life' was inexorably coming to an end – even if 'the end', already underway when I was born in the 1950s, seemed to have no beginning.

It was striking that many of my older interlocutors repeatedly spoke in this vein when looking back over their own experience of village life, pointing to numerous changes in sociality, institutions, livelihoods and lifestyles. This meant that my study of this particular locality was caught up in a more pervasive nostalgia for English rural life, an orientation that I was determined to avoid. Eviatar Zerubavel uses the term 'sociomental topography' to describe the affective power of collective memory and to investigate *how* we remember as well as *what*.[2] Applying sociological insights to the social contexts within which we access the past, he suggests that particular communities require a collectively shared orientation to the past in order to shape group identity and forge a sense of affiliation. I found the term useful in thinking about rural life in the twentieth and twenty-first centuries because, for one thing, it evoked the social geographies of places in relation to each other, drawing attention to the salience of collective memory operating on different scales: personal, local, regional, national and beyond. At the very least, the experience of living in another country offered glimpses of other sociomental topographies that I might not have had if I had stayed in the United Kingdom. The haunting imagery of 'a giant graveyard' is not uniquely applicable to the British countryside, even if the relationships between urban, suburban and rural work differently in the hinterlands of New England.

The end of an era

How poignant it sounds to proclaim that a 'way of life' is over, its material, social and ethical groundings removed from under its feet, not in sudden motion, like the proverbial rug, but gradually over the years so that its vanishing is almost imperceptible until too late. There is inevitably a tragic sense of loss evoked by the news that human subcultures are literally dying out not just in our lifetimes but in front of our very eyes, or, in this case, behind our backs. Reflecting on the disappearance of something in England called 'village life', author Richard Askwith declared that the point of no return was passed, unnoticed, some time ago. 'Most of us have been vaguely aware of such developments for years,' he wrote in his book *The Lost Village*. 'But the thought that struck me, and has continued to gnaw at me since, was that so much change and loss in such a short space was tantamount to a social tidal wave, in which a whole way of life – and a whole class of traditional country-dwellers – had been swept away'. [3]

Askwith's claim that the 'lost village' summons up the ruins of a collapsed civilisation deserves close scrutiny. When the particular, threatened 'way of life' – resting, in this case, on the notion of a traditional English ruralism – bears a significant, deeply rooted connection to the country's national identity, this sense of loss can generate powerful emotions, exacerbating a melancholic relationship to the past. His powerful evocation of the countryside as 'a giant graveyard, haunted by the ghosts of a lost tribe that had once imagined that its lifestyle would last for ever' could refer to the ruins of any ancient empire. Askwith himself made this connection, adding that the people who inhabit the countryside today are

> a new breed, adapting the physical remains of rural England for the purposes of their new, post-rural society – in the same way that, in the fifth and sixth centuries, post-Roman Italians broke and baked the marbles of antiquity to make plaster for their pre-medieval huts. [4]

Do these images of ghosts, graveyards and ruined empires amount to little more than effective literary hyperbole or do they work on a deeper psychological level? Set against this dramatic, epochal, meta-landscape, the interviews and documentary evidence supplied in analyses like *The Lost Village* risk being trapped within a rather morbid, ironically traditional, discourse of inexorable decline, feeding a strain of melancholic debate about what constitutes 'the national' and even the 'post-imperial'. [5] This makes it difficult to write about social, economic and cultural change in a small place in England outside this particular register.

The focus on the *rural* separates and then marginalises the contemporary experiences of people living outside the country's urban centres. It perpetuates the notion that there is a significant difference between urban and rural ways of life, as though this degree of generational transition – the end of a way of life – is only taking place in 'the countryside' and is therefore more authentically tragic. In addition, the emphasis on 'the countryside' invariably falls on 'the country' as well, feeding a profound nationalism that is unable to escape a melancholic attachment to the past. These two tendencies deepen a pervasive mood of resignation that the country – that is, England – is being transformed by forces outside its control. [6]

The movements of power and history

It is hard to imagine a world that no longer has any useful meanings for the terms urban and rural. These freighted concepts still serve a valuable purpose in measuring the underlying economic and political transformations that cannot always be read on the surface. They can be put to work in constructive and creative ways to unravel all manner of cultural, social and geo-political disjunctures. But that task requires a certain amount of clarification before it can cut through the thickets of nostalgia, melancholy and regret. Introducing a collection of essays intended to re-imagine the relationship between town and country, Anthony Barnett and Roger Scruton tried to resituate the debate by suggesting that there were fundamental connections between the economic, social and cultural changes happening, not just within the country but also in the context of the whole planet: 'The changes to our countryside result from forces which are changing our cities in equal measure, and these forces lie deep in the modern condition'.[7]

In another context, Stuart Hall reflected on the 'massive internal diversification of social life' in a country which was experiencing the unsettling effects of 'globalisation, the decline of Britain's economic fortunes and world position, the end of empire, the rising pressures to devolve government and power, the growth of internal nationalisms, local and regional sentiment, and the challenge of Europe'.[8] He pointed out that ethnic minority migrant communities, invariably associated with urban life, had frequently become the 'symbolic bearers of a complex pattern of change, diversification and "loss"', becoming 'the most convenient scapegoats'.[9] And the telling absence of ethnic diversity within Britain's rural communities only affirmed that this was where an endangered but homogenous 'imagined community' might still be found.

The cultural historian Patrick Wright has consistently analysed the insularity of this discourse on the disappearance of rural England. More importantly, he has simultaneously demonstrated a radical methodology that links articulate protest against the ravages of industrialisation and modernisation to the task of investigating the complex ways in which small places have registered the impact of social, economic and cultural transformation. In an interview discussing his own attempts to write about England, he said, 'I don't expect my localities to reveal much until I have been there many times over a number of years ... I like to see the movement of history and of power in a place before I start guessing at the dimensions of it'.[10]

In addition to relocating to another continent entirely, my decision to spend time on this investigation brought its own rewards. After almost a decade of research it became clear that things continue to evolve, but not always in predictable ways. In fact, one solution to the ideological problems outlined above has been to conceive of the project as a history of the present as much as a documentary of the recent past.

Under the gooseberry bush

The revelations of my comings and goings relate to many different aspects of daily life in my village, but for the purposes of this essay I will use just one interview as a template. Frank Dyer was born there in 1912, some forty years before me. The first time we met, in the summer of 1999, we took a stroll through the village and he explained how things had changed. As we walked I had a strong sensation that he was seeing things that weren't there any more, and he constantly searched for evidence of how things used to be:

> When I was a boy, I was playing with my ball and there was a hole there. And I threw my ball and it went in there, never came back. It's in there somewhere. The ball belonged to me. I never got it back.

Displacements

I remember it was a warm July day and we covered a stretch that was scarcely more than 300 metres long. Between us we struggled to recall people who had long since died or left the area. On this side was a hedge where a man laid out sheep cages that he constructed with his own hands; here was a rope-maker, but that was even before Frank's time; in this house was a harness-maker; there was a well over there and another one here. And here, where this house stands, there was a field that belonged to old Mr So and So. Listening to the tape some time later, I heard the sporadic crunch of our footsteps meandering this way and that, occasionally punctuated by the cheery greeting of a passer-by. In my mind I was able to take this walk again, and though I knew a different history from Frank's, I could retrace our steps, mentally turning my head as I recognised where we were and what we were looking at.

Since we were both born in that place we were both natives of a sort, but the half century that separated us in age reduced the overlap in our memories. As we moved new houses out of the way and restored some old ones, Frank described a way of life based on a local economy that was already residual when he left to work in another village in the 1930s. His sense of time was different, having known long hours of labour in tasks that required skills almost forgotten in this day and age: 'I was taught by the old gardeners in them days to trim a hedge as if, if you could lay a table cloth on top, you'd done a good job.' He pointed to a hedge that he considered to have been badly trimmed. 'That shouldn't be seen. See that one? That's how it should be, like that.' He showed me the correct way to clip the twigs, laying a leaf over the top of each one to conceal the ugly stump. Though the effect is dramatically different, the untrained eye would not notice. 'See what I mean? I mean they look a lot better but it's the time. There's a right way and a wrong way to do everything, isn't there?'

Frank's longevity and incredible powers of recall enabled him to contribute rich material to several formal and informal projects commemorating local history. His hand-drawn map, for instance, has become part of the archive of this tiny place, and photocopies circulate among residents interested in piecing together its knowable past. Listening to his reminiscences of family and social life in the village – Frank's grandfather had been headmaster of the local village school – it is even possible to imagine a continuity between a stratified but predominantly agricultural community that existed at the start of the twentieth century and the more attenuated enclave of middle-class, mainly retired residents who live there today. His testimony, together with his readiness to describe vivid, sensual and narrative fragments in relation to a particular place, provides an invaluable sense of duration.

The priceless evidence available from this 'long view' can be interpreted in many ways, whether put to use in compiling collective oral histories or simply held in trust as a community resource. Such material helps to sustain a common-sense belief that 'everything is different now'. More critically, it puts on record the fact that Frank's generation was born into a social universe that was itself interpreting the unsettling effects of change, however they were recognised in the wider world or brought home to the village. As he pointed out the traces of extinct livelihoods

– the house where the rope-maker once lived – or recalled the dramatic effect of new technologies – the dust raised by the first motor cars as they drove through the village, spoiling the women's washing that hung everywhere on lines – Frank revealed how his childhood memories were also informed by notions like progress, modernisation and a declining 'way of life'.

Such conversations about the past can often contain latent details which, when discovered, can alter – or certainly question – any simple account of inexorable change more effectively than heavily signposted transformations. One small incident occurred during the course of my own encounter with Frank that symbolised the 'fits and starts' of oral memory as a technique capable of binding individual and collective accounts of the past. He had been born at the opposite end of the village from me, in a row of small terraced dwellings constructed in the 1880s for agricultural labourers and their families. As we neared the house, Frank suddenly recalled that there had been a gooseberry bush nearby which had been fruitful when he was a child. He rummaged around in the hedge for a few minutes, and then to my astonishment announced triumphantly that the plant was still there.

It was only later that I realised that this same gooseberry bush, concealed just where he left it seven decades earlier, opposite a majestic oak tree and half hidden by long grass, was offering itself as an interpretive device to measure the social ecology of village life in ways that were not over-determined by the ponderous scales of decline and progress.

A flash of recollection, awakened by the poignant thought process of revisiting the pleasures of childhood, led to an unexpected rediscovery of material evidence, almost like buried treasure. The gooseberries had been forgotten – why else would the bush have been submerged by the undergrowth? Those particular children who enjoyed the fruit had grown up and mostly moved away, but somehow the bush had survived. Now, each time I pass that stretch of road I wonder if Frank had been mistaken. Perhaps in his eagerness to find material proof of his childhood in that particular spot, he had seized on a leaf that looked similar, feeling gnarled, thorny branches that reminded him of the prickly nature of gooseberry bushes.

Knowing that I am perfectly capable of checking for myself, I realise that this is not the point. Frank's spontaneous act of remembering and rediscovering indicated the value of aligning human and non-human life forms in a complex, haphazard, imaginative, and rhizomorphic account of economic, social, environmental and cultural history.

The Akenfield problem

Before Frank and I set off for our stroll we sat in the garden of my parents' house drinking tea. I asked him where he had worked and he told me about his employment with a poultry company with which he had served as a young man right up to his retirement. In 1936 he had started on a hatchery site where they were pioneering the use of new incubating equipment to produce day-old chicks. In the early 1940s the company acquired more local farms and grew corn crops, and

Frank moved on to a different site within the same area. In 1945 he returned to the original hatchery where he was a foreman until 1963. It was a brief account, a few dates here and there, but the difficulties of interpreting this story of a working life outside the conventions illustrated by Askwith's study seemed insurmountable.

My uncertainty about how to represent Frank's career was exacerbated not just by the conventions of writing about the erosion of English country life, but more specifically in the wake of a particular book which has set the tone for rural research within the past few decades. In 1969 Ronald Blythe published a compilation of oral memories taken from conversations with three generations of residents in a village in Suffolk which he called Akenfield.[11] Recounting experiences that spoke both within and about the locality, the book offers glimpses of an authentic English rural life that illuminated patterns of transition far beyond Suffolk – the testimonies of young men queuing up to offer their services to the British army in 1914 in their desperation to escape agricultural servitude being one striking example. As a result, the book became a classic study of a disappearing world, its appeal travelling far beyond the country itself.

In 2006 a sequel to *Akenfield* was published: *Return to Akenfield: Portrait of an English Village in the 21ˢᵗ Century*. This time the research was carried out and written up, not by a native of Suffolk but by a young Canadian author, Craig Taylor. Fascinated by the original study, he decided to find out how much had changed – or remained the same – in the generation living in the village since the book was published. 'I grew up in Western Canada, thousands of miles from Suffolk,' he explained, 'but like so many readers I was taken by the vividness of Blythe's book and the way it prised open this far-off world, a place with its own songs, its own traditions of planting and harvest, and even its own breed of horse'.[12]

Taylor begins with an interview with Blythe, using his predecessor's method of walking around in the same place holding a 'natural conversation'. Blythe told him how he came to write the book. Having settled in the area as a writer, he was approached by publishers from London and New York who had a proposition.

> Village life was changing all over the world, they said, and they wanted to do a series of books about it together. They would send a Russian writer to the French countryside or a French writer to Russia, that sort of thing. Mostly the books were to be written by sociologists. When they came to me and said that I should do one about Britain, I told them I was not a sociologist remotely, nor had I heard of the term oral history at the time. Besides I'd seen outside the window of this house all my life. What was interesting about it?[13]

Blythe contemplated moving to Wales to do something different, but found it hard to get inspiration. One wet and windy afternoon he went for a walk and decided to visit the local nurse who was an acquaintance. 'Once she started speaking about her own life, another person emerged … I wrote it down and that other person emerged.' Blythe continued to do the rounds, simply encouraging individuals to talk about themselves and then listening as they opened up. 'My only real credential was that I was native to its situation in nearly every way and had only to listen to hear my own world talking.'[14] The result was not intended as a 'spectacular' description of an idiosyncratic place: 'Akenfield' could be anywhere. 'The book was meant to be not a special village but any village,' he told Taylor; 'it was just a pattern of the world into which I was born'.[15]

Blythe's collected and edited conversations do not dwell on the transformations that have taken place, but a sense of history emerges naturally as the participants reflect on their own life courses. Taylor headed for the village some forty years later with a mission to seek out how much things had changed in the intervening years. Immediately he found himself noting the unremarkable, banal details of everyday life and turning them into evidence that the English village had entered the 'contemporary' world. 'But some changes were obvious,' he wrote in the introduction to the book:

> The two shops and the post office mentioned in *Akenfield* are gone, converted to private houses, and the vicarage sits empty behind the disused tennis courts. A street built in 1976 to house British Telecom workers at their new research centre in Martlesham wouldn't look out of place in any London commuter town. On the back of the cutlery in the pub's bright dining room is that telltale sign of contemporary life: IKEA. And just a few days before I arrived, the village was wired for broadband Internet access.[16]

By drawing attention to visible changes Taylor suggests that some things can be read at face value, and readily slotted into a conventional script about the dubious teleology of modern life. However, the fact that the village had only just acquired Internet access alerts the reader to the uneven pace of modernisation, and the idea that Akenfield is only now, in the last few days, 'catching up' with the rest of us. It would not be unfair to mention that Taylor grew up reading the original *Akenfield* in a country that has a strong post-colonial relationship to England. This England was an old country in which the idea of authentic and deep-rooted rustic traditions retained an enduring appeal.[17] Having spent several years investigating social transition in a place that I once knew as a native, I am fully aware of the dangers of projecting my own culturally-formed fantasies back on to the place. This only serves to underline the difficulty of finding a way to interpret and measure social change without becoming aligned with 'powerful feelings' that lead to banal generalisations.

Taylor ends with a further conversation with Blythe in which the older man offers his verdict on the improvement and loss in the quality of life since he wrote *Akenfield*.

> No, there's not a lot to envy about the old days. But something has been lost … people don't look at the fields now … They do other things … It's just modern life.[18]

Blythe's reluctance to sentimentalise the rural past by stressing the physical hardships is countered by his lukewarm assessment of 'modern life'. 'They're living urban lives in the countryside – not just here but all over the place … It is the normality of the new comfort.'[19]

Displacements

Those oral testimonies that garner evidence of recognisable 'ways of life' from a passing generation have tremendous value as independent social documents. However, as Hall suggested, the powerful feelings of nostalgia, melancholy and disillusionment evoked by a portrait of rural England in decline can become instrumental in promoting an unhealthy nationalism, resistant to more cosmopolitan modes of understanding not just how and why life might be different now than it used to be but, more importantly, what the future might look like too.

The customer is always right

The long-surviving gooseberry bush that Frank rediscovered on our walk must have been a sign pointing out how to bring the village back into the world, but it took a few years more years of reflection to understand its significance. The materiality of the bush was a hint that perhaps things don't change as much as we think they do. Or at least we might think that things have changed, only to find much later that there has been a continuity, only visible with hindsight.

When Frank and I walked through the village we did not discuss the poultry farm tucked away behind the imposing hedge of Leylandii trees just off the main thoroughfare. I had hoped to interview him about his experience of working there, but it turned out that he had been based in another site about ten miles away. Both farms had been owned by the same company, so there were connections, but I was a little disappointed that he could not tell me more about this one. In any case, I wanted to know what it was like to work in the rapidly developing poultry industry and to be part of a continuous experiment with raising ever cheaper and more profitable protein. Although Hampshire was associated with poultry farming before the 1930s, it was on an entirely different scale from the mass production sites that developed after 1945.

Like many of my informants, Frank had mentioned the contrast between the daily diet in the 1930s and 1940s, governed by seasonal rhythms as much as economics, and today's taken-for-granted availability of chicken and egg products. 'Before the war, the winter egg was the dearest egg,' he told me.

> And then prices went down probably during the summer when there was so many about… And you see all they had at Christmas time was just cockerels, you know, but not, there wasn't a broiler trade all through the year like it is now.

I had another interest in the local story of poultry farming because my father, a struggling market gardener in the early 1950s, embarked on broiler chickens for a few years and I had many memories of my own in that department. The trail that I wanted to follow started with the early Anglo-American stations and led to a vast network of sites each catering to different stages of hatching and rearing. I had already discovered that the concealed plant behind the tall hedge was then owned by Poultry First, which was multi-national in scope. Rather than dwell on the outward and more obvious signs of social transition in the village, I decided to focus instead on the transformation of food production that was continuing relentlessly out of sight.

By chance Frank came to meet me equipped with material evidence of his achievements with the firm that he used to work for. He proudly handed me a photocopy of a back issue of *Sterling World*, dated September 1964, and one of the leading publications of the British poultry industry at the time.[20] Inside was an article mentioning Frank by name, with his photo alongside, but instead of paying tribute to his work as a foreman in the poultry sheds, it spoke of his new role in landscaping the grounds of an adjoining site. It turned out that his skills as a gardener were legendary and, on his retirement in 1963, he was given the task of planting and maintaining a beech hedge lining the route to the new hatchery. While this aspect of Frank's life-story offered sociological insights into work-related themes, it was only when I looked through the pages of *Sterling World* that I was struck by the wealth of cultural information that emerged from this glimpse inside the fevered world of egg production.

One example in particular caught my eye. The entrepreneurs of the new trans-atlantic food industry were nonplussed by the lack of enthusiasm shown by British consumers faced with white eggs. In an article entitled 'Brown eggs or white…? A matter of economics' I learned:

> At present we have the frustrating situation that if brown eggs are offered to [the British housewife] at the farm gate she is willing to pay up to a shilling a dozen extra for them; but if they are offered to her as Lion-stamped eggs in the shops she expects them for the same price as white eggs! Moreover, she is becoming increasingly insistent on the inclusion of a proportion of brown eggs in every shop sample or pre-pack.[21]

The battle between the consumer, or in their words, the British housewife, and Britain's new chicken champions was premised on the fact that the White Link hybrid was better at churning out white eggs than its cousin, the brown egg layer. A series of sums illustrated that the margin in favour of the White Link was four shillings and two pennies per bird. But while profit is the driving force behind any industry, the article revealed the psychological warfare needed to break the consumers' association of certain foods with small-scale, free-range production. The British housewife, particularly in the 'better-class shopping areas of Greater London and the Home Counties', clearly knew what was good for her, but the industry was determined to change her mind: 'it will be an uphill task trying to break into a market which has been so completely monopolised by the farm-gate producer for so long.'

The author's irritation with the reluctance of more discerning consumers to buy mass-produced eggs rather than ones they could trace to locally reared chickens stands out in stark contrast to the advice that shoppers are inundated with today. Contemporary food culture in Britain engages unevenly with ethical and moral dilemmas about the sourcing, quality and volume of food, as well as the treatment of animals in the global food production chain. But another article in *Sterling World* revealed the dispute caused by the controversial application of new technologies invented to maximise profits. One writer reviewed the economics of intensive methods of production, answering specific criticisms of the new system of battery cages for laying hens. Discussing the accusation that intensive methods were guilty of mental cruelty, he suggested:

> We know that birds are affected by mental stress – or at least something approaching this kind of condition in the human species. This must be obvious from the existence of a 'peck order' … We must assume that this behaviour presupposes some mental process akin to thinking or reasoning, stimulated by a dislike of being bullied and a desire to escape from the recognizable cause.[22]

His conclusion was to urge the industry to 'think a little more on the living nature of the creature which gives us our livelihood and ponder much more on environment, management, and the interrelation with production'.[23]

This measured assessment of the dangers of intensivism was countered by another piece in the magazine which asserted that, 'Birds laying in battery cages appear to have a feeling of well being which is necessary for high egg production'.[24]

An interview with Alfred, whose career in poultry farming began in the 1950s when he joined my father in his new enterprise, revealed what it was like to witness the constant pressure to reduce costs in the interests of making a greater profit. 'When we started off there were 11,000 chickens in 12,000 square feet: one and a quarter square foot per bird. We finished with 0.5 square foot per bird. In 12,000 square feet we had over 25,000 birds … it became factory farming.' He explained how it was that the savings were forced on them by the rising cost of feed and other expenses. 'I never felt it was cruel,' he reflected thoughtfully, 'though they could have been much more comfortable.'

> They are very sensitive creatures, and it is unnatural, but they don't know any different. If you opened the doors they would run away from the light. There were times when they jumped off the lorry and crept into the hedge, but they could be easily caught in the first couple of days till they got used to the light.

Although many working in this relatively new industry were able to rationalise new methods as inevitable outcomes of a competitive sector, there were others who were becoming alarmed. In 1967 dairy farmer Peter Roberts, who lived nearby, founded an organisation called Compassion in World Farming (CIWF) in order to launch a campaign against raising chickens in battery cages. The organisation's mission to improve the lives of farm animals everywhere led to the growth of transnational networks of similar campaigning groups. As a result of their coordinated campaigns, the barren battery cage was banned within the European Union with effect from 1 January 2012.[25]

By fixing an eye on the chicken, rather than the actual farm, or even on the farm workers, all manner of insights into social attitudes, values and practices can be gleaned which connect the space of the village as a site of production, owned by a multi-national corporation, to a world-wide community of consumers dependent on protein for their existence. More importantly here, these observations are able to disrupt the artificial binary of urban-industrial and rural-agricultural. The rise of industrial production in rural areas, for example, confounds the false notion that villages and factories (and unions, takeovers, buyouts and multi-nationals) do not fit together, while the industry's attempt to change consumers' behaviour still requires extensive propaganda that milks powerful pastoral concepts such as 'natural', wholesome and farm-fresh.

But even more articulate than the chicken, the egg is also able to provide valuable object lessons on the history of everyday life. In his book on the place of sugar in modern history, Sidney Mintz admits that 'the prosaic quality of the subject matter is inescapable; what could be less "anthropological" than the historical examination of a food that graces every modern table? And yet,' he continues in his introduction, 'the anthropology of just such homely, everyday substances may help us to clarify both how the world changes from what it was to what it may become, and how it manages at the same time to stay in certain regards very much the same.'[26] Having studied the legacies of sugar production on communities in the Caribbean, he discovered that by focusing on sugar itself he was able to explore a far more satisfactory and complex account of how this particular commodity reached into and connected the lives of societies in different geographical locations across such a broad sweep of time as 'modern history'. By taking a food-centred approach to the anthropology of English village life, using the egg as a mediating device, it becomes possible to situate Frank's oral testimony (and the material provided by many other residents) within a very different framework of social, cultural and economic history.

From slimming to superfood

We have seen how the colour of the shell was a decisive factor in changing consumers' tastes, and how gendered this project was. By tracing the history of egg eating – from the seasonal patterns of pre-1939 Britain to the rationed one-per-person every three weeks in the immediate post-war period, to the increasing year-round availability from the mid-1950s onwards – a picture emerges of the way that a population can be persuaded to change its diet within a matrix of need, supply and not so subtle social engineering addressed to the question: why are eggs so good for us? The information is readily available on the pages of the Egg Marketing Board's website, but even here this is shown to be a sensitive process with often unpredictable peaks and troughs.

Advertising campaigns – like the celebrated 'Go to Work on an Egg' slogan – effectively increased demand in 1957, while health scares about cholesterol in the 1960s and 1970s diminished it. In 1988 the statement by Tory minister Edwina Currie that British eggs were likely to be contaminated by salmonella had a drastic effect on consumption which fell by 60 per cent overnight. The publication of Delia Smith's phenomenally successful *How to Cook* in 1998 increased sales, and this was followed by the extraordinary impact of the Atkins Diet, which promoted a high protein intake. In the light of new claims that obesity presents a greater and more immediate threat than climate change, demand for eggs appeared to be rising further after US research indicated that eating two hard-boiled eggs for breakfast was instrumental in successful weight-loss diets.[27] British egg eating is also affected by numerous economic factors – escalating global wheat prices, the dramatic rise in egg production in China and Brazil, fears about the pandemic of avian flu and the increased costs associated with improving animal welfare. The United Kingdom was one of several countries that managed to switch production methods to comply with the new law and Lion eggs (produced in 'higher welfare colony cages') are currently marketed under the slogan 'Britain's Pride'.[28]

This brief list illustrates how the egg floats around in a constellation of powerful meanings about food and culture, governed by economics and biopolitics in a deeply divided and unequal world. In terms of production, the fate of the egg can offer ways to interpret the experience of the poultry farmer in England within a pattern of marginalisation being experienced by farmers and peasants on a global scale, providing a transparent link in a chain that connects over-consumption in some parts of the world with scarcity and famine in others.[29] As with sugar, a focus on this 'homely, everyday substance' is able to reveal all kinds of things about what changes and what stays very much the same.

Returning eight years later to the village where I last saw Frank, I paid a visit to the poultry farm to see what further developments had taken place. The buildings had an unkempt appearance, and although the plant was being cleaned between flocks, residents of the village were complaining about the increase in rats as a result of cutbacks in pest control. On making inquiries I discovered that Poultry First no long existed, and the firm that ran this site was part owned by a 'sister' company in Germany. The manager of the local office told me that when she joined in 1999, the same year that I interviewed Frank, she was told by fellow workers that they looked back fondly to the good old days in the early 1990s when the industry was still expanding. When I asked her if the company hired Eastern European workers she told me that they did not at the moment, although if I wanted proof that they worked in the area I should go to the local Tesco store and see the shelves designated for Polish food.

One of the main employers of new migrant labour force, it turned out, was Vitacress, a rising multi-national located in another village nearby. Watercress is a longstanding local crop that I remember as a child since it flourishes on the particular characteristics of gravel river beds in the area. Having been elevated to 'superfood', along with green leaves such as rocket and 'baby' spinach, it was now enjoying its turn to make an impact on the national diet, albeit in more class-specific ways than the humble egg. The political economy involved in picking, preparing and packing those bags of health-giving salads only added to the value of food as an object of inquiry. Following the trail of the cheap chicken and the ethical egg, the resilience of this ancient nutritious product might provide yet another signpost that points beyond the clichéd dichotomy of 'desirable villages and charming scenery' and 'the ruins of a collapsed civilization'.[30]

Notes

1   Richard Askwith, 'Elegy for Britain's vanishing village way of life', *Daily Mail*, 18 April 2008.
2   Eviatar Zerubavel, *Time Maps*, pp. 2–3.
3   Askwith, *Daily Mail*.
4   *Ibid.*
5   I wrote about this in 'The ins and outs of Anglo-Saxonism: the future of white decline' in M. Perryman (ed.), *Breaking up Britain: Four Nations after a Union*, pp. 133–49. See also Patrick Wright, 'Last Orders', *Guardian*, Saturday, 9 April, 2005.
6   Patrick Wright, 'Real England? Reflections on Broadway Market'. OpenDemocracy 23 April 2008, www.opendemocracy.net/node/36320/pdf (accessed 31 July 2012)
7   Anthony Barnett and Roger Scruton (eds), *Town and Country*, p. xiii.
8   Stuart Hall, 'The multicultural question', pp. 229–30.
9   *Ibid.*, p. 230.
10 'Writing the obituaries: an interview with Patrick Wright, interviewed by Manfred Pfister', *Soundings*, 8 (1998), p. 15.
11 Ronald Blythe, *Akenfield: Portrait of an English Village*.
12 Craig Taylor, *Return to Akenfield: Portrait of an English Village in the 21st century*, p. 14.
13 *Ibid.*, p. 6.
14 *Ibid.*, p. 13.
15 *Ibid.*, p. 7.
16 *Ibid.*, p.14.
17 Robert J. C. Young, *The Idea of English Ethnicity*.
18 Taylor, *Return to Akenfield*, pp. 228–9.
19 *Ibid.*, p. 229.
20 *Sterling World*, 1964.
21 *Ibid.*, p. 29.
22 *Ibid.* p. 9.
23 *Ibid.*
24 *Ibid.*, pp. 30–1.
25 Peter and his wife Anna, who also raised poultry on their farm in Hampshire, had become increasingly concerned with the animal welfare issues connected to the new systems of intensive farming that began to take hold in the 1960s. They were unable to convince any of the major animal welfare societies to campaign against factory farming, so decided to do it themselves and CIWF was born. See www.ciwf.org.uk.
26 Sidney Mintz, *Sweetness and Power*, p. xxvii.
27 'Obesity "as bad as climate risk"'. BBC News, Sunday, 14 October 2007. http://news.bbc.co.uk/1/hi/uk/7043639.stm (accessed 31 July 2012)
28 www.legaleggs.com/page/production (accessed 1 August 2012)
29 'The end of cheap food', Leader, *The Economist*, 6 December 2007. www.economist.com/opinion/displaystory.cfm?story_id=10252015 (accessed 31 July 2012)
30 Four years later, in 2012, the situation in the village was different again. The prospect of the site being abandoned as a casualty of the global economic crisis had rallied the inhabitants of the village to plan how to pre-empt unwanted development in its place. The egg might be disappearing from view as a driving force in the story of this particular village, but it will doubtless retain a ghostly afterlife in the fabric of the community.

Bibliography

Askwith, Richard, *The Lost Village* (London: Ebury Press, 2008).

Askwith, Richard, 'Elegy for Britain's vanishing village way of life', *Daily Mail*, 18 April 2008.

Blythe, Ronald, *Akenfield: Portrait of an English Village* (Harmondsworth: Penguin, 1969).

Barnett, Anthony and Roger Scruton (eds), *Town and Country* (London: Jonathan Cape, 1998).

Hall, Stuart, 'Conclusion: the multicultural question', in B. Hesse (ed.), *Un/settled Multiculturalisms: Diasporas, Entanglements, Transruptions* (London: Zed Books, 2000).

Mintz, Sidney, *Sweetness and Power: the Place of Sugar in Modern History* (New York: Elizabeth Sifton Books, 1985)

Taylor, Craig, *Return to Akenfield: Portrait of an English Village in the 21st Century* (London: Granta Books, 2006)

Wright, Patrick, 'Writing the obituaries: an interview with Patrick Wright, interviewed by Manfred Pfister', *Soundings*, 8 (1998), pp. 14–48.

Wright, Patrick, 'Last Orders', *Guardian*, Saturday, 9 April, 2005.

Wright, Patrick, 'Real England? Reflections on Broadway Market'. OpenDemocracy, 23 April, 2008, www.opendemocracy.net/node/36320/pdf.

Ware, Vron, 'The ins and outs of Ango-Saxonism: the future of white decline', in M. Perryman (ed.), *Breaking up Britain: Four Nations after a Union* (London: Lawrence & Wishart, 2009).

Young, Robert J. C., *The Idea of English Ethnicity* (Oxford: Blackwell, 2007).

Zerubavel, Eviatar, *Time Maps: Collective Memory and the Social Shape of the Past* (Chicago, IL: University of Chicago Press, 2003).

If the shoe fits: appropriating identity?

Brenda Cooper

The shoe

I could not take my eyes off the shoe.

Maud Sulter: *SYRCAS*, 1994

It appears in this photograph by Maud Sulter, from her 'SYRCAS' series of suggestive images. The shoe felt so familiar, as if Sulter had been the photographer of my family in Lithuania and provided an opening into my own story and aspirations. I wanted that shoe to help me to tell my own story. Should I be able to use it to do that? The shoe reminded me of the boots worn by my grandmother, my Bobba, in a photograph taken with my mother when she was a small girl in a park in Lithuania, before they boarded the ship headed for South Africa, to escape the persecution of Jews in Eastern Europe.

From South Africa ...

From the beginning of my becoming politically aware as a white South African, I have tried to dissociate myself from that Jewish past. The conservative Jewish community in which I grew up in the Eastern Cape refused to recognise the parallels between Nazi Germany and Apartheid South Africa. Instead of identifying with the Eastern European Jewishness of my history, I immersed myself in African art and literature. Albeit that South Africa was where I was born and I had no other home, being white meant that I could not call myself African with any simple sense of entitlement. I have imagined other worlds through the visions of African artists, like Sulter, with her mixed parentage of Ghanaian father and Scottish mother. Over the years, I have understood my life through African thinkers, poets and novelists. Despite being white, I identified with the movement of Black artists and writers and joined them in the project of restoring the record of their creativity to the archives of the mainstream. I taught and researched African writing over nearly three decades at the University of Cape Town as a politics of opposition to its absence in the curricula of apartheid South Africa. The point was not to eulogise but to engage with African and diasporic writers, thinkers and intellectuals, an engagement that apartheid had done its best to prevent. To this end, I published books on the first, second and third generations of mainly West African fiction writers in English and their migrations from Africa to Europe. It was important to keep in simultaneous focus the existence of many heterogeneous Africas, alongside the forces of cultural imperialism, which extended over much of Africa as a whole. Many Africas and one Africa; and also hybrid Africa, which understands cultures as the product of movements, trade and mixture, a syncretism which mixed up European and African cultural threads, trends and influences. This meant that while my research and teaching became invested in an identity that focused on Africa, far from the Lithuania where my mother was born, it also helped me to understand how identities are fluid and composite.

What all of this meant was that as I engaged in the politics of making visible to my South African students the wealth and variety of African culture and intellectual thought, I also took from this the possibility of a new identity for myself. In the face of my family's racial prejudices and my own identification with Africa, I used literature to discard my Europeanness: both the Russianness of my grandfather, my Zeida, and the Eastern Europeanness of my Bobba. I tried to colour the whiteness of my family and black-out the Jewishness of my past, in favour of being part of the place where I was born, a place that I could not claim in my own voice, given my position of white privilege in the context of apartheid.

Something has changed recently and I am now questioning my use of the stories and images of black writers for the first time. What is different is that up until now I have not used black artists and writers to tell my own story of white South Africanness. What I taught, and wrote about, was black fiction, such as West African experimentation with Magical Realism, the consequences of the exodus of African writers to Amsterdam, Glasgow, London and New York and how this impacted on the development of a global African form of English. Now I am writing the story of my family's migration from Eastern Europe to South Africa and my own, temporary but lengthy, relocation from Cape Town to the northwest of England. Extracting Sulter's shoe to tell this story risks putting whiteness at the centre of history yet again. This white centring has always been at the expense of black visibility in the ghastly zero sum game of race wars. This is why Lubaina Himid, who worked closely with Maud Sulter, says that she makes images of black women because she wants to 'take back the art which has been stolen'.[1] And Himid resents 'white people [who] keep seeing themselves at the centre of other people's pictures where they absorb the efforts and energies of others'.[2] Sulter herself criticises 'trendy Londoners' who 'pilfer our culture our foods our sounds'.[3]

To Salford

My new-found space in Salford, Greater Manchester, where I now live, far from the intensities of Cape Town, has proved to be creatively hospitable in unexpected ways. The displacement of my intellectual life from the university setting, in which all my writing has taken place up until now, makes me rethink my worlds outside of the codes of writing imposed by the academy. Here I have been able to write differently, supplementing words with the visual and exploring rhyme, rhythm and poetry. And yet, this question of the appropriateness of writing my own life story into the lives of writers and artists from the diaspora remains an open one.

At the same time, it is liberating to write outside the framework of race, that still dominates the post-apartheid South African scene. It feels easier to write my own story here in Salford. The political urgencies of South Africa had seemed to prohibit it and make it self-indulgent. Here in England the melodramas of race meld more easily into broader questions of privilege; the Black British African diaspora makes the malleability of cultures palpable; Jackie Kay is a key influence, rather than Chinua Achebe or Ama Ata Aidoo. Here racial lines feel to me more blurred. Helen Oyeyemi, for example, whose Nigerian parents moved to London when she was four years old, gives us a white character as her alter ego in her novel *White is for Witching*.[4] This is to anticipate the fiction of Esi Edugyan, to which I refer below, who was born in Canada of Ghanaian parents and who echoes Maud Sulter in her preoccupation with a broad view of prejudice that encompasses Jews as well as Blacks in Nazi Germany in her novel, *Half Blood Blues*.[5]

Being far from home has brought to mind that this African diaspora of Sulter, Himid and Edugyan might have some intersections with the Jewish diaspora of my grandparents – Russian on one side and Lithuanian on the other. Maud Sulter's Ghanaian father and Scottish mother and Lubaina Himid's English grandfather on one side and grandmother from Zanzibar on the other, resonate with the migrations and cultural translations of my own grandparents.

With the wider view made possible by the move to Salford, at the end of my career of teaching, I find myself rethinking my lapsed Jewishness and my whiteness. It feels as if I cannot take on the task of self-representation when I enter into Sulter's artwork, unless I do so in my own skin. And, in fact, Sulter herself enables a broader and more nuanced portrait of oppression and violation to emerge, one that cuts across race. It is important not to take this point too far, however, since Sulter did focus much of her art and her poetry on the question of representing herself in the guises of other black women whom history had forgotten. Race may seem to matter less here, but it still matters.

Maud Sulter's guises of self-portrayal

In a series of large, ornate photographic portraits, Sulter depicts the Muses in the guise of black women, such as Alice Walker, Lubaina Himid, Dorothea Smartt, and others who posed for her. In the series, called Zabat, 'conventionally imaged in the history of Western art as white women, they are here portrayed by Black women writers, artists, musicians and strategists'.[6] In Sulter's own guise as Calliope, the Muse of epic poetry, Sulter becomes Calliope and also Jeanne Duval, the poet whose talent was negated by Charles Baudelaire. In the narrative accompanying the image of Calliope, Sulter imagines Jeanne Duval pondering 'that if you are Black and female the chance of one's poetry being attributed to one in later life is slim'.[7] Moreover, 'first you think they wooed you for your beauty', but you begin to realise 'It's your fucking talent they were after. That casual request for help with a rhythm or a rhyme soon after appears in print under some fuckers nom de plume and you are done for.'[8] Calliope declares that all she cares about 'is getting [her] name back on [her] poetry'.[9] While masks and guises that are assumed for the purpose of self-representation within the fraught context of race may be complicated, for Maud Sulter, taking on the identity of Jeanne Duval, the Caribbean Creole mistress and muse of the poet Baudelaire, is a clear-cut political statement. By doing so, she defies the erasure of Duval from history. For Sulter, this erasure becomes exemplary of the deletion and marginalisation of black women in general, and herself in particular.

Incensed by the erasure of Duval from Gustave Courbet's famous painting, *The*

Painter's Studio, after Baudelaire had instructed the painter to airbrush her out, Sulter writes:

> So now this painting, which is so central to the history of modern art, hangs prominently in the Musée d'Orsay in Paris. If you catch the light in the right place you can still see Duval's silhouette gazing at Baudelaire.[10]

Sulter's work is not a critical re-reading of an image. Rather, in a series of extraordinary portraits which merge Duval and Sulter, she brings Duval back into history. In the surfacing and constructing of palimpsests of erased pasts, historical and political knowledges are produced. What is significant here is that Sulter does not masquerade as Jeanne Duval, she *becomes* Jeanne Duval.[11]

Maud Sulter: *Jeanne Duval,* 2003

After an interview with Sulter in 2003, Vicky Allan of the *Sunday Herald* reports that 'the only subject [Sulter] seems really happy to talk about, to fill in with details, is Jeanne Duval, her muse'. She quotes Sulter as saying:

> I felt very strongly about how she'd [Duval] been described in historical texts, because all of them couldn't be true. They presented these great extremes. Either she sat there and never said a word, or she was loud. She was an idiot, didn't have a brain cell and yet Baudelaire would say she'd helped him edit his poems. He'd write to her to take care of 'my photographs and my writings'. You don't leave these things with someone who's unreliable. If your writing is the most important thing in your life, you probably leave them with the person you trust most in the world.[12]

The interviewer is wrong, however, to call Duval Sulter's muse. She was *Baudelaire's* muse, and musedom is abhorrent to Sulter, especially when the subject 'serves as a catalyst for ideas and representations in the work of others',[13] as was the case in Angela Carter's 'Black Venus' story. On one occasion, Carter asked Sulter what she thought of her story, in which Duval is her protagonist. Sulter recalls her response: 'I found I did not have much to say.'[14] Why is Sulter so tight-lipped in her disapproval? Would she also deny me, and my Bobba, also white women, entry into her frame? Perhaps it is not a matter of race, but rather the nature of Carter's depiction which is problematic. Carter's Jeanne Duval is a victim, who is depleted by her mixed-ness. Carter's Duval 'had always been too poor to be able to afford the luxury of acknowledging a humiliation as such. You took what came.'[15] I cannot visualise Sulter taking whatever came, or thinking that Duval would have been too poor to acknowledge the humiliations to which she was subjected. Worse, for a writer of her sensitivities, Carter romanticises a powerful African purity of which she imagines Duval has been robbed – 'The splendid continent to which her skin allied her had been excised from her memory. She had been deprived of history.'[16] I share Sulter's objection to the image of Duval as the product of colonial parenting by a grandmother whose own mother had died aboard some ship and 'another woman of some other nation … suckled me'.[17] Carter disparages here the interracial mixing, which Sulter celebrates. Carter's particular politics of representation offended Sulter. In taking on the guise of Jeanne Duval in the present, Sulter recovers, remakes, her existence in the opening up of an alternative future. This becomes the politics of surfacing palimpsests.

Excavating palimpsests

Palimpsests are the traces and remains of texts, stories and paintings that have been erased by history. Within the context of African and diasporic cultures, these traces become the surviving evidence of the existence of peoples and places that have been buried by dominant narratives. Excavating these traces is at the heart of the postcolonial literary theory that I taught at the University of Cape Town. And so Sulter searches 'into the hidden pockets of History. She excavates shafts that are rarely talked about and she investigates how the hiding is arranged, and even staged.'[18]

The stratigraphy of the palimpsest incorporates multiple layers of histories and offers itself as world within worlds. In *The Moor's Last Sigh*, Salman Rushdie calls the palimpsest 'a Babel of politics'.[19] In creating a fictional place, *Palimpstine*, with obvious echoes of the nation with which this rhymes, he transforms what is buried into a vision of poetic and political possibilities:

> Place where worlds collide, flow in and out of one another, and washofy away. Place were an air-man can drowno in water, or else grow gills; where a water-creature can get drunk, but also chokeofy, on air. One universe, one dimension, one country, one dream, bumpo'ing into another, or being under, or on top of. Call it Palimpstine.[20]

This imagined place, a kind of Palestine, with all its politically fraught and violent undertones, is revealed from beneath the rubble. Through a similar strategy, Sulter creates her SYRCAS series of photographs, which are 'large-scale, matt-laminated, cibachrome colour prints, mounted in raw oak frames', which 'are immediately striking but there's much more to them than first meets the eye'.[21] And, 'Sulter uses the medium as a starting point from which to build the layers of meaning and inventive image-construction which have characterised the black photographer's work over the past 10 years.'[22] This work uses digital techniques to recombine elements of the image and to expose the buried past of Africa's contribution to European history and culture. Jane Richards goes on:

'SYRCAS' is a fascinating series of large-scale constructed images which mix classical painting, technicolour post-card photography (of German landscapes), sculpture and black-and-white cut-outs of African masks and icons – to present Sulter's overall picture of the African presence in European history and culture.[23]

Sulter's digitally composited photograph (page 121) inserts new figures into a traditional European mountain landscape. The face of an African boy is set rigid in the rock, like a fossilised reminder of Africa's forgotten place in the history of Europe. He is perhaps Lubaina Himid's Kwesi, who has been imprisoned in his rename of Henry. Lubaina Himid made one hundred painted portrait cut-outs in which she returned their names to each one of these people, names which had been lost because their European owners, could not and would not learn their African names.

My name is Kwesi
They call me Henry[24]

Lubaina Himid: *My Name is Kwesi,* 2004

127

Maud Sulter: *SYRCAS*, 1994

In another work, an African mask seems to float above the landscape, in front of the Alpine snow-capped mountains and fir trees. The shape of the mountain shadows the mask, reversing the conventional power structure and rendering the African mask more solid and permanent than the European mountain.

It is certainly more majestic, rising beyond the frame of the image and hovering in the air like a god. And everything is enfolded in the unreality of reflections of water and sky and chocolate-boxed romantic settings, which are as staged as they are beguiling. This is a Europe in which Africa is rendered visible, its magnificence somehow challenged by the floating presence of the African mask in its midst.

While this mask is the homogenised Africa of European invasion, 'writing back' to Empire, the Africa Sulter portrays is a more complex one, with its own fractures, differences and power struggles. The African mask in this image embodies more than meets the eye. It is a Sande mask found in large parts of West Africa and unusual in that a Sande society is an organisation of women, who own the masks. It signifies the power of women; however, this is a society also associated with female circumcision or cutting. Like Alice Walker, who wrote a controversial novel against female cutting, Sulter would, no doubt, be highly critical of this African practice.[25] While those Germanic mountains, with their allusions to Africa, may also be the site of genocide and prejudice, concealed beneath their visual perfection, Sulter's choice of mask suggests that the oppression of women cuts across race and space. There is an example of one such mask in the Victoria and Albert Museum, which Sulter knew well; indeed many of her photographs are housed in that museum.[26] This Africa, within a Europe that would erase it, is as politically ambiguous as the ornate, subtly threatening figures in her other work (page 121). It is also the case that Europe in the period of the Nazi regime in Germany, upon which Sulter focuses, saw the persecution of Jews, gays and gypsies, along with black people. These connections provided an invitation for me to bring my Jewishness and my Africanness into conversation.

Portraying myself

Sulter's focus on the Holocaust and on the persecution of Jews and Blacks is related to her fascination with the German photographer August Sander. His photographs of the everyday world of a wide cross-section of ordinary German people appealed to her. This was particularly true of his Zircus series of 1926, in which there was 'the wide inclusion of people of African descent (and of course many portraits of "Persecuted Jews")'.[27] She was especially intrigued by 'young black women who were obviously also part of the troupe'.[28] In his 'Circus People' (1930)[29] a black man and woman figure among the circus performers. Sulter works to uncover the story that she suggests may lie behind Sander's photograph. This she does by way of a cryptic story of her own, entitled 'Blood Money', which is the back story of her own Circus/SYRCAS series.

Sulter's poetic story concerns the life of a young Cameroonian girl called Monique, who ran away from home to join the circus in Germany; here she met and fell in love with Kwesi, who 'was an African too, but German'.[30] Here is another Kwesi, like Himid's cardboard cut-out boy and also perhaps like the African figure buried in the rock in Sulter's photograph. The refrain that structures 'Blood Money' is 'Close your eyes and imagine a German.'[31] Kwesi is a German, but he is persecuted in Germany where he is not recognised as a citizen. He is sent to his death in a concentration camp, for being black and for being a communist, along with 'the gypsies and jews and gays and the others'.[32] Recognising that prejudice and its dreadful consequences also occur in other times and places, Sulter explains: 'In the light of the current and increasing racial attacks and the horror of "ethnic cleansing" in Bosnia and Rwanda, I felt compelled to look back to Germany's hidden history – the "ethnic cleansing" of the Holocaust.'[33] Sulter refers to 'Blood Money' as a poem; but it is really a poetic micro-fiction, a narrative, which she cannot make rhyme, as if the genre falters when humanity ceases to be humane.[34]

August Sander's pre-war German circus of mixed performers becomes Sulter's focus, where the 'clown' is the tragic victim of prejudice wherever it occurs. This is why her series of photographs is entitled SYRCAS, which is Welsh for circus, another interesting twist. The exhibition is staged in Wales and the catalogue is written both in Welsh and in English. While Sulter levels her critique at continental Europe, she is perhaps also aware that places like Scotland, where she grew up, and Wales are themselves involved in complex relations of politics within the United Kingdom:

> Sulter's new exhibition is loosely based around the concept of a circus, but was called 'SYRCAS' to fit in with the Welsh-speaking gallery for which it was commissioned. As Sulter explains: 'What is interesting is that the "S" is so much closer to the letter "Z" which starts the German word for circus – "Zirkus".' This, as it turns out, is a clue: the German connection is crucial. Deep at the heart of this body of work is the largely unacknowledged persecution of black people in the Holocaust.[35]

The question of the fate of Jews and Blacks in Nazi Germany also is addressed in Esi Edugyan's *Half Blood Blues*, a recent diasporic novel. The form and substance of this novel resonate quite closely with Sulter's project. Edugyan was born in Canada of Ghanaian parentage, a link with Sulter's own Ghanaian background. Edugyan describes in an interview how she came to this theme:

> I was living in Germany at the time, acutely aware of my difference -- being a black woman from Canada. At the same time I'd been reading about the so-called 'Rhineland Bastards' – the half-black children of France's colonial soldiers from Africa stationed in the Rhineland after the close of the first World War. I began imagining their lives in Germany, as both outsiders and insiders, and this naturally led to my wondering what must have happened to them during the 1930s, with the rise of Nazism. This is where my interest in the novel came from.[36]

Like Sulter, Edugyan is well aware of the persecution of black people in Europe and committed to recognising too the persecution of marginalised and stigmatised groupings more broadly. As she puts it in the novel:

> Remember, there was no on-paper legislation against blacks, so they were often admitted to work camps on trumped-up charges and under various crimes. Some were interned as Communists, or as Immigrants, who wore the blue badge. Or as Homosexuals, who wore the pink badge, or as Repeat Criminals, who wore the green badge, or Asocials who wore the black badge. Even more obscuring is that the Asocial group included the homeless, pimps, pickpockets, murderers, homosexuals, and race defilers, so that it's even more difficult to figure out who among them was black. These people are lost in the dark maw of history.[37]

'Lost in the dark maw of history' echoes Sulter's determination to find these lost people, even if it means, in Sulter's case, reinventing them in the guise of her own body. In *Half Blood Blues*, a group of musicians of varied ethnic origins gets caught up in the war. The Nazi officials dismiss blacks and Jews as 'Jewkikes!' and 'Niggerkikes!'[38] Hiero, one of Edugyan's musicians, is a German, like Kwesi. The Nazis loathe 'black Krauts … a Mischling, like our boy here'.[39] Perhaps Hiero, whose name is short for Hieronymus, was named for the artist, Hieronymus Bosch, suggesting an association with his images of a circus of horrors, ironically called a garden of delights. The group flees to Paris to escape the Nazis when the Germans invade. Hiero is doubly doomed, both as a black domestic alien in Germany and as a German enemy alien in France. (His father had been 'a colonial soldier from Senegal, one of them sent to occupy the Rhineland by the French government'.[40])

A certain music drives the narrative, the half-blood Blues of its title. If Sulter's poem is a micro-narrative, then Edugyan's novel is a musical score. It describes a sublime music that the ragbag bunch of 'mixed blood' fugitives manage to cut into a vinyl record, resisting the violence and injustice of the war. One might perhaps say that this music in the words of Edugyan, as with the images in the photographs of Sulter, is the counter-language of an 'other' history. It is the language in which, for example, the aging Louis Armstrong depicted in *Half Blood Blues* can only tolerate Jewish matzos for his weak stomach. 'Armstrong et matzos' becomes something of its own rhythmic refrain of hope.[41]

Armstrong eats matzos and the shoe fits!

Once again, I cannot take my eyes off the shoe. It seems to be of a different order from the statements embodied in the masks and the mountains; it seems more readily detachable from the image; it seems to be inviting me into the picture. This double process of the imperative of digging deep, to expose that which has been airbrushed out, and also taking what is already at the surface in the form of the montaged shoe, is in fact written into Sulter's methods. That is to say, she employs both the palimpsest and the montage, the inclusion of strange, discordant objects into the composition:

> [I]n SYRCAS Maud Sulter reverts to an early making practice of hers – that of montage; the gathering and reusing of images which in turn are remade into personal visual statements.[42]

In other words, in addition to the traces of deleted pasts, of power, exploitation and pain, Sulter's evocative composite photograph includes objects cut and pasted from other contexts and experiences that do not readily lend themselves to inter-pretation, but do seem to offer themselves for expropriation. The shoe invites me as a viewer to tell my own story. The shoe that so reminded me of my Bobba's encourages me to consider my lapsed Jewishness. It had always seemed to me that my African identity was somehow in opposition to my Jewish one. Perhaps I was partly right, and also partly wrong, about the exclusivity of identities.

Sulter was born and bred in Scotland but was diasporic in her exploration of her blackness and search for her Ghanaian father – the presence of Africa in Europe. I, born and bred in South Africa, had my Eastern European Jewish descent inscribed in invisible ink on my whiteness – the presence of Europe in Africa.

And so I return to the space that Salford has enabled. Here I may take some distance from the anti-apartheid project, and see myself as an African Jewish in-habitant of an imaginary land of multiplicity 'where worlds collide ... and wash of away'.[43]

Instead of claiming Sulter's past, I claim my own. I recognise myself in my Bobba as I try on Maud Sulter's shoe, and become creole in my African home. This traffic back and forward across continents, negotiating various boundaries, enables a kind of writing that captures alternative histories. It also allows for fan-tasy and story-telling within academic writing. An opening is suggested by what I read as an image of a floating carved door upper left in Sulter's photograph, giving me, the sense that I was passing through a portal between worlds.

I enter the photograph, I try on the shoe. The shoe fits! There is no prince in the wings as my prize. This is not the usual Western fairytale, but a different story from another tradition, connecting Maud Sulter and my Bobba through the image of the shoe, and allowing me to become myself.

> Fly back Jimmy. Fly back and wait
> at the mountain top where family will

> meet again someday; the Brethren and
> the Sistren, to decide the naming
> of the Sun. In our own tongue.[44]

The world is created anew through a new language, unlike the one that silences them:

> I am learning that tongue
> and becoming a sistre
> A white sister.

Kwesi was liberated from where he had lain, petrified in granite. I looked again at Maud Sulter's work and felt the connection, for my own history, between Table Mountain and a far-away park in Lithuania. And lest this all sounds too seamless and sweet, it is a fantasy, within which the issues are all tangled, the politics shifting and the outcomes unpredictable. Maud Sulter's refrain in 'Blood Money' sums it up: 'There's no way I can make this poem rhyme'.[45]

Postscript

I presented a version of this paper at a conference in Leeds, where Lubaina Himid was present. When I claimed the shoe for my Bobba, Lubaina raised her foot, and demonstrated that in fact the shoe was *hers*! She was indeed wearing one very similar to the one in the image. The shoe, it seems, is in reality Sulter's acknowledgement of Himid's own footprint in her art. This caused great hilarity at the conference. However, I defended my view that the montage opened up possibilities of interpretation for the viewer. I stood by my claim to the shoe. Himid, with great humour and grace, acknowledged my right of ownership. In fact, she herself suggests as much in the catalogue for these images: 'you must provide the key to unlock the mysteries of the human soul. Ultimately you are left quite alone to invent your own ending.'[46]

Thanks to Lubaina Himid for permission to reproduce Maud Sulter's and her own work.

Notes

1   Deborah Cherry, 'On Zabat', p. 52.
2   Lubaina Himid, in Griselda Pollock, 'Territories of desire: reconsiderations of an African childhood', p. 77.
3   Maud Sulter, 'JACARANDA a Cafe', p. 64.
4   Helen Oyeyemi, *White Is For Witching*.
5   Esi Edugyan, *Half Blood Blues*.
6   Cherry, 'On Zabat', p. 51.
7   Sulter, *Jeanne Duval: A Melodrama*, p. 59.
8   *Ibid.*, p. 59.
9   *Ibid.*, p. 60.
10   Sulter, *Jeanne Duval*, p. 22.
11   *Ibid.*, p. 41.
12   Vicky Allan, 'Looking in the mirror: she's a muse, a photographer and an artist', p. 18.
13   Sulter, *Jeanne Duval*, p. 14.
14   *Ibid.*
15   Angela Carter, *Black Venus*, p. 5.
16   *Ibid.*, p. 8.
17   *Ibid.*, p. 8.
18   Maria Lind, 'In the margin of margins', p. 42.
19   Salman Rushdie, *The Moor's Last Sigh*, p. 226.
20   *Ibid.*
21   Jane Richards, 'PHOTOGRAPHY/A cut above the rest'.
22   *Ibid.*
23   *Ibid.*
24   Lubaina Himid, *Naming the Money*, p. 24.
25   See Alice Walker, *Possessing the Secret of Joy*. I base this supposition both on probability and on the fact that Sulter selected Alice Walker to be photographed as one of her Muses, Phalia, indicating her admiration for Walker's writing.
26   See Victoria and Albert Museum (online), 'Beauty secrets: a Sowo mask'.
27   Himid, 'A brief introduction to the magical world of Maud Sulter's photoworks', p. 33.
28   *Ibid.*, p. 34.
29   See Fraenkel Gallery, 'August Sander: works'.
30   Sulter, 'Blood money', in *SYRCAS*, p. 35.
31   *Ibid.*
32   *Ibid.*
33   Sulter, in Richards, 'PHOTOGRAPHY'.

34 Sulter, *SYRCAS*, p. 35.
35 *Ibid.*
36 Christian DuChateau, 'Author plays the "Half-Blood Blues"'.
37 Edugyan, *Half Blood Blues*, p. 55.
38 *Ibid.*, p. 98.
39 *Ibid.*, p. 260.
40 *Ibid.*, p. 210.
41 *Ibid.*, p. 287.
42 Himid, 'A brief introduction', p. 33.
43 Rushdie, *The Moor's Last Sigh*, p. 226.
44 Sulter, 'Delete and enter', p. 74.
45 Himid, 'A brief introduction', p. 35.
46 *Ibid.*, p. 32.

Bibliography

Allan, Vicky, 'Looking in the mirror: she's a muse, a photographer and an artist', *Sunday Herald* (8 June 2003), p. 18.

Carter, Angela, *Black Venus* (London: Vintage, 1996).

Cherry, Deborah, 'On Zabat', in Maud Sulter, *Jeanne Duval: A melodrama* (Edinburgh: National Galleries of Scotland, 2003).

DuChateau, Christian, 'Author plays the 'Half-Blood Blues', *CNN* (6 March 2012), http://goo.gl/mKLgf. Accessed online 16 August 2012.

Edugyan, Esi, *Half Blood Blues* (London: Serpent's Tail, 2011).

Fraenkel Gallery, 'August Sander: Works', *Fraenkel Gallery (online)*, www.fraenkelgallery.com. Accessed online 16 August 2012.

Himid, Lubaina, 'A brief introduction to the magical world of Maud Sulter's photoworks', in Maud Sulter, *SYRCAS* (Wrexham: Clwyd County Council, 1994).

Himid, Lubaina, *Naming the Money* (catalogue) (Hatton Gallery, Newcastle: University of Newcastle upon Tyne, 2004).

Lind, Maria, 'In the margin of margins', *Portfolio*, 19 (1994), 42–3.

Oyeyemi, Helen, *White Is For Witching* (London: Picador, 2009).

Pollock, Griselda, 'Territories of desire: reconsiderations of an African childhood', in George Robertson *et al.* (eds), *Travellers' Tales: Narratives of Home and Displacement* (London: Routledge, 1994).

Richards, Jane, 'PHOTOGRAPHY/A cut above the rest', *Independent* (23 August 1994), http://goo.gl/R819R. Accessed online 16 August 2012.

Rushdie, Salman, *The Moor's Last Sigh* (London: Vintage, 2006 [1995]).

Sulter, Maud, 'JACARANDA a Cafe', in *As a Blackwoman* (London: Akira, 1985; reprint, Hebden Bridge: Urban Fox, 1989).

Sulter, Maud, 'Delete and enter', in *Zabat. Poetics of a Family Tree* (Hebden Bridge: Urban Fox Press, 1989).

Sulter, Maud, *SYRCAS* (Wrexham: Clwyd County Council, 1994).

Sulter, Maud, 'Blood Money', in *SYRCAS* (Wrexham: Clwyd County Council, 1994).

Sulter, Maud, *Jeanne Duval: A Melodrama* (Edinburgh: National Galleries of Scotland, 2003).

Victoria and Albert Museum, 'Beauty secrets: a Sowo mask', *Victoria and Albert Museum (online)*, http://goo.gl/rLKvE. Accessed online 16 August 2012.

Walker, Alice, *Possessing the Secret of Joy* (London: Vintage, 1993 [1992]).

Dust and mangoes: plain tales and hill stations

Margaret Rachel Beetham

The presenter of the television programme on the Dead Sea scrolls was showing some of the fragments found in earthenware jars. They had been discovered by chance in some desert caves. Dust had preserved them. Dust was what they crumbled into. The task of reconstruction was immense. The scrolls were a million-piece jigsaw puzzle without a picture to work from. All those pieces, each with a couple of letters, half a letter, a mark which might be an insect trail or might, the presenter said, be 'a crucial punctuation mark – a jot or a tittle'. That was in the Bible, something like 'till heaven and earth pass away, one jot or tittle shall not pass away'.

Rachel switched off the television and thought ruefully that if her head were not so full of bits of the Bible and quotations from here and there she might have more space for what was in the newspaper, which she had been reading and which had now dropped to the floor. But as it was, Bible sayings and lines of hymns would suddenly came from nowhere to her lips. She would find herself making coffee and singing 'Abide With Me' or humming a tune which turned into 'What a Friend We Have in Jesus' as she put out the rubbish.

It was no wonder. From earliest childhood her world had been saturated with hymns, Bible stories and sayings. Even the family jokes, the word plays and puns which her father delighted in, were Biblical or vaguely ecclesiastical. Like the one about the maid who asked her mistress, 'Is it true that we come from dust and go to dust?'

> 'Yes, the Bible says so.'
> 'Well, Ma'am', the maid replies, 'There is someone either coming or going under the spare room bed.'

Like so many adult jokes told at the dinner table, Rachel had not understood why that was funny.

On family walks, when her father had to drop behind to do what her mother called 'paying a visit', he would shout, 'Remember Lot's wife.' Looking back was

---

This is an edited version of chapters from a book-length work the author is currently completing called *Home is Where*, which is a lightly fictionalised account of her early childhood and schooling.

dangerous. But, like Lot's wife, she could not help herself. She wiped the salt from her eyes and picked up the paper again. The pamphlet she had found this morning at the Library fell out onto the floor. 'Oral History Project', it said in large letters. 'If you are over sixty, come and tell your story'. 'Tell your story,' they said. It was all the craze now, the confessional culture, the assumption that it was good to tell all. But, Rachel thought, memory wasn't like that. There wasn't a story, just fragments, snatches of song, a dot-to-dot puzzle. A handful of dust. Memories rose up unbidden just as the old hymns rose to her lips.

How dust motes danced in the light coming from the glass roof! They rose and fell – an intricate movement. The child in the high chair watched, rapt. Was it a memory or had she made it up, that sense of being outside time?

Rachel had asked her mother about it once. 'A glass roof?' her mother had said. 'Goodness! Can you really remember that? It must have been when you were one – nearly two. I know because it was up in Kodai. We stayed that hot season in a house called Merton Lodge which had a glass conservatory-sort-of-place where we used to eat. We only stayed there one year as it was a barn of a place, even though we shared it with two other families. The year after that we stayed in another house when we went up to the hills. It was East House, I think.' Yes, Rachel thought to herself, it was just one of those houses they had lived in briefly during the annual migration to the hills. Every year this move from the plains – red, hot, dusty – to the green hills – cool, smelling of pine and eucalyptus.

'I to the hills will lift mine eyes, from whence doth come mine aid.' It was her father's favourite psalm, his deep voice ringing out in the metrical version, the rich inheritance of his Presbyterian upbringing. 'The Lord thee keeps, the Lord thy shade on thy right hand by day.' Shade in the day time could save your life. That is why, if you could, in the hot season you escaped to the hills. The bus with its open windows would rattle along the road, sounding its horn and spreading a cloud of dust behind it – on the mud huts with their palm roofs, on the lines of women walking with bundles on their heads, on the cattle standing in the shade of a banyan tree or nosing in a pile of rubbish. Then the steep climb up the ghat; dusty red sand turning first to scrubby bushes, then to green trees, the bus tooting its horn and chug-chugging round the steep bends, under the cut walls of cliff with white painted signs, 'Horn Soundly'.

When the bus engine boiled over, as it always did, everyone got out and walked about, peering down the steep, unguarded sides to the shola thousands of feet below. Invisible in the green tree tops, spread out like a lumpy blanket far below, black-faced monkeys called, 'who-who? who-who?'. Then, at last, the bus was rattling up through the bazaar at Kodai, as evening came down and kerosene lamps were being lit in the little open shops. The air tasted clean, everyone laughed and talked more quickly, drunk with coolness and altitude. Happy to be together, to arrive, to be in the hills. From whence doth come thine aid.

Then a few weeks later, came the journey back, down into the heat and red dust of the plains. The missionary houses in the hills would be closed up for another year, and the older children would stay on 'in boarding' so they could carry on going to school – as Rachel started to do when she turned eight. The boarders would make the trip down the ghat in October for the long holiday. Every year there was this migration up to the hills and back. Then every five or six years, that longer voyage back 'home' on the great liners of the P&O. Always the sense of the other place, the other home. Here we have no abiding city.

Rachel came back to the present and looked across to the bay window of her room where the large trunk, the one her mother had called 'the tin liner', sat – massive and heavy – with its brass corners and lock. It carried the remains of old labels, sometimes pasted over each other and worn through to show the earlier lettering; Bombay, Madras, Southampton, Tilbury, Colombo. Still visible on the lid were the traces of the words 'Not Wanted on Voyage' which her mother had stencilled neatly onto it in white paint all those years ago when she and her new husband had set off on the boat to start their lives together as missionaries to the church in South India. When was that? 1936? 1937? The trunk took up a lot of space, but Rachel would not get rid of it.

She had also inherited her parents' cabin trunk ('Wanted on Voyage') with its hoops of bent wood which had become hers when she was travelling to and from her boarding school in England. It just fitted under the spare-room bed, where it sat now, gathering dust. Coming and going. Story of their lives, Rachel thought.

Her mother's parents had also been missionaries in India. Mum was sent 'home' when she was seven to go to boarding school, just as Rachel and her sisters were sent when their time came – to the same school, founded in the 1830s 'for the daughters of missionaries'. Unto the third and fourth generation, Rachel thought. We were the last of that line, thank God. That particular pattern of child migration had gone now, though not of course, those wider and more brutal colonial legacies of families divided, children left behind by parents seeking sanctuary or work, children sent alone (sometimes hidden in the backs of trucks) or accompanied across the seas, though more often now in the air than in the great liners of the P&O in which Rachel and her family made the three-week voyage from India to that strange place called home.

I was lucky as well as privileged, Rachel thought. I didn't get sent back to England away from my family when I was seven. I could go to school in Kodai for a few more years – even if that meant boarding. At least I was in the same country. I had a Mum and Dad, and I did see them again after we were sent to England, even though it was not for many years – those long years of my growing up when we were in different continents, different worlds, with only a thin line of blue air-mail forms connecting us.

Typing 'Kodai' into Google brought up a range of tourist websites.

> Kodaikanal or Kodai is often referred to as the "Princess of Hill stations" and is a popular tourist destination…
>
> Being one of the most well known hill stations of India, the sylvan beauty on the upper palani hills lines its south near Madurai in Tamil Nadu. With its rocks, woods, lovely lake and bracing air, Kodaikanal is an ideal hill resort…[1]

The picture looked just like the old postcard Rachel still had in her desk.[2]

She scrolled down and found:

> Kodai is situated at an altitude of about 2,133-m high ... Established in the year
> 1845, Kodaikanal then saw settlement by American Missionaries who later set
> up a school run on American lines,

But, of course, the 'hill station' was an invention not of the Americans but
of the British Raj, most famously at Simla or Shimla, the Himalayan station to
which the Government all moved from the capital, Calcutta, in the hot season and
whose sexual and imperial politics Kipling satirised in *Plain Tales from the Hills*.
Being in South India, Mum and Dad should, Rachel supposed, have chosen to go
to Otticamund (Ooty, as the Brits called it), the southern equivalent of Shimla,
where in the hot season all the officials moved from Madras, as it was called
then. (The power to name, Rachel thought. Sticks and stones are nothing to it.)
Yes, Mum and Dad should have sent us to the 'English' school in Ooty, but they
didn't. Did that go along with them supporting the Indian National Congress,
having Indian friends, not employing an ayah and refusing to join the English
Club? The Kodai house where the family spent the hot season when Rachel was
nine was near 'The Club'. Walking home from school, holding her younger sister's
hand, Rachel would hear the yaw-yaw tones and the thump of tennis balls coming
from the other side of the high hedge. But she never saw what lay on that other
side. Years later she discovered that her mother had refused to join, even though
she had been an outstanding tennis player at school ('Just what we need in the
Club, don't you know'). So was that why Rachel and her sisters went to 'a school
run on American lines' where Rachel learned that the British were Imperialists in
red coats and that they had been defeated by the brave Americans, led by George
Washington who never told a lie? It was to cause her some confusion later at her
English boarding school, which was run on lines laid down in late nineteenth-
century Britain, but in those May days in Kodai it was just how things were.

May was mango season. Mum always said the best place to eat mangoes was a punt on Kodai Lake. Then you could lean over the side of the boat and let the juice run down your chin and over your hands. These were not the huge green fruit which began to be flown into British supermarkets from South America as the twentieth century aged and died. These were the yellow mangoes of India, which appeared in the bazaar in May. 'Mangoes', Dad would say, 'are like the girl with the curl in the middle of her fore'id.

> When they are good they are very, very good,
> and when they are bad they are horrid.'

An over-ripe mango tasted of petrol but a just-ripe mango was as sweet as a May morning in Kodai.

Then the South Indian plains shimmered in the heat, but up in the hills it was cool with the faint scent of eucalyptus in the air. There was a holiday from school. Not the long holidays from October to January when school closed and all the children in boarding went down to the plains, but the short one when the missionary houses were taken by different families. Daddy came up to Kodai for 'a little break', as did lots of aunties and uncles. Mum told Rachel that her 'real' aunties were at home in England, but that was just one of those confusing things adults said which only made sense many years later. Now, Rachel thought, coming back to the present, some of her African and Indian friends called her 'Auntie', a mark of respect for older women which metropolitan Britain had never adopted.

The Kodai houses were smaller than the bungalows on the plains. Instead of verandahs and tatties they had windows with glass in them. There were no poles on the beds because you didn't need mosquito nets in Kodai. The houses smelt funny when you first arrived, damp and shut up. Everything smelled different up here from down on the plains. Rachel loved it, the cool of it and the smell of trees and damp – just as she loved the heat, the dust, the smells of the plains – but differently. Each of the Kodai houses was special in its own way. East House had a corrugated tin roof, so when it rained you could lie in bed, listening to the drumming sound and snuggling under the blanket. You needed a blanket in Kodai. It took a few nights to get used to the weight of it and the smell of damp wool, which never quite went away. It rained in the hills. On the plains the ground was parched and even the tanks had nothing to show for the last monsoon but the cracked surfaces of dried out mud behind the bund.[3]

There were enough dry days in May for expeditions: walks to places like Pillar Rocks, where through the drifting mist you could look down, down to the plains and where Rachel once saw what she was sure was a tiger paw print. There were picnics at streams with pools where you could paddle and the grown-ups could swim, places called 'Neptune's Pool' and 'Whiffey'.

'Whiffey's a funny name for a pool,' Rachel said to Daddy on one of their walks.

'It's not its real name. I think perhaps a tiger or a jackal had left a bit of a dead animal near there once and someone called it that and the name has stuck. It's a joke name, a bit like calling the tracks up from the Lake near Rock Cottage "Consumption Ghat" and "Sudden Death".'

'But that's their names,' Rachel had said.

Going from the tourist websites to Google Scholar she found:

> Offering, as they did, a climate more akin to a warm British summer than that of the 'plains', these hill stations became places of holiday and recreation in which the British elite could create versions of the Britain they remembered or imagined they remembered. They planted gardens and parks with imported plants. They built houses on the model of British homes and mock gothic Victorian churches like those being erected in the suburbs of English cities.

And this:

> British colonial life in India thus moved between two locations: 'the plains', hot, noisy, restless, and 'the hills', green, cool and restful. Though rooted in the natural

differences of climate and topography, this was a culturally constructed opposition and one not available to the Indians who were needed to service the British and who lived, often in cramped quarters, around the bazaars … However, thanks to Bollywood, these landscapes are now familiar to millions, the common property of the Indian imagination.

Rachel thought of the bazaar with its little shops on both sides of the steep road and the jumble of huts around it, of St Peter's Church with its gothic spire, and of all the houses built around the lake with names like Claverack, Netherlocharbour, Bide-a-Wee and Windsor Lodge. Then there was Bryant's Park, which Rachel now realised had been modelled on a European urban park with flower beds and walks laid out in formal patterns and special plants brought from all over the world, just as the rhododendrons of India were being taken back to bring that touch of the exotic to the parks and gardens of Britain. Rachel's friend Catriona came back from a visit to Kodai last year and told her the sholas all over those hills were being overwhelmed by eucalyptus trees. They had spread out from Bryant's Park, where they had first been planted as decorative imports. Grown-ups said they liked the Park, though they rarely went there, but Rachel and Chris thought it was boring. There were no proper bushes where you could make dens and you weren't allowed to climb the trees. The scrubby shola of mimosa trees and lantana bushes behind Rock Cottage was more fun and more deliciously scary, since it was from there that at night the call of the jackal pack would rise in its spine-tingling crescendo.

The year the family stayed in Rock Cottage when Rachel was seven, nearly eight, she started piano lessons after school once a week. Mum said she was old enough to walk home on her own on those days. 'I'll try to come out to meet you half-way when I can,' she said. At the school gate Rachel would meet the halva man carrying his glass box. He would open up the legs of the box and rest it on the ground while he squatted beside it, chewing betel. You could see the sweets; pale squares of Mysore pak, and golden jellabies jewelled with flies. Rachel looked, but she never had any money and, besides, you were not allowed to buy sweets. She would smile at him and walk fast.

To get to Rock Cottage from School you had to go past the gate of the Park and climb the short steep path called Consumption Ghat, but first you had to walk round an arm of the lake. There the water buffaloes lay in wait. Sometimes they were sunk down among the water-lily pads, only their nostrils and black eyes showing above the water. More often they grazed by the road, swinging their huge horns from side to side as they walked, their grey skins wrinkled. Rachel would slide past, hardly breathing. Once when she was coming back from school on her own after a piano lesson, she saw her mother across the lake. She was in a red dress, carrying the baby. Rachel felt a surge of relief. She waved and walked boldly past the great grey beasts, who took no notice of her, as usual. But the woman kept walking and did not wave back. As Rachel got closer she realised that it was not her mother but a woman she did not even recognise, someone who turned into the Park. Rachel pretended to wave to the empty road beyond and ran past. She never spoke about the water buffaloes, but the huge beasts lurked in her dreams.

The Lake was at the centre of Kodai, a watery starfish stretching its arms into every corner. Sometime it was quicker to row than to walk. Rowing boats were fast and wobbly, but for a lake picnic you needed a punt. Daddy loved punts. 'A punt on the lake!' he would say, 'What a good idea! Come on you two,' he would say to Rachel and Chris, 'come and help choose a punt.' The boat house was dim and cool. It smelt of the lake. Rowing boats and punts lay tied up on the dark water, and between them were gangways of wood where you walked out to climb into the boat your daddy had chosen. 'That one', he would point, and the boat-boy would get cushions and paddles or oars and a boat hook and jump into the boat, which bobbed around while he arranged cushions. Daddy gave the boat-wallah money and pushed out. You had to keep your hands inside while Daddy pulled the punt along the line of boats, hand over hand, until suddenly you were out into the dazzle of the lake. There were Mummy and the little ones. You could lean over and splash your hands in the cool, green water or even sit at the back and try to paddle.

Punts were flat with cushions where you could sit and eat the picnic Mum had brought. That was when the mangoes tasted best. You could let the juice drip down and wash your hands afterwards in the water. Daddy said they had punts in a place called Cambridge in England, except there they had poles instead of paddles. How punts, with or without paddles, came from Cambridge to Kodai was not a puzzle to Rachel. It was just how things were.

Rachel's birthday was in June and marked the end of the hot season, when even Mum and the other aunties went down to the plains. Daddy had gone already. The year they were in Rock Cottage, just after Rachel's birthday, Mummy began to get out the trunks and to sort things ready for packing as usual.

'Now you're eight, you are old enough to stay up in boarding when we go down to the plains.' Mummy said.

'But Mummy...'

'You'll have your friends and it won't be long until October when you can come back for the long holidays.'

'Can Chrissie stay, too?'

'Christine is too little and she has only just started school. I know you'll be a big brave girl.'

Her first night 'in boarding' Rachel lay awake and could not go to sleep. She was in a big room called 'a dorm'. The other girls were asleep. A light came in from the corridor and made shapes in the dark room. She got up very quietly and tip-toed, so as to make no noise, over to the window. It was dark outside, a moonless night with no stars, but there was a light from a house across the valley – just one. If Mummy or Daddy or Chrissie looked out of the window they might see it. They were ten minutes' walk away. They were months and months away. Tomorrow they would go down to the plains. She was here until the big holidays in October. Rachel thought she could just walk out, go up the road, open the door and climb into bed next to Chris. They would cuddle down under the blanket and be safe. But she couldn't. Time stretched out. Something large and hard rose up in her throat. She walked carefully back to bed and lay down with her face in the pillow.

Was that when she began to write letters? Rachel tried to remember. It must have been. The start of all those many years of the weekly letter written from boarding school, and the letters arriving – sometimes a typed one from Dad and always, every week, a letter from Mum. She never missed. After all, she had spent her life writing letters, starting from when she was sent home from India herself to go to boarding school. That's how they all kept in touch. Now, of course, no-one wrote letters. They went on Facebook or emailed or texted, as Rachel did. Everyone had mobile phones. She had read somewhere that there was more than one mobile per adult in sub-Saharan Africa. It was a statistic she doubted, even though she knew that her friend Adela, who had fled to Britain from Rwanda after the genocide and spent long years trying to avoid being sent back, had two mobiles with which she kept in touch with survivors back home. The personal letter, like so many of Adela's family and friends, was dead. All Rachel's dead had been letter-writers, and she herself had written hundreds – no! thousands – of them over the years.

She thought of those long Sunday afternoons at boarding school in England where you sat on your bed in silence and wrote home, except that, of course, you were at 'home' and the parents to whom you addressed the flimsy blue air-mail forms were somewhere other, which felt like home but had no name. 'Dear Mummy and Daddy...' Even if Mum sat down and wrote back by return it would take at least a month to get a reply, by which time you had forgotten what had felt so urgent. There was a phone call once a year at Christmas, the only time in the year Rachel or her sisters ever used this strange black instrument. Back then in the 1950s you had to book these international calls in advance and you had to be somewhere with a phone. It was always an awkward occasion because the whole call had to take two minutes and what could you say to fill up the time? 'Hello, Mummy. Are you having a nice Christmas?' Letters, for all their drawbacks, were easier.

When in their spry old age her mother and father decided that they didn't want to be a burden to anyone and it was time to take themselves off into sheltered housing, they went through the house in which they had spent the years after leaving India. Her mother gave all the uncracked cups to the Salvation Army, keeping the chipped ones for their own use. Her father gave away most of his precious library. When Rachel went to help them sort out the house, they gave her the old 'tin liner' with its palimpsest of labels, its 'Not Wanted on Voyage', and also bundles of Rachel's old letters to them, secured in elastic bands; blue air-mail forms in her schoolgirl hand, envelopes from the early years of her marriage, letters she had written to them over all those long years of separation.

'We thought you might like them back,' her mother said. 'We won't have room for them now.' But Rachel couldn't bear to read them. She stuffed them into the other trunk – the cabin trunk – under the spare-room bed. No longer coming and going, the trunk had now become for her something like the Jewish genizah, a place in the synagogue – she had read – where texts too sacred to destroy or throw away were stored and allowed to decay gradually, sinking back into dust. Some-time, perhaps, before she died, she would be able to take them out and read them. She had a few of theirs, too; Mum's neat writing in blue-black ink (no ball-points then) and a few typed letters from Dad which left a slight purple stain on your hands because he made multiple copies for all the family using carbon paper. She had taken out one or two of these and read them before folding them carefully and putting them back into the trunk.

'Did Mum and Dad give you back your letters?' she'd asked her sister at Christmas.

'Yes.'

'Have you read any of them?'

'No. Just threw them out. I don't want them cluttering up the house.'

'I am sure she is right, but I find it hard,' Rachel confided to her brother later. 'I've kept all the old letters, but I am not at all sure I'll read them, and besides,' she had hesitated, 'the one thing I am sure of is that, whatever they say, it's unreliable.'

'Yes, The Pravda style of letter-writing.' He had grinned 'Everything on the collective farm is working perfectly.'

They had laughed ruefully. Letters were no more reliable than memory. You had to read the gaps, glimpse the water buffalo walking, huge and silent, along the margin of the lake. One day perhaps, Rachel thought, I will take them out and be surprised.

Meanwhile, she was sorting the photos she had inherited on her mother's death. They were all stored in a wooden box which Mum had taken with her even into the nursing home where she spent her last year after Dad died. On the top of the box were three or four green photo albums. Rachel took them out and sniffed them. They smelled of dust. In those early days of her marriage Mum had stuck photos carefully into the albums with special photo corners ('so fiddly') and had written neat captions underneath: 'The Church of Scotland Tea Party, 1937', 'Bungalow, Chingleput', 'Picnic at Neptune's Pool, May 1941'. Rachel turned the pages carefully. There were not many photos of those early years when film was expensive and hard to get. There were a few of Kodai and of special occasions: christenings, the visit of some ecclesiastical dignitary, a picnic on the lake. There were none of ordinary life down on the plains. Besides, these small black and white 'snaps', taken on Mum's old Box Brownie, gave no sense of what stayed so strongly in memory: the colours, the heat, the lingering smells of spice and shit, the snatches of music drifting over the walls of the compound from the city, the dust.

Every morning down on the plains you would wake inside the white tent of the mosquito net to the sounds of an Indian dawn; the caw, caw of the rooks and near at hand a sweep, sweeping; the sweeper with her bundle of twigs. She was bent over the work, which left circular patterns in the dust outside the house, until people walked on it and left imprints of toes and heels or sometimes the mark of chupples. Every leaf, every twig, every piece of paper or cigarette-end was precious. Nothing could be thrown away.

Not a hair of your head shall be lost.

Then the sweeper would come up the back stairs to empty the pots with all the wee and poo in them. If you met her she would pull her sari over her head and step back. She was an untouchable. Even the least of these, my brethren.

Did the sweeper live in the go-downs along with Big Tambi's and Moses' family? Rachel did not think so. She could not remember. Big Tambi was the best at jumping. He could jump off the second step onto the cold concrete floor of the dining room. He was two years older than she, and Rachel learned from him most of the bazaar Tamil which was the only version of the language she knew and with which sometimes she and Chris shocked their parents' more sedate visitors. Tambi and Rachel and Chris played on the veranda of their big bungalow. It was (she found a photograph) a colonial mansion. Her family ate sitting at a table on chairs and slept in beds with mosquito nets; Tambi's family sat on the earth floor to eat, and slept on thin mats, which were unrolled in the evening and laid out all together on the floor of the family's one room. That was just how things were.

But God loved everybody. She knew that. Each evening they would say their prayers. 'Thank you God for everything, food and clothes, and please bless Daddy and Mummy and Big Tambi and the Aunties. Amen.'

Her parents said their prayers every morning and evening. She had inherited her father's prayer book. The pages just inside the covers were marked with the traces of dead insects, caught by her father who used to clap the covers of the book shut onto the more persistent mosquitoes and other flying creatures which interrupted evening prayers – snap! There they still were, brown marks on the page – like the marks on the Dead Sea scrolls.

At mealtimes there was grace. 'Thank you for the world so sweet. Thank you for the food we eat.' Even ragi congee, which was the staple for breakfast, was better than nothing, which she knew was what many had for breakfast, and there were always bananas. Even now, more than sixty years later, her friends joked, they had to make sure they had a good supply of bananas if she came to stay. She hadn't seen an apple until she was seven or eight. Perhaps Eve had taken not an apple but a banana from the tree of knowledge. Wouldn't that make the story quite different?

Sometimes they sang a different grace,

> Lord I would own thy tender care and all thy love for me.
> The food I eat the clothes I wear, are all bestowed by thee.

Once, a visitor (there were always visitors), after hearing that grace sung, said, 'I wouldn't like to blame God for the clothes I wear.' And all the grown ups laughed. Children in the go-downs went about naked for the first couple of years – a piece of string tied round a swollen belly. None of them wore shoes, not even chupples. Consider the lilies of the field. They toil not, neither do they spin and yet…

The house was full of going and coming, the lilt of Tamil, the chatter of Indian English, the yaw-yaw tones of visitors from Britain, men in shirts and trousers, men in white dhotis, men in cassocks. Sometimes a group of village women squatted on the veranda wanting justice because – being untouchables – they had been denied access to the village well, or bringing some family quarrel which the village punchayet could not resolve. Her father would come out and joke with them in Tamil and they would screech with laughter, shifting on their haunches and moving the betel in their mouths so they could shoot a stream of red spit over the edge of the veranda into the dust.

That was on the front veranda. Visitors did not come to the back veranda, which faced the go-downs. Moses worked there in the kitchen. The sweeper would pass after her work, salaaming and pulling the sari over her head. Sometimes, if there were lots of important visitors for dinner, the punkah-wallah came. The punkah hung above the dining table, a heavy strip of weighted cloth with a rope which ran out through a high hole in the wall to the outside veranda. The punkah wallah would sit cross-legged on the veranda floor, his back against the outside wall of the dining room, rhythmically pulling and releasing, pulling and releas-ing the rope, fanning the diners inside while he chewed on his betel. Sometimes, allowed to slip down from table while adult talk went on, Rachel and Chris would go and squat beside him, or sit cross-legged and lean against the wall, as he did, chatting in snatches of their bazaar Tamil. The sun beat down beyond the veranda, a wall of heat and brightness. When did they get an electric fan? She could not remember.

Moses still survived, a white-haired patriarch of uncertain age, whose grand-children were computer programmers in Chicago, Sidney and Mombai. The others were all dead now – her parents, the punkah wallah, her sister.

Dust thou art and to dust thou shalt return.

How to make sense of it? The unthinking privilege beside the commitment to love everyone as children of God. How did her parents make sense of it? Her father's predecessor had refused to allow any Indian to sit down in the house. Her parents not only invited Indians into their home but had Indian friends. Her father spoke wonderful Tamil, everyone said, not like the mangled missionary-speak which was the butt of jokes (like the one about the sermon in which the father did not fall on the neck of the prodigal son and embrace him but rather fell on his donkey and laid an egg, all because those English could only make one 't' sound with their clumsy tongues). The colonial administrators were on their way out. The last English Collector had lived down the road in a huge mansion. None of the British managers of the local mills allowed their girls and boys to play with the local children, as she did. Her father's early letters back to his family in Eng-land, one or two of the ones she had reread, struggled to describe what he called 'race prejudice' (racism, of course, was a concept yet to be given a name), and how it disfigured even the Church which taught that God loved everyone. And yet, and yet…

Rachel looked absent-mindedly through – rather than at – the suburban Man-chester street beyond her window. Just as she found it impossible to read her old letters, she found it impossible somehow to go back. All her friends went to India now, mostly to the North but a few to Kerala, and one friend had even gone to Tamilnadu and visited the great temple whose gopurums had defined the city-scape of Rachel's memory.

'Come with us to India next winter,' Isobel had said over the phone. 'We've found this great hotel near the beach in Goa. Really cheap. What do you mean, "Goa isn't India"? Oh, well! Suit yourself.' She'd put the phone down.

Rachel couldn't explain to herself, let alone to her friends. India hovered before her like the figure of the woman across the lake she had mistaken once for her mother, as she had walked back from school past the water buffaloes. If she went closer, she knew the figure would turn into a stranger.

Her Sikh neighbour came out of his house and got into his mini-cab.

No! It was early June now. It was the mango season. She would go out and walk into 'Curry Mile' in Rusholme. She would walk past the sari shops, the pyramids of sweetmeats in the Sweet Emporium, past the take-away selling hallal pizza, and at the greengrocer's on the corner she would buy a box of those perfect yellow fruit sold here as 'Pakistani mangoes'. She would eat them and let the juice run down her chin.

Afterword

The autobiography or memoir has a long history as a genre, going back at least to St Augustine's 'Confessions', and in recent years has flourished, spawning a variety of sub-genres: the celebrity biog, the misery memoir, and so on. As we all live longer – at least in the rich countries of the global North – more and more of those who have never written anything longer than a shopping list or an email, as well as those who have written professionally, are turning to memoir, sometimes under the rubric of 'life writing'. Yet, for a feminist, starting to write a reflection on her life is not straightforward. Feminist critics have consistently sought to situate their knowledges and specific histories within the dynamics of power and difference – whether of gender, race or class. This means the feminist memoir cannot treat the 'I' as self-explanatory. Besides, as many critics have pointed out, autobiography is always more or less unreliable. Memory is partial, but so are letters and diaries. Yet, they are what we have. If the memoir moves to publication, there are ethical questions of how far it is right to represent not just the living but the dead, who can't come back with a, 'No, it wasn't like that at all'. All this informs the way I have written, in particular the use of a non-linear, fractured narrative method.

I would like to say that in the light of these complexities I deliberately chose to write in the third person, but the truth is that I found I could only write 'otherwise', coming at the subject sideways rather than directly. Writing in the third person enabled me to be more truthful – always, of course, within the limitations of my own view. It released me into a different space in which to speak the experiences of my early life.

That early life might, I thought, be of interest beyond the circles of immediate family and friends. My parents went to India as missionaries of the Church of Scotland in the 1930s. They were at the end of a tradition of British Protestant mission which stretched back in a continuous line to the late eighteenth and early nineteenth centuries. This long history was exemplified in my family, as in several others we knew. My mother's father had left southwest Ireland in the 1880s, also to go as a missionary to India. My mother's best friend, Mary Hulbert, was the fourth generation of her Indian missionary family. The wider histories of what the churches called 'foreign missions' are marked by similar continuities as well as change (allowing unmarried women as missionaries being among the most radical). When in the late 1950s my father gave up his post, believing that it should be held by an Indian, it marked the end of that long tradition, one which has profoundly shaped not only the countries which were part of the British Empire but also the economies and society of metropolitan Britain and what Raymond Williams called its 'structure of feeling'.[4]

My experience was quite close to that of my mother and her siblings, and indeed of the generation of missionary children before them. They had all spent their early childhood in India but were sent 'home' to go to boarding school in England. My mother, the youngest of a large family, did not leave India until she was seven, unlike one of her elder sisters, who was just two. The school they attended was founded in the 1830s to give 'the daughters of missionaries' a suitable education. Though I was twelve, rather than seven, when I came back to that foreign place we had been taught to call 'home', I attended the same school in the same buildings and with much the same ethos as when my mother had been there. Even the colour of the school uniform was the same. The major difference from my mother's time was that the letters we wrote every Sunday to our parents could now be sent by air, so they took ten days rather than three months to arrive. The experience I shared with my mother vanished in the 1960s and is more or less incomprehensible to my children.

Within the broad category of memoir or autobiography the 'missionary life' had a special place during the nineteenth and early twentieth centuries. I have several examples on my bookshelves, including perhaps one of the last of the genre, my father, Lesslie Newbigin's, autobiography, *Unfinished Agenda* (1985). But these were public accounts, in which family life and in particular the experience of children could only be spoken of in formulaic terms. My – admittedly partial – knowledge of the vast outpourings about missionary activity in the religious press of the nineteenth and early twentieth centuries has yielded almost nothing which addresses the effect on, and affect for, missionary children of their early life experience. These experiences of childhood migration and separation they shared with the children of colonial administrators, business men and soldiers, but they were inflected by particularities of class, wealth and a different relationship with 'native' culture, one marked by the contradictory impulses of identification and separation, which also marked missionary activity in general. Postcolonial scholars, too, have not generally thought children's experiences worth attention, though that has recently begun to change, notably in Elizabeth Buettner's work (2004). We are still to allow the voices of the child refugee or asylum seeker to be heard through the cacophonies of war and forced migration.

I understand and indeed have been complicit in these silences. The experience of migration, separation and loss of a loved and familiar world I share with many others in colonial and postcolonial modernity. However, though I was a privileged white child, I have never been able to speak about it even to my close friends or colleagues. The reasons for this are complex: the difficulty of acknowledging loss, the embarrassment of comparative privilege, a perceived hostility to any kind of expressions of faith within those parts of the academy where I have spent most of my working life. All of these contributed. This writing, however inadequately and indirectly, seeks to explore that childhood experience which has been absent, not only from my personal narrative but also from the wider histories of colonialism and postcolonialism.

Notes

1 The websites 'quoted' are my own pastiche of similar sites rather than direct quotations, as are the articles supposedly from Google Scholar. I have, however, drawn on Dane Kennedy (1996).
2 All photographs are from my family collection.
3 The best source for that rich hybrid language of the Raj which has bequeathed so much

to Standard English is Colonel Henry Yule and A. C. Burnell's *Hobson-Jobson* (1994). I hope the Hobson-Jobson terms used here are self-explanatory.

4 Raymond Williams, *The Long Revolution*, pp. 64–88 and *passim* through much of his work.

Bibliography

Buettner, Elizabeth, *Empire Families: Britons and Late Imperial India* (Oxford: Oxford University Press, 2004).

Kennedy, Dane, *The Magic Mountains: Hill Stations and the British Raj* (Berkeley, CA: University of California Press, 1996).

Kipling, Rudyard, *Plain Tales from the Hills* (London: Macmillan, 1888, 1890).

Newbigin, Lesslie, *Unfinished Agenda: An Autobiography* (London: SPCK, 1985, updated St Andrew Press, 1993).

Williams, Raymond, *The Long Revolution* (Harmondsworth: Penguin, 1961, 1965).

Yule, Henry, and A. C. Burnell, *Hobson-Jobson: A Glossary of Colloquial Anglo-Indian Words etc.*, ed. William Crooke (Sittingbourne: Linguasia, 1886. British Edition, 1903; New British Edition, 1994).

III
Poetics

Bliss: opera's untenable pleasures

Monica B. Pearl

This is an essay about pleasure, to which opera, for me, is not incidental.

What *is* incidental: my knowledge of opera, my musical knowledge.

As someone committed to scholarship, I am invested in believing that if I don't know something, I can correct that; I don't mean I could take on any talent: I am not hubristic, not in this way at least. But I am practical. I am able to suppose that with some earnest application and attention (i.e., studying), I could learn about music. For the most part, I have chosen not to. I have not closed my ears or eyes to what knowledge might infiltrate, but I have not sought it out. This makes my knowledge incidental. And visceral.

That is the idea.

I know how ridiculous that sounds. A scholar, after all.

When I say visceral – I mean emotional, even physical: not cerebral, in other words. Not words, in other words.

I am not alone.

Many writers who love opera try to describe the ways that their love of opera is like – love. Though usually love is not the word they use. Adoration, sometimes; obsession; passion.

Or sex.

These writers invariably include the physical component of love in their descriptions: that the desire and pleasure felt in the engagement with opera is akin to the feeling of desire and pleasure felt physically.

There is an embarrassment of examples. Not least in the many references to the *jouissance* of the experience of opera, a nearly untranslatable French word that contains the feeling and understanding of the English word for pleasure but includes the suggestion of climax. It is the perfect word for the inarticulately undone.

For example, Terry Castle comments: '[f]ar from seeing opera (as [Catherine] Clément does) simply as an institution devoted to the ritualized "undoing" and debasement of the feminine, I consider it a much more complex and subversive cultural phenomenon, precisely because of its power to evoke homoerotic *jouissance* in its female fans'.[1]

Richard Miller, in his rendering into English Roland Barthes' *The Pleasure of the Text*, translates *jouissance* as bliss.[2]

Also, consider the title of Michel Poizat's book: *L'Opéra, ou Le Cri de l'ange: Essai sur la jouissance de l'amateur d'opéra*.[3] The book's methodology is to approach 'opera in much the way we sometimes approach dreams',[4] and Poizat's translator has similar difficulties: 'Occasionally I translate *jouissance* as "bliss" or "ecstasy," but because neither of these terms quite conveys the literal and metaphorical senses of orgasmic experience expressed by the term, or its transgressive aspects, usually it remains untranslated in this work.'[5] 'In English,' notes Richard Howard, 'our words for our pleasures ... come awkwardly when they come at all'; 'we lack *jouissance*', he says, 'and *jouir*.'[6] It is tempting to suggest that if we lack the words we lack the experience. In French our pleasures are multiple; in English monolithic.

However, opera is democratising: it renders us multi-lingually speechless.

I am willing to use bliss and pleasure somewhat interchangeably here, in the way that some of the translators helplessly have to. But Roland Barthes is not. The function of the word *jouissance* and its connotation of ineffable physical pleasure for him is that it marks the borders of text and self. We must bear in mind that Barthes refers to texts of words only – the written word, not music – when he makes the distinction between a '[t]ext of pleasure: that text that contents, fills, grants euphoria' and a '[t]ext of bliss: the text that imposes a state of loss, the text that discomforts'.[7]

I am perhaps joining a pantheon of opera adorers' confessions, penning this essay. There are so many: composed encomiums, scriven panegyrics to the exaltations of opera and the hopelessness of adjuring words to approximate or approach them. Even if I were to circumscribe my own feelings by assuming a more scholarly tone, I would just be joining a different level of the pantheon – for there is no scholar that I have come across who can contain her (or his) breathlessness when writing about the art – no matter how sober or scholarly she starts out.

We find in Carolyn Abbate's *In Search of Opera*, for example: 'In opera, certain arias can convey a sense not that they are being sung, but that they instead are reaching out to give life to a moribund body, making it sing.'[8] And in case we haven't heard her slight stretch beyond scholarly restraint to the rhapsodic, she tells us that her love of opera is 'an enduring obsession'.[9] And in Heather Hadlock's very impressive and mainly prosaic monograph on Offenbach's *Les Contes d'Hoffman* called, perhaps already revealingly, *Mad Loves*, she offers this poetic possibility: 'maybe all music sleeps in a green casket until we raise the lid and peer inside at the rich treasures that our imagination, our creative energy ... will animate once more.'[10]

Several written tomes on opera burst through the attempt at circumspection and openly struggle to find ways to equate or understand the relationship between opera and sexuality. Margaret Reynolds comes out and says, simply, that 'opera is about sex'.[11]

Most writers, even if they do not refer to the sexual aspects of opera, in responding to opera nevertheless manage to describe their response in physical terms. Note, for example, the title of Robert Levine's book: *Weep, Shudder, Die*, in which he writes: 'Properly performed, and properly listened to, these finely tuned if unlikely – indeed, improbable – moments should and will transport us to a sphere way above our quotidian lives, to a place where we cry and/or shudder.'[12] The body is undone by opera.

And there are no words to describe it. 'Bliss is unspeakable,' Barthes says, 'interdicted.'[13] '[P]leasure can be expressed in words,' he insists, but 'bliss cannot'.[14] Koestenbaum at the end of his long disquisition on opera wonders if perhaps he ought not to 'know better' than, 'struggling against [his] own naïveté, to put into words the emotions that overwhelm [him] when [he] listen[s]'.[15] As we hear over and over again, the experience of opera, at its finest and most exalted, is an experience beyond articulation, beyond poetry, beyond scholarship, beyond expression. So why bother? This essay is obviously, as I hope I have made clear from the beginning, a futile exercise. One has capitulated to words after all, shattered though one is: 'a sort of gurgling, burbling semi-idiot', as Castle puts it so embarrassingly and accurately.[16]

Opera seems to induce in its rapt listeners a desire and pleasure like no other; in contravention of psychoanalytic orthodoxy, sex and sexual desire are, here, perversely, perfectly, the metaphor for understanding other pleasures. While in the world of psychoanalysis (which is to say: the world) everything is a metaphor for sex; in writing about opera, sex becomes the metaphor for opera's pleasures. Catherine Clément reminds us that in 'the opera, just like in psychoanalysis, everything counts'.[17]

Der Rosenkavalier

In a review of Koestenbaum's book *The Queen's Throat*, Hadlock laconically sums up one classic ecstatic moment in opera when she writes of the duet 'Mir ist die Ehre widerfahren' in Richard Strauss' *Der Rosenkavalier*: what opera 'fan's catalogue would miss the two-soprano bliss of the Presentation of the Rose?'[18] Koestenbaum himself worries that when listening to *Der Rosenkavalier*, 'we might perish from ecstasy'.[19]

Many writers are drawn to this opera, drawn to try to explain the ecstasy of the singing in key moments of the work. Two key moments in particular are the Presentation that Hadlock refers to, and also the trio that melts into duet at the end. Another moment is the Marschallin's aria in the first act, a lament over ageing and the inevitable loss of love. Clément comments: '[the] marschallin's long German monologue in *Rosenkavalier* seemed sublime to me, from the moment I learned that she was describing there her childhood and the wrinkles now appearing at the corners of her eyes.'[20]

Richard Strauss' 1911 opera *Der Rosenkavalier* takes place in 1740s Vienna. It opens in the aftermath of a night of lovemaking between the Marschallin, a soprano, and her young lover Octavian, usually a mezzo-soprano (though sometimes another soprano). The opening scene is the Marschallin's grand bedroom – more specifically, her bed (Slavoj Žižek calls his whole chapter on *Der Rosenkavalier* 'The morning after'[21]). Though there is discrepancy in their ages – Octavian is only seventeen and the Marschallin perhaps mid-thirties (but decidedly represented as middle-aged in this opera) – they are clearly in love. Octavian cannot bear to take his leave of her, but she insists he go. When he is gone, however, she immediately regrets pushing him away, calls desperately for him to return, one last kiss. It is too late, her servants inform her, trying to rush after him; his horse has taken him away as swiftly as they have ever seen.

The Marschallin contemplates her visage in the mirror, her age. Meanwhile in this initial scene the Marschallin's oafish older cousin, Baron Ochs, has prevailed upon the Marschallin to suggest a messenger – a Cavalier – to present a silver rose as a ceremonial proposal to marry the young (very young: fifteen-year-old) Sophie, whose father's *nouveaux riches* will underwrite his noble title. Ochs and his desires – he flirts with Octavian disguised as Mariendel, a chambermaid – are presented as a starkly pathetic contrast: the mercenary marriage proposed and the love scene just witnessed. We will witness an even more drastic contrast in a moment.

Scene Two opens with the Presentation of the Rose, a sublime encounter in which Octavian, whom the Marschallin has proffered as her emissary to appease Ochs, falls in love with the trembling young Sophie even as he proposes marriage on behalf of another man. If you do not know this duet, see Koestenbaum again, above, on what it might do to you to listen to it.

In a chapter of his book called 'Operatic orgasms' (one really does wish we had 'jouissance' instead, after all), Sam Abel describes, in a subsection called 'Making love in the afternoon', what it is like for him to listen to a recording of *Der Rosenkavalier*. Abel takes three pages to describe listening to the final trio of *Der Rosenkavalier*. He opines that '[e]verything that happens in the previous three hours, that is, the entire plot of the opera, is a prelude to these last ten minutes'.[22] After two paragraphs of explaining how he *prepares* for the opening notes of the trio, he tells us:

> Now the three singers begin their inexorable climb up the scale to the tops of their registers. They hit high note after high note, dropping down a little in pitch after each new high, only to climb even higher in the next phrase, barely giving me time to recover between them. The ever-building music washes over me in closely harmonized waves, each one more intense than the last. Wave after wave, the harmonic tensions get denser, the orchestra louder, the instrumentation more dominated by the strings, until I can no longer separate strings from voices. The words are gone; the plot is gone; only the sound of voices blending with the orchestra remains.[23]

He describes ever more acutely the physical response he has – his heart, his back, his stomach, his buttocks. It is a decidedly sexual reaction. 'If I smoked,' he says after the music dies away, 'I would light a cigarette.'[24] 'For me,' he tells us, 'these are the most dangerous ten minutes in opera – and the most beautiful.'[25]

Clément takes three pages also to describe this opera: 'The curtain rises on a bedroom. Full of night love smells. The opera takes place between the sheets. Bodies are undressed; you see their skin as they awake; underwear is scattered about and pillows are everywhere.'[26] But Clément understands that that gorgeous final trio is not just bliss – for how can there be bliss without entwined suffering? Opera is built on this very idea – unfettered joy would have no resonance: 'Three female voices singing on their own behalf, each has its own discourse in a moment that has stopped to weigh all three destinies. The three voices are amplified to the point of ecstasy: an ecstasy for one, a shared ecstasy for the other two.'[27]

Operatic ecstasy is not only different from pleasure; it can be conceived as the 'enemy of pleasure': We are reminded that 'Lacan's *jouissance* unavoidably evokes orgasmic pleasure, but it is a sexual pleasure that sex can't give; indeed, it pushes pleasure beyond itself, to the point of becoming the enemy of pleasure, that which lies "beyond the pleasure principle".'[28] Pleasure might suffuse us, reconstruct us, make us feel whole, but *jouissance* is far more disruptive than that, even violent: it has been described as sadistic,[29] as narcissistic,[30] and as masochistic.[31] *Jouissance* does not sustain us; it dissolves us.[32]

'In opera,' Clément tells us even more succinctly, 'sweetness is deceiving.'[33]

Clément is right that this trio is ecstatic. Johanna Fiedler includes the trio among other heightened operatic moments in an account of 'an operatic orgy' in which one might 'wallow'.[34] It is also very sad. Oedipal: at the end the Marschallin walks off regally, taking her place as the elder beside Sophie's father, the 'parents' now to the relinquished young couple. Octavian's anguished maturity – recognising that he must allow her to let him go, to love Sophie – is heartbreaking, and exquisitely beautiful.

Are these sensual descriptions surprising? Have I said that for these lovers of opera sex is a metaphor for opera? Did I mention that Reynolds says that we go to the opera for sex? Let me quote her at length:

> Everyone knows that opera is about sex. It is no accident that the opera house is furnished with velvet plush, gilded mirrors, naked cherubs, and powdered footmen, for these are the trappings of the brothel, and we go to the opera house for sex. Opera lovers are all roués. They know how to savor, how to spin out refined pleasure, how to surrender with apparent abandon, and how to contrive, calculate, cost, and regulate their pleasure. Opera is not natural, not contemporary, not real; it tells us nothing about our lives, nor does it have any truck with the trivia of the everyday. In this consecrated place we give ourselves over to the contrivances of art. And the pleasure that art offers is sophisticated and curious. It thrives on arcane rules, is wholly cerebral in the locus of enjoyment, while it is yet strangely, powerfully, connected to the senses so that the body really does feel when the mind is most deeply engaged. As I say, we go to the opera for sex.[35]

Of the initial Presentation of the Rose, Koestenbaum writes: 'the two women seal with a duet their instant infatuation. Drugged by the music, I overvalue passion; I don't ask its name.'[36] If we arrived at the opera house with a sturdy sense of our gender, or of our sexual proclivities, he warns us, we will be dismantled; we are rendered promiscuously impassioned by the blind recklessness of ecstasy it creates in us. It is not the trouser role, *per se*, that is conceivably transgressive, it is that we feel ardour regardless of who is wearing what or courting whom. Perilous pleasures, indeed. 'When the silver rose arrives,' maintains Koestenbaum – faith in the dictum that the trouser role is the man's role now in shreds – 'Sophie falls in love with a woman.'[37]

Others experience this same crisis of gender conviction at the opera. In speaking of the trouser role more generally – about *Fidelio* as well as *Le Nozze di Figaro* and *Der Rosenkavalier*, Žižek wonders if, for example, it is possible 'to speculate that at a deeper libidinal level, Marzellina loves Fidelio because she is secretly aware that "he" really is a woman'.[38] 'The silver rose', Koestenbaum instructs us, '– and opera itself – carry the charge of an unspeakable and chronology-stopping love':

> When Octavian enters ... Sophie speaks for the listener. 'This is so lovely!' I sigh, hearing the soprano's excitement and orchestral explosion announcing Octavian's arrival. The music provokes my exaltation and also comments on it; this vocal and orchestra climax justifies my devotion to swooning and obliteration.[39]

Koestenbaum then also, like Clément, speaks of the smell of the opera, so immersed are we in our senses provoked: 'Smelling the rose ... I become clandestine, insurmountable.'[40] 'The listener may well ask,' he concludes: 'who am I, and what is my gender, if this vocal outpouring elects me as its recipient?'[41]

After all, that is what undoes us: that we are so licentiously receptive to what bliss might enter us. 'Sophie's and Octavian's lines finally come together to describe ecstasy in a double movement that hypnotizes the police.'[42] Koestenbaum no doubt means the police who arrive in the penultimate scene within the opera, but one cannot help but imagine that it is our own superegoistic policing that is undone. In other words, whatever the defences (and identities) with which you normally fortify your emotional battlements, you carry them to the opera at your peril: don't be too attached; as one crosses the threshold one's tethers are already fraying.

Barthes contributes this about the policing of pleasure: 'No sooner has a word been said, somewhere, about the pleasure of the text, then two policemen are ready to jump on you: the political policeman and the psychoanalytical policeman: futility and/or guilt, pleasure is either idle or vain, a class notion or an illusion.'[43] It is an 'old, a very old tradition,' Barthes sighs resignedly: 'hedonism has been repressed by nearly every philosophy'.[44]

It is ourselves doing the policing, Koestenbaum reminds us: 'Opera can offer no more piercing reminder of our emotional penury than by suddenly flooding us with sentiment we must suppress.'[45] Jeanette Winterson also describes the futility of constraint at the opera when she writes: 'In the end it is all about feeling. I think we spend quite a lot of time trying to control our feelings, only to find ourselves hopelessly overwhelmed when we least expect, or least want it to happen.'[46]

Susan Sontag describes in her journals attending in Paris in 1958 'a mediocre *Der Rosenkavalier*' that nevertheless has her 'riding the crest of erotic fantasy, the tide of the familiar gorgeous music'.[47] Forty-two years later she is still undone by it. 'With a fired-up look on her face', Sontag tells her interviewer 'that she went to the opera last night and cried at the end':

> 'What did you see?' I ask.
> 'Something I've seen many, many times: *Der Rosenkavalier*. It's the same tired production that's been at the Met for 20 years, but Renée Fleming was singing the part of Marschallin for the first time – making her debut, I think, in that role. And when that sublime trio began at the end, I started to cry, like I always do.[48]

The beginning of Reynolds' essay on the trouser role in opera offers us an epigram:

> Some time since I knew a woman I desired. We were friends. We were polite. I did not want to behave politely with this woman, but how to translate my rude lust into ruder action? How to make her understand? She was wise in these matters, but cautious. I was a novice, and, moreover, my circumstances required discretion . . . so I invited her to *Der Rosenkavalier*.[49]

If we are unsure about the aphrodisiacal qualities of opera – and the inner policing it dissolves – let us look to the end of the essay to see how this strategy turns out:

> We sat in the darkness of the stalls, and she watched the stage, and I watched her. She smiled as the curtain rose on Octavian's naked back; she smiled at the Presentation of the Rose. She laughed as Baron Ochs lost his wig, applauded his ignominious departure. She wept at the trio. Afterward, in the darkness of the street, she kissed me on the mouth. She says I kissed her. Who knows? *Non so più cosa son, cosa faccio* … [Cherubino sings this in *Le Nozze di Figaro* declaring her (I mean, his) love for all women: 'I do not know anymore who I am, what I do …'].[50]

Coming out

Even when writers are not actively comparing their experience of opera to sex, they nevertheless reveal their love of opera in sexual narratives. Many writers capitulate to the urge to tell their operatic coming out story – that is, how they came to love opera. For so many of them it was through records; though whether through recordings or the experience of attending the opera, there is invariably an experience of surprise – conversion: falling in love.

Koestenbaum's 'first three opera sets, talismanic [were] purchased by my grand-parents for my tenth birthday:

> *Carmen*, the Richmond/London budget set…
> *Aida*, the Toscannini version…
> *Madama Butterfly*, with Anna Moffo.'[51]

Although he stopped listening initially, 'midway, because [he] couldn't find the melodies',[52] he later fell for Moffo, in a story that – like the gay coming out story – has a recognisable narrative: first there is resistance, even boredom or contempt, then love – impassioned, ineffable adoration:

> I made it far enough through the first act to be struck, when Anna Moffo entered, with a sensation I've tried to describe before, and may never adequately name. Her timbre was separate from its surroundings. Her voice wasn't the canopy, the column, the architrave; gravely self-sufficient, it seemed not a copy of life, but life itself, and, like a breathing property, it entered my system with a vector so naïve, unadulterated, and elemental, so unpolluted by the names I would later impose on the experience, that my drab bedroom shifted on its axis.[53]

Although Koestenbaum says he 'waited eleven years to listen again to the *Butterfly* recording', he 'knew the ability to respond was stationed in [his] body, waiting for reveille'.[54]

Castle describes acquiring 'a 1964 Deutsche Grammophon recording of Alessandro Scarlatti's chamber cantata *Il Giardino d'Amore*, featuring Brigitte Fassbaender as Venus and the American soprano Catherine Gayer as Adonis'.[55] Castle admits that although she was 'impressed by Fassbaender's strange androgynous timbre and the precocious skill with which she and Gayer wove their seductive vocal lines', she was not initially overwhelmed. Later she acquires a 'reissue of the Scarlatti cantata on compact disc … in the new "silver" format, with the sound immeasurably cleaned up and the voice projected with a presence so direct and intimate as to be startling'; it was, she confesses, 'a revelation'.[56] She came to think of it as 'a miniature epiphany' – 'akin to those moments in Iris Murdoch novels when two characters who have known one another for years – without feeling the slightest emotional attraction – suddenly fall wildly and improbably in love'.[57]

The performance artist John Kelly describes it this way:

> One summer I was visiting a friend at his house on Fire Island … we were sunning ourselves on a waterbed mattress when a giant sound came pouring out of the house, a sound that made my ears ring, and my heart burst. At that point I knew virtually nothing about opera, but this voice, this singing, this *sound* touched me deeply and I had no idea why. It was *The Art of Maria Callas*, a stereo recording made late in her career, which introduced me to the art of opera. This collision of music, language and expression got my spirit to soar, and conjured feelings of times and places lost and regained, vast and yet familiar, like some kind of spirit guide had refocused me on all my past lives that were suddenly clamoring for attention. I was hooked.[58]

Lawrence D. Mass in his book *Confessions of a Jewish Wagnerite* explains that 'It was Gene', his best friend from adolescence, 'who first introduced [him] to opera'.[59] 'Initially, we became familiar with a few popular works through recordings we both owned: *Carmen* (Stevens, Reiner), *Turandot* (Nilsson, Bjoerling), *Don Giovanni* (Siepi, Price, Nilsson, Leinsdorf) and *The Barber of Seville* (Merrill, Meters, Leinsdorf).'[60] And then the now familiar transformation: 'Then came the brand new Solti/Nilsson recording of *Tristan and Isolde*, the first in stereo. We were both instantly and utterly seduced.'[61]

For the fictional Judge in Patricia Duncker's novel it was through live performance. But the pattern of imperviousness, even irritation, followed by revelation is similar:

> The Judge crouched in her seat, baffled by the action and the incoherence of the music. Yet everything unrolled according to her prejudiced expectations: forbidden love, desperate conflicts of loyalty and trust, she loves this one but has to marry that one, who is this one's lord and master. So far, so predictable. But the music unsettled her nerves; a monolith of sound, oddly broken and discordant. Each theme she picked out modulated, mutated, dissolved, escaped, so that

she could never keep hold of the threads ... She could hear the danger rising, rising. And so two conflicting emotions bubbled within her: anger and irritation at being forced to listen to something that she neither liked nor understood, and hypnotised fascination.[62]

And after the interval:

The last act of *Tristan and Isolde* is about waiting, waiting in impatience and frustration, waiting, waiting for life to ebb, waiting for the dawn, waiting to see the one you love for the last time, waiting for death. And the music makes you wait. Was it simply the effect of the champagne? The Judge felt the tension easing from her jaw and shoulders. She let the cashmere shawl slip down across her back. Let go. *Let go of everything. Like loosening a rope. Is that the right metaphor? Yes, let go.* And this was her undoing.[63]

This fictional example serves me well; like Duncker's Judge, live performance was my undoing too.

My first visit to the opera was sudden and unexpected – precipitous. I was twenty-four years old, and living in New York. My mother had tickets for *Il Barbiere di Siviglia* at the Metropolitan Opera. Though she didn't mention them. Having acquired them several months in advance, she had forgotten it was Thanksgiving, and her companion for the evening couldn't get out of family entanglements to attend. My parents were divorced, and my father was somewhere with his new wife. My sister was living in Harrisburg, Pennsylvania – far from New York – and had other plans, so my mother and I were deciding among our options.

I lived on West 13th Street then, and my mother was nearby, still in my child-hood home, in New Jersey. Contemplating the kind invitation from Margot, my manager at the bookstore (Shakespeare and Co. downtown) where I worked, who was holding a dinner for stragglers in her apartment in Brooklyn, my mother mentioned that, oh, she happened to have two tickets for the opera if I was interested. It was an early curtain, and we would still have time to get to El Rio – the sadly now defunct landmark Spanish restaurant in the meatpacking district, our eclectic selection, ultimately, for Thanksgiving dinner. 'But why hadn't you mentioned you have opera tickets?' I remonstrated. 'Oh,' she demurred, 'I didn't think you would be particularly interested.' She had nearly forgotten she had them. 'Don't dwell' was always her advice about mistakes or disappointments.

(One might gather from this essay that I have never fully absorbed this counsel.)

They are the best seats I still have ever occupied: first row of the Grand Tier. The event, the opera, was wonderful. Kathleen Battle and Leo Nucci were singing that night, skirmishing it out in that glorious duet 'Dunque Io Son'. I enjoyed it, yet it wasn't quite my apotheosis. Though that was only weeks away. It is perhaps worth noting that the little used subtitle of this opera is *L'inutile precauzione* (*The Futile Precaution*).

When my friend Lisa had a fight with her boyfriend on the eve of Christmas Eve, she asked me to take his place. As a birthday present, her father and his spouse had presented her with opera tickets – Orchestra, aisle seats, stage left, near the front – for the Christmas Eve performance of *Le Nozze di Figaro*. Her father's significant other, a singer who specialised in comprimario roles, was singing Don Basilio that night.

Yes, I said. Even though I had another engagement after that – at midnight. I was meeting my mother and my sister at Carnegie Hall. *Figaro* ended at 11.30pm; I had less than half an hour to sprint from Lincoln Center to Haydn's Farewell Symphony.

This was the moment; this evening was the transformation.

It emerged sitting next to my friend, hearing Anne Sofie von Otter, as the importunate page Cherubino, singing her supplication to the graceful, preoccupied, and momentarily moved (really: unsettled) Countess. This was my undoing. I was transfixed. Near tears. Breathless.

It was bliss. One wants to say 'the beginning of bliss', but bliss has no time – here it always was.

Under the audience's applause after this rapturously sad and seductive aria, Lisa leaned over and whispered to me, 'Monica, you're swooning.'

Cherubino declaims that aria kneeling before the Countess – 'Voi che sapete.' In this unlikely scenario, the young page momentarily seduces the Countess, who otherwise really does not even notice her (um, him), who only dwells on her husband's (in)attentions. That it momentarily transfixes the Countess suggests the power of seduction, and the power of the beauty of the voice, diegetically, within the very world of the opera – but also, oh, on us. On me. I was ensorcelled, smitten – undone.

You who know what love is, Ladies, see if I have it in my heart … It is new for me. I understand nothing.

And now of course I can see, it was the conversion, the falling precipitously in love reported by nearly every opera lover describing his or her headlong plunge; it feels like a transformation, but in hindsight it was also always there: anticipated, *planted*, always already in us, poised to dehisce.

Boredom

Let us take a moment to compose ourselves, to step back from my exemplary undoing by considering another less besotted aspect of opera, something that might seem like the opposite of bliss, but perhaps is better understood as its paradoxical underside: boredom. Those who do not adore opera usually say they are bored by it.

But it is not only those who do not love opera who experience boredom. The composer Ned Rorem reminds us that, for example, 'there is much to dread in *Rosenkavalier*'.[64] *Der Rosenkavalier* is an opera that is not only full of plangent laments and declarations. It is also farcical. German farce: not always funny, sometimes tedious. I might have neglected to mention that *Der Rosenkavalier* has its dull and annoying moments, as when Octavian disguises himself again as Mariendel, the chambermaid, to pretend to provoke a seduction by Baron Ochs in order to expose his lechery so that Sophie's pledge to marry him might be dissolved.

In any opera, no matter how dramatic or scintillating, there are potential *longueurs*, extended moments when one's mind wanders. All that time, money and effort – and one is willing to squander one's attention and attendance on, who knows what: deadlines? bills? Or sometimes even on reverie – that last kiss, that longed for next touch. But either way, in those moments, where has the opera gone…?

Yet are we really distracted from the opera in that time, or are these *inspired* distractions – distractions that only this music, these voices, could compose? If there is boredom in listening to *Der Rosenkavalier* it is likely to come from the restiveness of waiting, waiting for the glorious moments. Koestenbaum explains why we need those intervals, why it cannot all be the suffusing sweetness of those climaxes. When he writes that Strauss' opera might cause us to perish from ecstasy, he does so in the context of the threat of utter annihilating abandon into pleasure: 'If *Der Rosenkavalier* were consistently ambrosial,' he writes, 'we might perish from ecstasy, or tire of it, or learn to distrust it.'[65]

Barthes tells us, '[b]oredom is not far from bliss: it is bliss seen from the shores of pleasure.'[66] Indeed, he tells us (parenthetically, as though too absurd or perilous to contemplate) that it is bliss itself that can incite boredom: that '(bliss does not constrain to pleasure; it can even apparently inflict boredom)'.[67] Boredom, after all, might be remedial; it might be the ancillary antidote to our constant undoing: in the moments of boredom or distraction we are momentarily recomposed. Like breathing, in, out, throughout the opera: we frondesce; we collect ourselves back together.

Pleasure and boredom can even derive from the same feature. One of the things that produces the greatest pleasure in opera, for example – repetition – might also produce boredom: that phrase, those notes, that opera…, *again*! One of the things that is most known (if still to many inscrutable) about opera fanatics is their wish to hear something – what seems like the same thing – many, many, many times. To have every version of a recording (see Terrence McNally's 'The Lisbon Traviata', where the protagonist is obsessed with hearing a recording of Maria Callas' *Traviata* performed in the Portuguese capital, although he has, and has heard, many other versions), to hear one's favourite soprano (say) sing the same role as many times as possible, no matter where in the world it takes one, or indeed to hear that role sung by as many different singers as possible. The repetition (and variety) can take many forms. But repetition is key.

Koestenbaum writes that he listens 'five times a morning [to] the record of Isolde's "Liebestod".'[68] Poizat recalls that '[a]fter attending a performance of *Orfeo*', the eighteenth-century salon hostess Julie de Lespinasse, wrote, 'I could listen to that aria ten times a day; it tears me apart, sends me into an ecstasy of sorrow. I have lost my Eurydice … That music drives me mad: it sweeps me away, my soul craves this kind of pain.'[69] *New York Times* classical music critic Anthony Tommasini, explains that '[f]or insatiable opera buffs, there can never be too much of a good thing'.[70]

This repetition does not sound like boredom at all; it is irrepressible ecstasy. If Barthes tells us that 'repetition itself creates bliss', he also tells us however that 'to repeat excessively is to enter into loss'.[71] For Koestenbaum it is opera's very repetition that recalls us to Freud's observations about the narrative work of mourning when he writes that: 'Operas are works of mourning; they repeat a task that failed the first time.'[72] Freud explains that the bereavement involved in the work of mourning is experienced and expressed as unvariegated and repetitive: in mourning 'the laments ... always sound the same and are wearisome in their monotony'.[73] The cure for mourning – or, rather, the signal that the work of it is done – is libidinal recathexis: in other words, love.

The end

So we know that while Reynolds has opined that opera is about sex, it is also, terribly, beautifully, about loss. Does opera tell us (or remind us) that love is always about loss? We might recall here that Barthes has made the distinction between pleasure and bliss by indicating that the text of bliss is 'the text that imposes a state of loss'.[74]

Even within the opera: in *Der Rosenkavalier*, Sophie, all the characters, must forget their bliss to have – well, narrative. After she has been presented with the rose she must make chaperoned small talk with this young man who is a guest in her home: 'in the ecstatic duet, a few moments before,' Koestenbaum observes, Sophie 'stared into runic secrets of erotic bliss and eternity that now she forgets so that the drawing-room comedy can proceed.'[75]

Bliss itself is not narrative, but requires – and produces – narrative; it is eternal, but fleeting; unalloyed yet frangible. Bliss after all does not mean happiness, or not only or always happiness, but rather the experience of revelling in strong feeling, even difficult or terrifying feelings. To do so creates a kind of pleasure because to feel strongly is enlivening, it is embodying, it fills out the flesh. 'For me,' Winterson contends, 'opera is a place where all the emotions can be fully felt yet safely contained.'[76] Opera contains and provokes every human feeling, but, as Clément soberly tells us, '[w]hen you leave it is all over':[77] 'The end of an opera is a work of mourning. It is ephemeral work, quickly absorbed by little actions. One has to get up, move around, put on a coat, leave, walk, go down the stairs.'[78]

Like Reynolds, I also once attended a production of *Der Rosenkavalier* with someone by whom I was beguiled. As in Sontag's experience, in mine Renée Fleming was also singing the Marschallin, and it was the 'same tired production' at the Metropolitan Opera. Susan Graham was not only singing Octavian but seemed to become him. My paramour that evening was ... how do I say this?... I can't really begin to describe her glamour and allure: her dress, her mastery of the heels she was in, her décolletage, her magnificent lipsticked mouth, her noble carriage. I sported my nattiest jacket, sharpest trousers. When I wondered out loud during the first intermission why everyone was looking at us, why we were such a site of attention, she said, in her inimitable quick and perspicacious way, it was because we are the alternative ending.

She meant, to them we were the ending to *Der Rosenkavalier* where the Marschallin does not leave the stage; the ending where Octavian renounces the new infatuation with Sophie for her great, original, true majestic love.

In one stroke she rendered the oedipal ending of the opera ridiculous. The passage of time, renunciation – why capitulate to *that*? (And, after all, while we're at it – forgive me – but who really wants Sophie? Doesn't everyone really want Octavian and/or the Marschallin? Even Ochs – that ox – prefers Octavian to Sophie; and it does not take much suspension of disbelief – or any – to imagine wanting Octavian even more in drag.)

Indeed we were the Alternative Ending that evening, and for a while after. But as in opera, as Clément has only just told us, 'when you leave it is all over. Outside it is chilly; it was a beautiful performance.'[79]

However, I take heart in understanding that the unfolding of events in *Der Rosenkavalier* is already an Alternative Ending. Part of what makes Cherubino's supplication to the Countess in *Le Nozze di Figaro* so sublime and tantalising is the impossibility of it. The Countess is overcome with the command and beauty of Cherubino's gesture, but after all, she is the Countess, he a page. But *Der Rosenkavalier* opens the 'morning after' (Žižek): the morning after a night of love between the page and the Countess in the form of Octavian and the Marschallin. The ending is nearly the same – the page and the Countess cannot end up together – too many differences: status, character, mainly age – but this time, in Strauss' version, while it is still the Countess who decides, it is a heartbreaking relinquishment. It is impossible, but for a moment, an utterly convincing moment, it wasn't.

Is this part of what breaks our hearts in opera: not the relentless extinguishments (the dramatic deaths and *les petites morts*), but the impossibilities that remind us relentlessly of possibility? Mourning is precisely the repetitive attempt to make it right – to change the ending. It never works. And then, anyway, suddenly, it does. Bliss is not the cure for loss, but it is ameliorative; not because bliss erases loss but because it offers us glimpse after glimpse of something else: plenitude. Not *merely* joy – but the possibility of everything.

Notes

1 Terry Castle, 'In praise of Brigitte Fassbaender (a musical emanation)', p. 269.
2 See Richard Howard, 'A note on the text', in Roland Barthes, *The Pleasure of the Text*, p. v.
3 Michael Poizat, *The Angel's Cry: Beyond the Pleasure Principle in Opera*.
4 *Ibid.*, p. ix.
5 *Ibid.*, p. xiii
6 Howard, 'A note on the text', p. v.
7 Roland Barthes, *The Pleasure of the Text*, p. 14.
8 Carolyn Abbate, *In Search of Opera*, p. 16.
9 *Ibid.*, p. xiii.
10 Heather Hadlock, *Mad Loves: Women and Music in Offenbach's* Les Contes d'Hoffmann, p. 16.
11 Margaret Reynolds, 'Ruggiero's deceptions, Cherubino's distractions', in Corinne E. Blackmer and Patricia Juliana Smith (eds), *En Travesti: Women, Gender Subversion,*

Opera, p. 132.

12 Robert Levine, *Weep, Shudder, Die: A Guide to Loving Opera*, pp. 21–2.

13 Barthes, *The Pleasure of the Text*, p. 21.

14 *Ibid.*, p. 21.

15 Wayne Koestenbaum, *The Queen's Throat: Opera, Homosexuality, and the Mystery of Desire*, p. 240.

16 Castle, 'In praise of Brigitte Fassbaender', p. 201.

17 Catherine Clément, *Opera, or the Undoing of Women*, p. 85.

18 Hadlock, 'Peering into "The Queen's Throat"', p. 270.

19 Koestenbaum, *The Queen's Throat*, p. 219.

20 Clément, *The Undoing of Women*, p. 17.

21 Slavoj Žižek, 'The morning after', in Slavoj Žižek and Mladen Dolar (eds), *Opera's Second Death*

22 Sam Abel, *Opera in the Flesh: Sexuality in Operatic Performance*, p. 30.

23 *Ibid.*, pp. 80–1.

24 *Ibid.*, p. 81.

25 *Ibid.*, p. 31.

26 Clément, *The Undoing of Women*, p. 108.

27 *Ibid.*, p. 110.

28 Leo Bersani and Adam Phillips, *Intimacies*, p. 60.

29 Maud Ellmann, 'Bad timing', in Shaun Whiteside, trans., *Introduction to Sigmund Freud: On Murder, Mourning and Melancholia*, p. x.

30 Lauren Berlant, 'Neither monstrous nor pastoral, but scary and sweet: some thoughts on sex and emotional performance in *Intimacies* and *What Do Gay Men Want?*', p. 269.

31 Bersani and Phillips, *Intimacies*, p. 68.

32 Berlant, 'Neither monstrous nor pastoral', p. 264.

33 Clément, *The Undoing of Women*, p. 110.

34 Johanna Fiedler, *Molto Agitato: The Mayhem Behind the Music at the Metropolitan Opera*, p. 2.

35 Reynolds, 'Ruggiero's deceptions', p. 132.

36 Koestenbaum, *The Queen's Throat*, p. 218.

37 *Ibid.*, p. 218.

38 Žižek, 'The morning after', p. 209.

39 Koestenbaum, *The Queen's Throat*, pp. 218–19.

40 *Ibid.*, p. 219.

41 *Ibid.*, p. 219.

42 *Ibid.*, p. 219.

43 Barthes, *The Pleasure of the Text*, p. 57.

44 *Ibid.*, p. 57.

45 Koestenbaum, *The Queen's Throat*, p. 221.

46 Jeanette Winterson, 'Introduction', p. 3.

47 Susan Sontag, '1/12/58', p. 182.

48 From an interview with Sontag. James Marcus, 'Desperately seeking Susan: a 2000 conversation with Susan Sontag'.

49 Reynolds, 'Ruggiero's deceptions', p. 132.

50 *Ibid.*, p. 149.

51 Koestenbaum, *The Queen's Throat*, p. 10.

52 *Ibid.*, p. 10.

53 *Ibid.*, p. 10.

54 *Ibid.*, p. 10.
55 Castle, 'In praise of Brigitte Fassbaender', p. 220.
56 *Ibid.*, p. 221.
57 *Ibid.*, p. 221.
58 John Kelly, 'Closet thrush', p. 38.
59 Lawrence D. Mass, *Confessions of a Jewish Wagnerite: Being Gay and Jewish in America*, p. 78.
60 *Ibid.*, p. 78.
61 *Ibid.*, p. 78.
62 Patricia Duncker, *The Strange Case of the Composer and His Judge*, pp. 102–3.
63 *Ibid.*, pp. 104–5; emphasis in original.
64 Ned Rorem, 'The *Rosenkavalier* diary', in *Settling the Score: Essays on Music*, p. 163.
65 Koestenbaum, *The Queen's Throat*, p. 219.
66 Barthes, *The Pleasure of the Text*, p. 26.
67 *Ibid.*, p. 52.
68 Koestenbaum, *The Queen's Throat*, p. 240.
69 Poizat, *The Angel's Cry*, p. 5.
70 Anthony Tommasini, 'Time travel at the Met, thanks to CDs'.
71 Barthes, *The Pleasure of the Text*, p. 41.
72 Koestenbaum, *The Queen's Throat*, p. 178.
73 Sigmund Freud, 'Mourning and melancholia', in Angela Richards (ed.), *On Metapsychology: The Theory of Psychoanalysis*.
74 Barthes, *The Pleasure of the Text*, p. 14.
75 Koestenbaum, *The Queen's Throat*, p. 219.
76 Winterson, *Midsummer Nights*, p. 3.
77 Clément, *The Undoing of Women*, p. 9.
78 *Ibid.*, p. 174.
79 *Ibid.*, p. 9.

Bibliography

Abbate, Carolyn, *In Search of Opera* (Princeton, NJ, and Oxford: Princeton University Press, 2001).

Abel, Sam, *Opera in the Flesh: Sexuality in Operatic Performance* (Boulder, CO: Westview Press, 1996).

Barthes, Roland, *The Pleasure of the Text*, trans. Richard Miller (New York: Hill and Wang, 1975).

Berlant, Lauren, 'Neither monstrous nor pastoral, but scary and sweet: some thoughts on sex and emotional performance in *Intimacies* and *What Do Gay Men Want?*', *Women and Performance: A Journal of Feminist Theory*, 19:2 (July 2009), 261–73.

Bersani, Leo and Adam Phillips, *Intimacies* (Chicago, IL, and London: University of Chicago Press, 2008).

Castle, Terry, 'In praise of Brigitte Fassbaender (a musical emanation)', in *The Apparitional Lesbian: Female Homosexuality and Modern Culture* (New York: Columbia University Press, 1993).

Clément, Catherine, *Opera, or the Undoing of Women*, trans. Betsy Wing (London: I. B. Taurus, 1997 [1988]).

Duncker, Patricia, *The Strange Case of the Composer and His Judge* (London: Bloomsbury, 2010).

Ellmann, Maud, 'Bad timing', in *Introduction to Sigmund Freud: On Murder, Mourning and Melancholia*, trans. Shaun Whiteside (London: Penguin, 2005).

Fiedler, Johanna, *Molto Agitato: The Mayhem Behind the Music at the Metropolitan Opera* (New York: Doubleday, 2001).

Freud, Sigmund, 'Mourning and melancholia', in Angela Richards (ed.), *On Metapsychology: The Theory of Psychoanalysis*, Penguin Freud Library, vol. 11, trans. James Strachey (London: Penguin, 1991 [1917]).

Gerstler, Amy (ed.), 'Introduction', in *The Best American Poetry 2010*, series editor David Lehman (New York: Scribner, 2010).

Hadlock, Heather, 'Peering into "The Queen's Throat"', *Cambridge Opera Journal*, 5:3 (November 1993), 265–75.

Hadlock, Heather, *Mad Loves: Women and Music in Offenbach's* Les Contes d'Hoffmann (Princeton, NJ, and Oxford: Princeton University Press, 2000).

Howard, Richard, 'A note on the text', in Roland Barthes, *The Pleasure of the Text,* trans. Richard Miller (New York: Hill and Wang, 1975).

Kelly, John, 'Closet thrush', in *Queer Voice*, exhibition catalogue (Philadelphia, PA: Institute of Contemporary Art, 2010).

Koestenbaum, Wayne, *The Queen's Throat: Opera, Homosexuality, and the Mystery of Desire* (New York: Vintage, 1993).

Levine, Robert, *Weep, Shudder, Die: A Guide to Loving Opera* (New York: Harper Collins, 2011).

Marcus, James, 'Desperately seeking Susan: a 2000 conversation with Susan Sontag', www.amazonia-book.com/sontaginterview.html. Accessed online 10 April 2012.

Mass, Lawrence D., *Confessions of a Jewish Wagnerite: Being Gay and Jewish in America* (New York and London: Cassell, 1994).

Poizat, Michael, *The Angel's Cry: Beyond the Pleasure Principle in Opera*, trans. Arthur Denner (Ithaca, NY, and London: Cornell University Press, 1992).

Reynolds, Margaret, 'Ruggiero's deceptions, Cherubino's distractions', in Corinne E. Blackmer and Patricia Juliana Smith (eds), *En Travesti: Women, Gender Subversion, Opera* (New York: Columbia University Press, 1995).

Rorem, Ned, 'The *Rosenkavalier* diary', in *Settling the Score: Essays on Music* (New York: Doubleday, 1989).

Sontag, Susan, '1/12/58' in *Reborn: Journals and Notebooks 1947-1963,* David Rieff (ed.), (New York: Farrar, Straus, Giroux, 2008).

Tommasini, Anthony, 'Time travel at the Met, thanks to CDs', *New York Times* (20 January 2012).

Winterson, Jeanette, 'Introduction', in *Midsummer Nights* (London: Bloomsbury, 2009).

Žižek, Slavoj, 'The morning after', in Slavoj Žižek and Mladen Dolar (eds), *Opera's Second Death* (New York and London: Routledge, 2002).

Graphic to surface: textual effects and criticism

Judy Kendall

The visual materiality of language can actually create meaning.[1]

Graphic or visual textual effects have been integral to textual production from its very beginnings, as the hieroglyphic tablets of Egyptian antiquity and the early ideograms of Chinese writing bear witness. And so it has continued in hand-written, printed and digital text: from the illustrations and illuminated scripts and scrolls of mediaeval manuscripts to the visually inventive novels of Laurence Sterne, Christine Brooke-Rose or Mark Z. Danielewski; the elaborate and sophis-ticated sequential combinations of text and images of Japanese manga; and the kinetic and interactive manipulations of text in the digital world.

The different visual possibilities open to textual effects are huge and can impact deeply upon how the reader/viewer sees, thinks about and assimilates text. Infor-mation received from the visual stimuli affects the reader's approach to the text. Crucially, this information is received before the process of reading is initiated. It could be called a process of *pre*-reading and is likely to push literary critics out of their comfort zones, as it is an investigation of the process of *pre*-writing, of what happens before a poem emerges on the paper or the screen – a key question for a creative writing academic like myself. Little exists in the way of established frame-works for such journeys within literary disciplines, although Glyn White's *Read-ing the Graphic Surface* and Joe Bray *et al*.'s *Ma(r)king the Text* have made some headway. As a result, when attempting to cover the groundwork and formulate the terms and language with which to discuss what is in effect a science of read-ing and writing, a researcher may well be attracted, despite themselves, to murky and forbidding disciplines – disciplines that focus on activities of the mind and the brain: psychoanalysis, psychology, cognitive and neuro-science. Picking and choosing appropriate elements from these diverse approaches, the researcher now acts like a creative writer putting together the elements of a new poem. Readers of such work may well find themselves making unlikely comparisons drawn from disciplines other than that in which they think the work resides. Disorientation is inevitable.

Neuro-science offers a convenient account of the process by which visual infor-mation is assimilated by a viewer. David Marr's model of the human visual system, published in 1982, outlines the different diverging stages of visual processing: 'in-formation about the shape of an object must be processed separately from information about what the object is for and what it is called', and 'the visual system can deliver a specification of the shape of an object even when that object is not in any sense recognised'.[2] This seminal model is supplemented by the hypothesis of neurologists Leslie Ungerleider and Mortimer Mishkin, published also in 1982. Ungerleider and Mishkin's basic distinction lies between the 'what' and the 'where' system in visual processing. This has been refined and modified by subsequent researchers, but their basic premise still endures: 'visual information takes different processing routes depending on what type of information it is'.[3] Different aspects of visual effects are processed separately and non-chronologically.

This separation of the different stages involved in the assimilation of what we see is clearly pertinent to the reading process. Sigmund Freud's very different model of the mind is also helpful, particularly his concept of *Nachträglichkeit*. Literally meaning 'afterwardsness', it highlights the ways in which remembered stimuli affect subsequent impressions. As Nicola King explains, *Nachträglichkeit* makes 'explicit the fact that memory, operating as it does in the present, must inevitably incorporate the awareness of "what wasn't known then"'.[4] In other words, it relates to the effect of interaction of successive acts of memory between different points along a time continuum.

Freud put it thus in a letter to Wilhelm Fliess:

> Our psychic mechanism has come into being by a process of stratification: the material present in the form of memory traces being subjected from time to time to a rearrangement in accordance with fresh circumstances – to a retranscription. Thus, what is essentially new about my theory is the thesis that memory is present not once but several times over, that it is laid down in various kinds of indications. (I postulated a similar kind of rearrangement some time ago [Aphasia] for the paths leading from the periphery...)

The letter continues:

> I should like to emphasize the fact that the successive registrations represent the psychic achievement of successive epochs of life. At the boundary between two such epochs a translation of the psychic material [takes] place. I explain the peculiarities of the psychoneuroses by supposing that this translation has not taken place in the case of some of the material, which has certain consequences.[5]

The phrases 'from time to time' and 'successive epochs of life' indicate that Freud is referring to large chunks of time – years or more. However, *Nachträglichkeit* also maps with ease onto the more immediate framework of visual processing and the reading experience, in which the process of perception affects the subsequent process of reading. What we read in the content of a page is affected by what we have previously seen when we viewed that page prior to reading it.

Of course, perception is not simply one 'act', so, to become fully cognisant of the reading process, it is necessary to trace in detail the stages of perception of visual textual effects. Similarly, there is no single 'act' of reading. Experiments in functional neuro-imaging, such as those of Petersen *et al.* in 1988, show that there are distinct and separate pathways in the brain for auditory information, visual information and semantic processing. Petersen's work reveals

> a direct information pathway from the areas in the visual cortex associated with visual word processing to the distributed network of areas responsible for articulatory coding and motor programming, coupled with a parallel and equally direct pathway from the areas associated with auditory word processing. Moreover, the areas associated with semantic processing [...] were not involved in any of the other tasks, suggesting that those direct pathways did not proceed via the semantic areas. [6]

Such research suggests that the reading process is not hierarchical (or chronological) but multi-layered. Each separate byte of information, each separate visual or textual effect, combines with others to produce a final, illusory, but apparently integral, impression in the reader's consciousness. The application of such research to consciousness, impressions and memories points towards an affective science of writing, embodied, irreducibly informed and shaped by the circumstances in which it occurs. The reader/viewer's personal experiences relating to their context, culture, gender and memories also become of importance in their assimilation of and response to visual and textual effects.

So, what are these specific visual textual effects and how do they combine to affect the reader's impression of the text? In an initial attempt to investigate these questions, I focused on one personal experience, the experience to which I had most privileged and unique access: my own. As part of my research, I decided to manipulate visually a draft chapter, 'Birds' Nests', of my next monograph, *Edward Thomas and Birdsong*. By doing so, I hoped to ascertain the specific contributions made by visual text effects to a piece of writing.

I avoided, however, choosing a completed piece since, commonly in my drafting processes, I tend to deliberately insert in later drafts various effects specifically designed to assist and underline a linear semantic argument. This was contrary to my purpose. I wanted to examine the widest possible range of contributions that visual text effects might make to a piece.

In harmony with the aesthetic experience of poetic composition, which, for me, regularly begins with notes of immediate and unconsidered impressions, I treated my visual remanipulations of text in the same way. For a similar reason, I tried to minimise my reflections, while writing, on the overall semantic content of the work, letting my focus rest instead on immediate local visual effects. Aesthetic considerations of space, rhythm, metre, echo, repetition and association led the way.

I first worked with the opening of the original textual draft:

> The nest material of 'bayonet-like reeds' in 'Birds in March' has become 'reeds/ Like criss-cross bayonets' and they are linked both to a place (where a bird sang), the past ('once'), and also, ominously, to the present and future, particularly that of a soldier-poet in 1916.
>
> 'Rain', composed a little earlier than 'Bright Clouds', on 7 January 1916, also

refers to broken reeds. The speaker, homeless and lying in a 'bleak hut', thinks of those who are dying or lying awake:

> Like a cold water among broken reeds,
> Myriads of broken reeds all still and stiff
> (Edward Thomas: *Annotated Collected Poems* [*ANCP*], p. 105)

I lifted the Thomas quotations from this, and subsequent lines, and rearranged much of what was left in an alphabetical sequence, overlaid with semi-circular nest-shaped quotations of some of the Thomas lines in a larger-size font. Finally, I introduced the piece with a slice of leftover text from the original draft:

Over twenty years later, buried in lines in Thomas's poem 'Bright Clouds', composed in early June 1916 are oblique and almost subliminal references to 'Birds in March'. The scene described in 'Bright Clouds' has many parallels with 'Birds in March', including a reference to a moorhen and

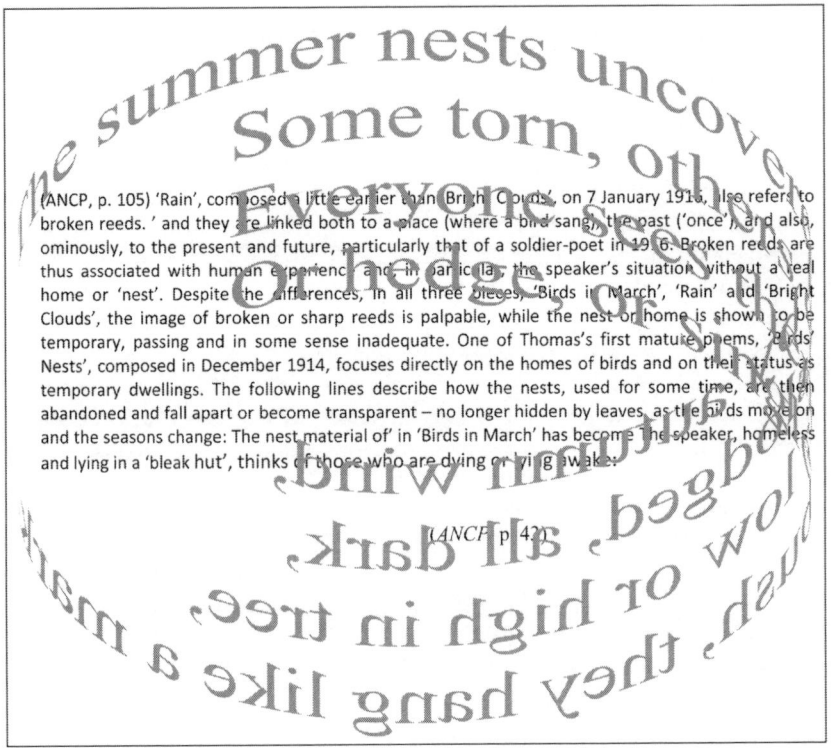

I placed some additional unused text in a new setting created by graph software. The result gave the poem fragments their own place on stage, as it were (illustrated on facing page).

After several days I had reworked just over one page of the fifteen-page draft into four pages of visual text. The time I had set aside for this experiment was run-

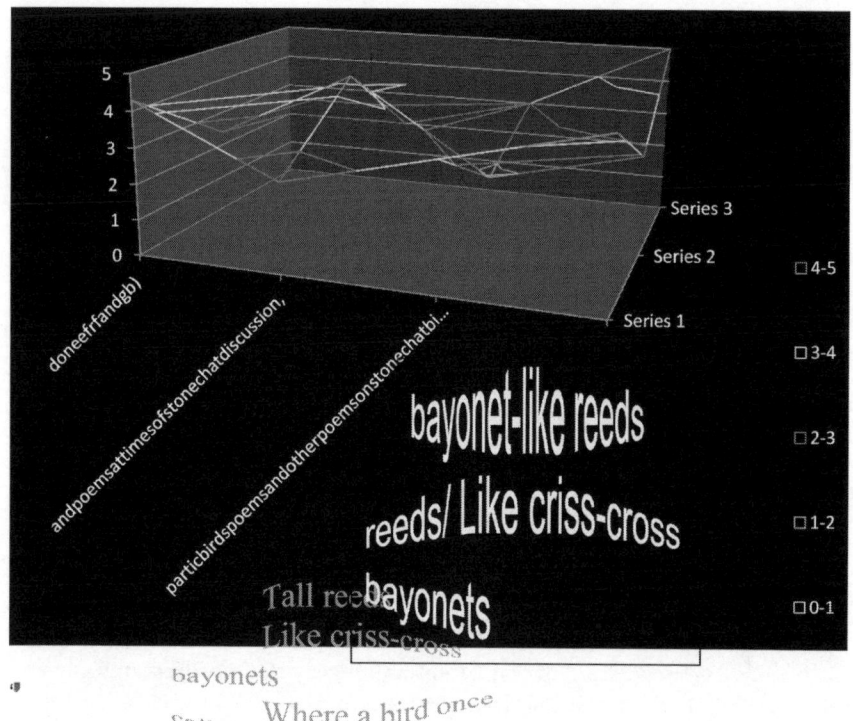

ning out, so I jumped several pages of the text version, to pages five, nine and ten, and added as a resolution a section on Thomas's sense of home as fleeting and his poetic rendition of a rook's sense of home and perspective. This was cheating since I was thinking in a more academic and logical, linear, semantic way – not visually.

My preference, had I world enough, would have been to travel on with the visuals and see where they led. Nevertheless there was sufficient material for some fruitful analysis to take place. Initially, this took the form of a preface to the manipulated piece, entitled 'Intention', which examined how the piece had changed as a result of its visual transformation.

Effects that I highlighted included a blurring of the order of the sections and changes to the order within them. In a number of cases, previously effective attempts at introduction, explanation, analysis and conclusion were rendered redundant by the visual display. The slice of explanatory text from the original draft, which had linked two sections together, seemed unnecessary in the visually manipulated version (see figure on facing page).

New and unintended effects also emerged. The isolation of Thomas's quotations as curved shapes allowed them to sing out, like birdsong. The piece had become aural. The visuals and words worked like musical notes – viewing them was like reading music. This sense of sound and song affected the way I ended the piece: I scanned the original draft for ways in which to tie up the now emerging references to nest and to song. It also affected the original intended purpose of the draft. Initially, I had deliberately excised references to song, planning to discuss these later in the monograph, but the simple act of lifting Thomas's quotations from the text reintroduced a strong sense of song, suggesting that this aspect was always there, hidden, at the edge of the senses, as birds so often are.

On page three of the visual text I included a boxed quotation from Thomas, drawn from page nine of the original draft. I set it in the middle of a second text about him, taken from page five of the original, and changed the point size of the font of each line of the poem so as to suggest different perspectives:

present, ideal or fleeting, homes that cannot be found, or are temporary, elusive,
The more expansive view offered by the rooks references to the environment,
physical | Over the land freckled with snow half-thawed | setting, and
other | The speculating rooks at their nests cawed | markers of
what | And saw from elm-tops, delicate as flower of grass, | constitutes
home for | What we below could not see, Winter pass. | a bird.
(*ANCP*, | | p114)

In this visual rendering, the quotation no longer fitted neatly, seamlessly and semantically into the prose, but drew attention to itself as a separate voice, which of course it was, since I had lifted it from a different section in a last-dash bid to cover pages I had no time to set visually. The quotation now disrupted the text in which it was set. It also rendered redundant the need to discuss perspective, laboriously present in the original but now experienced visually as we read. The immediacy of this experience was accentuated by the introduction of transcriptions of birdsong that were not in the original draft. I inserted these where they enhanced the look, sound or pace. My decisions were largely intuitive and directly related to my actual sensuous and aesthetic experience as I worked. What felt, looked and sounded right stayed. I did not seek out rational explanations for my choices – the sensuous experience was sufficient of itself.

The effect was (for me) remarkable. Reading the piece, I not only heard bird song, coming in and out of the text, as it might to my ears in a walk in a forest or field, but also heard a spoken voice, charged, like an oracle – 'spoken' perhaps because the visuals consisted of words, and, on the last page, of numbers. The inscrutability of these unadorned numbers also added to the sense of displayed, measured, deliberate, but coded meaning.

The numbers came from Thomas quotation page references. They were removed from the quotations as not relevant, useful or aesthetically pleasing. An academic habit prompted me not to delete them but to place them in a bunch at the end of the piece. In this form, when sandwiched between two verbal renderings of birdsong, their own potential as song was obvious:[7]

go back, go back, go back back back
but-I-DO-love-you
(*ANCP*, notes, p. 163). – **ref to Davies POEM Harvey elected bk?**
(*ANCP*, p. 43)
(*ANCP*, p. 58)
(*ANCP*, p. 64)
(*ANCP*, p. 81)
(*ANCP*, p. 82)
(*ANCP*, p.113)
(*ANCP*, p.114)
(*ANCP*, p.63)
[…]
kaah

Spaced on the page, this became unavoidable:

go back, go back, go back back back
but-I-DO-love-you

(*ANCP*, notes, p. 163). – **ref to Davies POEM Harvey elected bk?**
(*ANCP*, p. 43)
(*ANCP*, p. 58)
(*ANCP*, p. 64)
(*ANCP*, p. 81)
(*ANCP*, p. 82)
(*ANCP*, p.113)
(*ANCP*, p.114)
(*ANCP*, p.63)
[…]

kaah

My preface described this process of composition thus:

> by accident, I discover the list of numbers I had removed from one section of text and forgotten to delete seems to offer a suitable way of concluding the piece. The field notes of birders, twitchers, sometimes use letter and number codes to record experiences, sights and observations of birds, and is this any more or less valid than the more florid attempts of writers such as Thomas (although of course Thomas too kept and published his field diaries) or, indeed, a writer writing about bird writing like me?

This selection, isolation and visual manipulation of scraps of Thomas's writing, previously buried within the draft, comprised an act of care. They were celebrated, untrammelled by the explanatory prose that surrounded but no longer submerged them. Selecting bits of phrases that Thomas had written over the years, each a resurrection of the same or similar image, my visual manipulation presented them rising, bubble-like, from the page. The result was a focus on his lines, and an experience rather than an account of the changes and reinterpretations of the image. It was more 'firsthand'.

Out of this experiment a set of questions arise. Do my findings suggest that critical analysis of a poem hinders the act of caring for it? Does the visual manipulation of the poem allow for a different kind of caring to take place, bringing to the fore associations, meanings, emotional impact that are not otherwise noticed? And are these already present in the text or are they created by the visual manipulation of it?

A significant outcome of this experiment was my new awareness of the deep resonance of the image 'broken reeds' for Thomas ('for' in both senses of the word), particularly in their relation to home, whether possible or unachievable. The visual display of the various permutations of the 'broken reeds' image re-enacted for me the experience of influence on creativity, echoes of previous versions of an image reverberating in the mind as a writer composes. It also led me to consider giving 'broken reeds' more prominence in the monograph. Manipulating the text visually thus resulted in a shift in the emphasis of the semantic content of the previous conventional draft. Although my succeeding prose draft did not contain visual effects, insights received from the visual experiment affected and deepened it.

It is curious to observe that to write, as I just have, about what is going on in the poet's mind, presumably Thomas's, as he writes, seems fanciful in a text of prose, but the visual image of bubbles of 'broken reed' lines arising and passing away does not. It lets me say, or represent, what it is difficult to 'explain' convincingly. Do visual renderings allow not only for intuitive knowledge to arise but for us to present it to others? And how do such remanipulations affect questions of authorship? Do they constitute more profound changes than the vastly different permutations in page design that successive publishers might offer to the same text, with some extreme results, as in the case of later editions of Sterne's *Tristram Shandy* in which the particular typographic and positioning effects upon which Sterne was so insistent are lost, or later publications of Blake's *Songs of Innocence and Experience,* in which the illustrations, which he conceived of as united with the poems, have been excised?[8]

To investigate this subject further, I present here a second analysis, which comprises a close examination of visual textual effects in one short piece. I take as my subject the abstract that accompanied this essay, reproduced below. In my analysis I lay out the reasons behind the choice of effects, easily accessible through personal memory and awareness of habits of writing, since I, the writer of this essay, was also, at one time, albeit several months ago, the writer of the abstract:

As a poet-academic in the area of THE PROCESSES OF POETIC COMPOSITION; VISUAL TEXT; THE GRAPHIC SURFACE IN WRITING, CREATIVE OR OTHERWISE, I am increasingly aware of the ironies inherent in and obscurities resulting from presentation of my research by means of traditional *SCHOLARLY PRESS* or *ACADEMIC ABSTRACT.* In recent work therefore I have been exploring new ways in which to approach this material: ways that heighten the reader's awareness of the effects of visual text; ways that facilitate in the act of reading an informed experiential sense of process; ways that fall between the creative and the critical. The consequence has been a wave of interrogative demonstrations of process in the very moments of its coming up for air. The intent is to display graphic / textual surface in such a way that its inevitable plunge beneath the levels of perception is delayed until after conscious registration of its presence. This essay forms one such attempt.

Recourse in the course of such writing to my own and other contemporary writers' creative practice simultaneously informs and is informed by the description, analysis, and enactment of the processes under observation. Success is measured by the degree to which the writing illumines the writing.

Graphic features in this abstract include typography and layout. Small capitals mimic printed titles, but effect a smoother transition from lower-case to upper-case letters. Normal-sized capitals would have formed more of an interruption to the text, similar to the interruption capital letters create when used singly at the start of a sentence, but intensified when appearing in a row as a string of words, MORE LIKE HEADLINES THAN PRINTED TEXT.

The abstract also makes use of variations in typeface – Calibri and *ITC Edwardian Script.* A shift in the sizes of letters, like the choice of small capitals in lines one and two of the abstract, results in better flow and less interruption of the text. In contrast, ITC Edwardian Script was chosen precisely for its relative illegibility. Its presence allows the text to enact the obscurities referred to at a semantic level – how scholarly or academic approaches can throw a cloud over their subject-matter: the difficulty, depth, specificity and specialism of the enquiry risking a progressive obscurity, only accessible to a privileged and specifically educated elite. The counter to this tendency is offered by an approach which requires researchers to enact as they explore: process as argument.

The lexical 'or' in lines two and four evokes the borderline territory between the creative and the critical, the textual and the visual, a borderline that is negotiated, explored and demonstrated through the use of small capitals, font size and style. In line nine, 'or' is replaced by the more visual sign, '/', an intensely visual mark that, unlike the comma, works only when viewed. When reading, we combine 'o' and 'r' to spell 'or', but '/' cannot be spelt out. If the text is read aloud, we have to add an effect to replace the '/'. Unlike a comma which can be 'heard' as a pause or breath when reading aloud, '/' has to be substituted by movement, perhaps the word 'slash' or 'stroke', or the gesture of a stroke through the air, or, indeed, 'or'. This last, in particular, is an unsatisfactory replacement. In the text in question, '/' is more intense than 'or'. The choice of '/' reflects the charged semantic content, which in line nine starts directly to express the 'intent to display' the borderline area and to throw into focus the interplay, and contradictions, that run between the graphic surface and semantic levels of a text, where semantic and visual textual effects do not divide but elide as one.

The abstract is deliberately restrained in its use of commas to pick out the phrases in its lengthy sentences. Without commas, the reader, if needing to break down the sentences into more digestible units, has to resort to other methods. Visual effects in the layout point the way: judicious diagonal positioning of repeated words and phrases (the repeated 'ways that' in lines five to seven and the visually and aurally similar 'wave of' in line eight forming a steadily retracting diagonal evocative of the movement of an actual wave)

....

....

....

....

– only we are now reading the wave backwards, in reverse, as we travel down the different ways to the wave and into the sea; vertical positioning ('plunge beneath' in line ten coming under the surface 'coming up for air' of line nine)

coming up for air

plunge beneath

; and enjambment (transitive verbs are divided from their objects in the straddling of lines five to six and six to seven, echoing, in each case, the heady expectation expressed both visually and metaphorically in the breaking wave that is carved out in lines five to eight and named in line eight)

therefore I have

been exploring new ways in which to approach this material: ways that **heighten the reader's awareness** of the effects of visual text; ways that facilitate in the act of **reading an informed experiential sense of process**; ways that fall between the creative and the critical. The consequence has been a series of interrogative

. Such mimetic effects, the text graphically enacting its semantic content, are also mimetic of the process under scrutiny, of research that enacts as, and what, it expresses and explores. This is evident in the positioning of the full-stop at the beginning of the line in which the previous sentence starts (and of the semi colon near the bottom of the previous page – in my written copy of this essay at any rate, although I cannot control its positioning in print). This positioning calls attention to the punctuation mark's function as full-stop, alerting the reader to the requirement to pause, and encouraging a considered analysis of the reason(s) for that requirement.

If the reader does not pick up the poetic language/devices in the abstract will they be influenced by such effects? Is it immediately apparent on a first reading of the abstract? Does it subconsciously affect the reader? Clearly, the text's reception will depend on the reader's sensitivity to visual cues. Some readers will register these consciously. Others, missing them, will find the text frustrating, although this may encourage them to adopt a different approach. Yet others will need a critical analysis to make out the text's visual aspects.

Such obscurity is not such an issue in poetry, which is more often recognised and appreciated for its visual effects. This is particularly the case with traditional Japanese poetic forms, such as haiku and tanka. Working very strongly with space, they demand that we pay attention to that space. Consequently, most readers will not ignore the choice of line breaks, the decision not to use capitals or punctuation, the role played by space, in a tanka printed, as they often are, alone on the paper, an unseen hinterland framing the visible text, as in the contemporary example by Stuart Quine, reproduced overleaf. [9]

The setting of the tanka in Tahoma typeface, with the lines in centre position on the page, but not centred, and the proportion of top to bottom margins being roughly that of 1 to 2, were all directed to me by Quine. Accompanying the process of rendering academic writing into visual text is the realisation that techniques and considerations accompanying poetic works such as Quine's can also be used with other writing. Consequently, when reworking my monograph draft into visual text, I became aware of dealing with the prose text as if it were a poem. This does not happen in reverse. Visual effects, if they are any good, work best as visuals, not as part of an academic argument.

The extent to which this previous paragraph is true renders a traditionally academic approach problematic when applied to visual text. Commonly, scholars of visual text surround themselves with objects, such as physical books, illustrations, diagrams, and image devices to demonstrate the effects they are outlining. As the little piece of dense, if accurate, close analysis of the abstract pertaining to this essay so aptly demonstrates, it can become lengthy and difficult to write – and only write – about such effects. Diagrams help. However, reading the abstract itself takes far less time than navigating through the pedestrian parsing of its visual effects. Reading about the abstract's visual effects is almost impossible if there is no access to the abstract. The task is easier if the abstract itself is available, even as an endnote; easier still if it is included in a footnote; and easiest of all if it can be placed in full view on a facing page.

a new year begins...
wind in the chimney
rain at the windows
I sit within
a great becoming

Clearly, understanding visual textual effects requires us to prioritise looking as well as reading. If you have reached this far into this essay, you will by now be doing this. You may have just been puzzling at the reversed apostrophe in the previous paragraph, and uncertain, as you would not have been otherwise, whether this is accidental or deliberate.[10] Such a response also, of course, puts pressure on the writer to ensure that any merely accidental typographical errors are ironed out or exploited. But what about accidental effects the writer does not notice? And what about those that occur after the piece has left the writer's hands: an irregularity in the printing process perhaps, or careless handling by a coffee-drinking reader who then becomes an inadvertent creator/collaborator? When does the process stop, if ever?

Another reason for the difficulty of writing in a traditional academic manner about graphic, visual textual effects is the fact that not only are they '**visual**' effects, which require us to look rather than read, but also the effects they produce can be invisible. The enlarged '**visual**' in the previous sentence stands out because it is also emboldened. Simply 'visual' is more subtle and 'visual' more subtle still. We also have the choice of visual and **visual**. Each of these is a noticeable, clockable, effect, although it is conceivable that a reader might assume that visual is a vagary of the typesetting or of their tiring eyes, and discount it from any consideration, but what about when placement of words in the printed text ensures that 'visual effects' as a phrase is split down the middle and stretched across two consecutive lines, with the result that, as in poetry, a visual emphasis is placed upon 'visual' as the end of the line, since the distance that the eye takes to track back to the very beginning of the following line, or, more accurately, the mapping that the eye observes as it leaps in its usual wayward jerky movements across, round and occasionally up and down the text, taking it in in small discrete patches, one of which is unlikely to include the word **visual** at one end of a line while placing **effects** at the beginning of the next, renders it similarly unlikely that the reader initially, in that first moment of pre-perception, puts the two words **visual** and **effects** together either?[11]

And that last sentence is hard to follow, partly from lack of attention to **visual** effects. Try this:

Each of these is a noticeable, clockable, effect,
although
    it is conceivable that a reader might assume that

                                                        visual
    is a vagary of the typesetting or of their tiring eyes, and discount
    it from any consideration,
but
    what about when placement of words in the printed text
    ensures that   visual
effects   as a phrase is split down the middle and stretched across two
    consecutive lines
  , with
  the

result
that,
      as in poetry, a   visual
      emphasis is placed upon   'visual'
      as the end of the line,
since
      the distance that the eye takes to track back to the very beginning
      of the following line,
or,
more
accurately,
      the mapping that the eye observes as it leaps in its usual wayward jerky
      movements across, round and occasionally up and down the text,
      taking it in in small discrete patches, one of which is unlikely to
      include the word   **visual**
      at one end of a line while placing the word
effects   at the beginning of the next,
      renders it similarly unlikely that the reader initially,
      in that first moment of pre-perception,
      puts the two words   **visual**
      and
effects   together either?[12]

Here the visual effects are highlighted by their specific positions on the page. In fact it is likely that you will read it differently, perhaps scanning down rather than, or as well as, left to right, and picking out individual isolated words as well as blocks of text. In addition, words that indicate the thrust of the argument ('although', 'but', 'with the result that' etc.) are now placed to the left of the lines in the main text in order to help the reader thread through the trajectory of the logic. Such specific and unusual placement of words encourages the reader not simply to read the text but to view it and so to recognise and consciously assimilate the visual effect, which more normally remains unobserved and unacknowledged.

This relates to the difficulty of a conventional academic approach. It is doubly hard to analyse effects of which we are not in the first place conscious. Or, to rephrase that, to analyse effects the consciousness of which we do not acknowledge, since clearly we do see that a word is emboldened, at the end of a line, in a different font, right justified or not, but are not currently conditioned to register this as a significant indicator of meaning in conventionally laid-out prose, is doubly hard.

Let's return for a minute to your first reading of the abstract. Did you as reader notice the visual effects before they were analysed? And would you have done so more easily if they had been highlighted topographically on the page? If your answer to this last question is yes, then this is an indication both of the importance of visual effects and of our tendency as readers of prose to discount them.

It may have felt unsettling and disruptive to read process as argument before being aware of it. This was deliberate. The extent to which it felt disruptive is an indication of the extent to which you have been conditioned not to notice visual effects in this kind of layout. As readers and takers in of information we filter it, and as readers of prose, we have been conditioned to filter out visual effects. We may 'clock' them at some level, but we then pass them by.

Had I forewarned you of the effects about to be displayed, or set up specific signposts to steer you in your navigation and 'correct' reading of the text and realisation of the intentional nature of the effects, had I even included the abstract at the beginning of the piece, thus clearly highlighting my intent, rather than simply as a box in the text, you would probably have taken more notice of its content and seen at least some of the effects first time round. However, it was necessary not to alert you to the process as embodiment of argument until you had experienced it, so that you could become aware of the extent, or not, of your usual alertness to visual text as a possibility when reading.

Once again, poetry tells another story. Take a recent Issa haiku I translated with Wilhelm Wetterhoff. It began in English as

into the blue sky, birthcry rising sparrow

It was then transmuted into the slightly unreadable and space-expensive

i
n
t
o
t
h
e
b
l
u
e
s
k
y
b
i
r
t
h
c
r
y
r
i
s
i
n
g

s
p
a
r
r
o
w

Next it became

blue sky

^

rising birthcry

^

sparrow

finally[13]
and was/rendered as

blue sky

rising birth-cry

sparrow

The last version was presented as performance, visuals and sound accompanying each other.

The impetus for our decisions was a focus on the direction of reading and probable order of assimilation of the Japanese characters for a Japanese reader of the text. It was relatively easy, once we had recognised this as a driving force, to represent these features in English by means of visual effects, and, since it was poetry, we felt no pressure to explain or highlight such effects. We trusted that they would be accepted and understood, as part of a poem whether on the page or screen.

With prose, however, it is different. This is not to say that viewing does not take place. The visual effect is instantaneous. A reader has first to see the letter and word divisions and to recognise a text as a text, rather than as an amorphous and random scattering of ink, before reading. This is even more obvious in unusually shaped prose. A reader makes out the tail of the mouse that Alice follows in *Adventures in Wonderland* first, and then reads it as a tale. Perhaps what happens in conventionally shaped prose is that the visual effect of the text is registered and then dropped once the brain starts to tackle its linguistic meaning. (This differs from a good piece of visual text, where meaning and visuals interconnect so closely that they cannot be divided.)

When we read, the first stage of the process is viewing. This informs our later perceptions of a text as text. Hence, the emphasis in published works, designed for the untutored and unprepared eye, on presentation. To analyse visual effects successfully, it is required to lift the act of registering the presence of the effect into the forefront of awareness, delaying the moment at which the brain kicks in and filters out information it considers to be unnecessary to the **sense** of the piece. (At this point it is highly likely that you noticed the emboldened sense as **sense** in that line and also its deliberate position at line ending, and its accidental but judiciously coincidental placement at page ending).

However, since, for the most part, visual effects are unacknowledged and ignored, we lack or have lost the language with which to describe them. So, current work on visual text effects, such as White's *Reading the Graphic Surface*, or Bray *et al.'s Ma(r)king the Text*, quite rightly tend to focus on defining the terms in which to talk about these effects, listing and grouping them.

It is an open field. Exciting, but confusing. Here are some of the possible terms: graphic surface, surface visuals, visual effects, visual text, graphic text, visual textual effects. Or to put it another way:

```
graphic surface
        surface visuals
                visual        effects
                visual text
graphic                 text
visual                  textual effects
```

Which way of presenting this list of terms, visually, or as part of a prose sentence, is clearer? Why? Does each tell us something different? If so, why, how? The difficulty of this terminology surfaced in a recent discussion with Glyn White, coiner of the problematic term, 'graphic surface'. We had independently entertained similar doubts about this term. Rather than suggesting the differentness that is involved in reading a text through its visual textual effects, and its consequent value as an alternative mechanism for producing knowledge, understanding or perhaps just 'responses' to a text, the use of 'graphic surface' implies a hierarchical order in which a superficial 'surface' is set against a deeper, 'beneath the surface' academic reading. It is interesting, therefore, that in the visual rendering of the various proposed terminologies above, created before that conversation and before my awareness of this particular drawback of the term, I chose to place 'surface' at the surface. Accidentally?

Visual effects were not always unseen, invisible. The history of the book in Western Europe can be traced back to the elaborate golds, blues, reds and yellows of the illustrative emblems in illuminated manuscripts. Intriguingly, the history of my and any young Western reader's progress towards literacy also moves backward to visual art, and beyond that to the object it signifies: through, in my case, uninspiring Janet and John illustrations captioned by simple and often unilluminating texts; to picture books sporting only one word per multi-coloured and visually lavish page; to lessons involving letters and images – A for Apple, I for Ice cream, with an ice cream promised on completion of the letters.

We are talking here of the materiality of the text. In the case of a newspaper, for example, it is immediately apparent that its size is part of its meaning. A change from broadsheet to tabloid is a change in meaning. Broadsheets have been perceived as more intellectual in content than their tabloid counterparts, their greater size used to examine stories in more depth. A shift to digitalisation shifts the meaning yet again, allowing the reader to select only the article they intend to read and to miss the advert for pills next to it.

My first 'proper' book was *Arabian Nights*.[14] What I mainly remember from this first treasured book is the text, three lines to a page, illustrated with glorious blue and gold images, and also its size, shape and weight, and the thickness of the pages.

Unpacking a box in my new house, shortly after writing the above, I find this copy of *Arabian Nights* tucked into a corner. With this discovery, I am literally handed proof of the need to consider the effects of temporal dislocation on the reading process, through the passage of time from my younger self, five, to my current self, fifty-two, and through the process of writing this essay and searching for demonstrative examples. Looking at the book, I notice a number of discrepancies with my memory. Although blue and yellow, along with red, orange and green, feature on its covers, with the title in red outlined in yellow on a deep blue sky, the illustrations inside only use shades of red, orange and black. Rather than three, there are up to eighteen lines of text per page. Most pages carry illustrations, but several do not, and although there are three double-page full illustrations, there are also three double pages devoted only to text.

Why do I misremember this? Or is it a case of misperception, happening at the time of reading? Could the magic thinking inherent in the text, the enchanting transformations and vanishings, the (to me) exotic settings, have heightened the colours and expanded the illustrations? Could I have been responding, however hazily, to the powerful legacy that the original eighteenth-century French and English translations of *Arabian Nights* bestowed on Western children's literature?

Crucially, on the frontispiece, there is a very clearly handwritten, almost printed, note congratulating me on learning to read. It is from 'F. Christmas' (aka my father, easily identifiable to me now by the phrase 'hoping this finds you, as it leaves me, in the pink', a favourite of his). The note is dated 1965. I cannot remember now, and no longer trust my memories of this time anyway, whether I understood this to be from my father or from F. Christmas, but the acknowledgement of having learnt to read and the gift itself (our family was large and cash was strapped) suggest why I might now recall this book as important, although even as I write I have a vague memory that at the time I felt slightly insulted; the book was either beyond me – too much text – or, I felt, beneath me – disappointingly childish.

Glancing through the stories in it now, I read them as images of learning to read. There is Ali Baba's 'Open Sesame' and the glories and dangers he subsequently uncovers – everything being different as a result; Sindbad [*sic*] the sailor seeing 'what seemed to be a little field peeping out above the water', which, once he has landed on it, reveals itself to be a huge sea-monster who, by shipwrecking him, changes his life; and Aladdin, daring to accompany a stranger out of the known and familiar because he 'was always ready for an adventure', but also keeping his wits about him when the stranger tries to rob him of his lamp, and later, his princess – daring, but retaining awareness and independence as well.

When I was first developing my reading skills, the leap from image to text was, for me, a difficult one. A precocious reader, as my appetite for more sophisticated semantic content grew, I became dismayed at the lack of pictures on offer. From the range of library books that presented me with an adequately satisfying semantic content, I made my choices according to the quality and quantity of illustrations, and when reading used the pictures to anchor myself between the bouts of more challenging text. Thus, pre-teen, I was able to consume illustrated Jane Austen novels, her ironic intent completely passing me by, my interest being only in the romances experienced by her characters. Unquestionably I was too naïve for her wit, but the drawings of eighteenth-century lords and ladies in aristocratic drawing rooms set the tone. These illustrations framed the text and helped me through it in much the same manner as the illustrations of my *Arabian Nights* had promised to some five years earlier.

I say that the illustrations framed the text, but at times I acted in my selection of books and reading/viewing of them as if the text framed the pictures:

> Where does the frame take place. Does it take place. Where does it begin. Where does it end. What is its internal limit. Its external limit. And its surface between the two limits. [15]

Later in my career as a reader, and significantly I cannot recall exactly when this happened, text sneaked onto centre stage, although even now I still retain the habit, when my attention sags, of checking how many pages are left before the end of a chapter or a book, behaving like the readers of *Northanger Abbey* encouraged by Jane Austen to see 'in the tell-tale compression of the pages before them, that we are all hastening together to perfect felicity'.[16] However, the experience of reading has changed. When I deliberately sought out the pictures first, this tallied with my experience of vision, in which pictures are witnessed before text. Now I work harder to push text to foremost position. However, text is never first. Although it may become centre stage as we read, the process always involves earlier degrees of recognition of the depth and wealth contained within the graphic textual surface.

I am indebted to the members of my two reading forums on Writing Otherwise and Visual Text for the development of this piece: Kate Adams, Margaret Beetham, Brenda Cooper, Ursula Hurley, Glyn White and Janet Wolff

Notes

1 Richard Bradford, *Silence and Sound*, p. 171.
2 David Marr, *Vision: A Computational Investigation into the Human Representation and Processing of the Visual System*, cited in José Luis Bermúdez *Cognitive Science: an Introduction to the Science of the Mind*, pp. 49–50.
3 Leslie Ungerleider and Mortimer Mishkin, 'Two cortical visual systems', cited in Bermúdez *Cognitive Science*, p. 70.
4 Nicola King, *Memory, Narrative, Identity: Remembering the Self*, p. 11.
5 Jeffrey Moussaieff Masson, trans., *The Complete Letters of Sigmund Freud to Wilhelm*

Fliess 1887–1904, pp. 207–8 (6 December 1896).

6 S. E. Petersen *et al.*, 'Positron emission tomographic studies of the cortical anatomy of single-word processing', cited in Bermúdez *Cognitive Science*, p. 81.

7 At times it has been necessary to negotiate with the editors/publisher of my monograph to allow divergence from the usual conventions of text positioning on the page in order to retain specific visual effects.

8 See Glyn White, *Reading the Graphic Surface: The Presence of the Book in Prose Fiction*, pp. 24–30.

9 *Presence*, 46 (Summer 2012), p. 5.

10 Accidental, and questioned for exactly the reasons I state in an early showing of the essay, it has now been exploited to further my point.

11 See http://en.wikipedia.org/wiki/Eye_tracking for a diagram of typical eye movements when reading static text (accessed 5 December 2011).

12 An indication of the issues involved in creating and sustaining visual textual effects from draft to printed version is evident here, since, although in the initial draft the words in the text of the previous paragraph are identical to those in the visually manipulated version, the processes of redrafting, editing, typesetting and proof-reading render it almost certain that they will vary slightly, as I, the editor and the typesetter struggle to maintain the exact positioning of the discussed visual effects.

13 In one draft typescript of this chapter, 'finally' was inserted by hand because I had forgotten to include it. It was pointed out to me that this helps to confirm the sense of finality, since the last adjustments of a writer before going to print are often made by hand.

14 The particular edition of *Arabian Nights* I discuss here was published by the Children's Press in 1965.

15 Jacques Derrida, 'Parergon', in *The Truth in Painting*, p. 63.

16 Jane Austen, *Northanger Abbey*, p. 271. In a previous draft, the Jane Austen quotation, which I had lifted from elsewhere, appeared in eleven-point Calibri, the font of the previous text in which it had appeared. I had the choice of changing it to the font that I was currently using, twelve-point Times New Roman, or leaving the difference, signalling its provenance to the reader, and, perhaps, making the quotation marks themselves redundant.

Bibliography

Arabian Nights (London: The Children's Press, 1965).

Austen, Jane, *Northanger Abbey* (London: Oxford University Press, 1945).

Bermúdez, José Luis, *Cognitive Science: an Introduction to the Science of the Mind* (Cambridge: CUP, 2010).

Bradford, Richard, *Silence and Sound* (Cranbury, NJ: Associated University Presses, 1992).

Bray, Joe, Miriam Handley and Anne C. Henry, (eds) *Ma(r)king the Text: The Presentation of Meaning on the Literary Page* (Aldershot: Ashgate, 2000).

Derrida, Jacques, *The Truth in Painting* (Chicago, IL: Chicago University Press, 1987).

King, Nicola, *Memory, Narrative, Identity: Remembering the Self* (Edinburgh: Edinburgh University Press, 2000).

Marr, David, *Vision: A Computational Investigation into the Human Representation and Processing of the Visual System* (San Francisco, CA: W. H. Freeman, 1982).

Masson, Jeffrey Moussaieff, trans., *The Complete Letters of Sigmund Freud to Wilhelm Fliess 1887–1904* (Cambridge, MA: Harvard University Press, 1985).

Presence, 46 (Summer 2012).

Quine, Stuart, 'A new year begins …', *Presence*, 46 (Summer 2012), p. 5.

Thomas, Edward, *The Annotated Collected Poems* (Newcastle: Bloodaxe, 2008).

Ungerleider, Leslie, and Mortimer Mishkin, 'Two cortical visual systems', in D. J. Ingle, R. J. W. Mansfield and M. A. Goodale (eds), *Analysis of Visual Behavior* (Cambridge, MA: MIT Press, 1982), 549–86.

White, Glyn, *Reading the Graphic Surface: The Presence of the Book in Prose Fiction* (Manchester: Manchester University Press, 2005).

First person plural:
notes on voice and collaboration

Marianne Hirsch and Leo Spitzer

'You collaborated on a book?' 'And you're still married...?
My spouse and I could never write together!'
'How did you actually do it?' 'Did you write separate chapters?'
'Why did you want to do this?' 'What's your secret?'

Yes, it's true. Not only did we collaborate on a book, but we have also written articles together, co-taught courses and seminars, and, on many occasions, we've presented papers and given joint public talks. But it is our collaborative writing and publication of a lengthy book that elicits the raised eyebrows and incredulous chuckles. Although research scientists often work together in teams and publish papers signed by multiple authors as a matter of course, academic collaboration in the humanities, and especially interdisciplinary collaboration resulting in published work, is still viewed by many as sufficiently unusual to merit comment. And collaborative writing and publication by academic domestic partners occurs so seldom that it continues to generate astonishment and wonder.

Unlike novelists or poets, academic writers are rarely asked about their creative practices and strategies. We tend to be endlessly curious about a fiction writer's method of composition: Does she handwrite or type? Does he write in the mornings? For how many hours? How does she revise, by pen or computer? What energises his inventiveness? No one would think of asking academics these kinds of questions. We imagine academic writing to be cerebral and disembodied, produced within more-or-less agreed upon disciplinary conventions, and we therefore don't care to imagine academic authors at their desks.[1] If academics want to jar or shock their readers, they step out of expected practices and make their presence as authors, and their role in the construction of the text, visible. They remind us that there is a living person with a body – with desires, needs, and perhaps even with disabilities and biases – that is selecting, processing, and shaping the production of a scholarly composition.

This kind of presence inevitably becomes apparent when two people living together sign an academic work. As the eye-winking queries above imply, such collaboration immediately seems to remind readers of the personal embodied lives of the authors. They are a couple, but they are also two separate people. The practice of composition employed by them in the collaborative effort cannot simply be assumed; it leaves itself open to scrutiny. Who wrote what? How? Was work equitably distributed? What effects did writing together have on the couple's relationship with one another and with their domestic life? How, while trying to collaborate, did they negotiate life and work, marriage and career?

In our case, moreover, two additional risk factors enveloped the potential hazards stemming from collaboration. The first derived from our decision to employ the personal voice in our recent co-authored book *Ghosts of Home* – a voice we had both used in previous, single-authored, published works.[2] The second, from our desire to continue to write 'otherwise' and to participate jointly in what one might call a 'writerly turn' in academic work. This involves the foregrounding of the *act* of writing itself, conforming to Roland Barthes' description of reading as a form of writing and his definition of a *texte scriptible* or *writerly text*.[3] For Barthes, such a text breaks out of expected codes of representation to challenge the position of the passive reading subject by enjoining an active engagement and participation in textual production. It reflects writing (and, consequently, also reading) in the *middle* voice – in a voice that is neither active nor passive, neither transitive nor intransitive, neither altogether personal nor impersonal – one in which the subject is *inside* the writing, constituted *by* the writing. 'Today, to write', Barthes suggests, 'is to effect writing by affecting oneself.'[4]

It is in relation to this middle voice and our practice of 'writing otherwise' that we propose to discuss our collaboration and how we came to it – each in our own way.

LS: What marks us? What stays with us, indelibly, but also perhaps invisibly, and becomes a defining constituent in who we are and what we creatively represent?

When I now specifically try to identify aspects of my younger years that have stayed with me and affected my interests and approach as a historian, a sense of myself as 'outsider', as 'marginal', 'in-between', is fundamental. I was born in La Paz, Bolivia, a few days before the start of the Second World War to parents fleeing Nazi persecution in Austria.[5] I was raised within a community of German-speaking, largely Jewish, refugees who had been forced to abandon (through what we now call 'ethnic cleansing') lands in Europe with which they, and generations of their forebears, had long identified – lands into whose dominant culture they had attempted to assimilate. Anti-semitic displacement, the insecurities of refugeehood, alarming news from the European warfront, the silences of less fortunate family members left behind, revelation of the immense scale of the genocidal criminality that we've come to call the Holocaust – all these enveloped my childhood and left their indentations and notches on who I am.

I emigrated to the United States when I was ten years old. I acquired a new language here and, largely unconsciously, was North Americanised by yet another assimilationist process. I was educated, socialised, politicised to become part of the dominant culture in this country, and, over the years, I was fortunate enough to be rewarded by its institutions. But, having already been profoundly inscribed in childhood with the history and culture of a people who had been defined as 'other', and who had been persecuted and marginalised, I also never felt totally absorbed by this process. Despite the fact that I have now lived in the United States for most of my life, I have always been somewhat distrustful of the idea of a 'permanent home'. Anchored 'roots', as opposed to diasporic 'routes', make me nervous.

If I have to identify one key quality that I acquired over the years and that became instrumental in my efforts as a historian and cultural critic to analyse and explain aspects of the past – how persons living then, and in other places, understood their world – it has been empathy. George Mosse, one of the great émigré German historians of the generation of Fritz Stern, Peter Gay and Walter Lacqueur, observed that 'in order to empathize, a historian has to be the eternal traveler, the spectator, rather than being committed to a set worldview, least of all a nationalist belief system'.[6] I am of a later generation from that of these émigré German historians. But as with them, feelings of empathy – the predisposition to sympathise with the hopes, aspirations, and frustrations of the subordinated and displaced – were honed in me in my childhood environment and sensitised by a desire to connect to the lived experience of people and to remain, in every sense, intellectually as well as physically, an 'eternal traveller'.

And yet, even at my most empathic, I have certainly not managed to get 'inside the skins' of the persons or groups on whom I have focused. Nor have I been able to put myself in their places, or to perceive the world exactly as they perceived it. I have long acknowledged (and, indeed, have tried to make visible) the fact that my perspective as a historian – the orientation from which I examine the nature of individual and group confrontations with racism and other forms of exclusion and domination both in my written work and in the classroom – is an interpretation. And it is an interpretation that is not neutral. I have no problems declaring that I am not an 'objective historian' in the old sense. I abhor the omniscient narratives of historians claiming to stand above the fray. I am, I am not hesitant to admit, an engaged historian who, in so-called 'academic writing', uses the personal voice.

Indeed, for many years now, it has not been my goal as a historian to provide a seamless and impersonal narrative of events in which subjectivity and emotion are suppressed or left unacknowledged. For me, the voice (or, perhaps more accurately, the voices) of the historian, however interested, as well as the multiple voices and memories of the participants – the stories they tell and how they tell these stories – are as much part of the fabric of history as are written records and other archival materials. To take into account and reveal subjectivity and affect – to consider what is remembered as well as what is forgotten, fears as well as imaginings, the apprehension and misapprehension of events – complicates and restores a measure of contingency to history. It deepens our historical understanding and helps us to resist interpretive closure.

MH: Is all scholarship at its base personal, even if that fact is nowhere acknowledged? I have always thought so, though my early work did not betray it in any explicit way. But my dissertation on bi-cultural writers and texts mirrored my life, as did my second book on mothers and daughters, though both were written in purely academic language and scholarly convention. Even so, it took a great deal to begin to shed some of those conventions. I know I was fortunate to grow up as a scholar in a feminist environment that enabled and encouraged personal engagement and, eventually, also a turn to the autobiographical and the anecdotal.

In the 1980s, however, during the time that my work began to mature, that encouragement also came with the unfortunate concentration on identity categories – writing 'as a' (white, heterosexual, bourgeois, married, mother of sons, for example). I've always seen the personal turn not, as might be expected, as an instantiation but as a critical response to identity politics: fleshing identity categories into stories, giving them breadth, location and space, developing them over time, so that they expand and multiply, to the point of eventually disappearing. Embarrassingly, I must admit that I did feel I had to write 'as a' at the time, but also that it made me uncomfortable – the categories did not fit me, as, of course, they fit no one really. Personal writing, on the other hand, can reveal the complexities and contradictions of identity, its contingency and mobility.

My turn to the personal came in response to this discomfort with the politics of identity, and it came in a flash – with a call for papers I saw for a volume called *Displacements* edited by Angelika Bammer in the early 1990s. As I looked at the call, I immediately knew what I wanted to write, and it was not a scholarly article but an autobiographical piece about my emigration from Romania as a young teenager, and my immigration to the United States. At age twelve to thirteen, I suffered both cultural displacement and displacement from childhood to girlhood: how did those relate to each other? Which particular changes were caused by which of the two 'migrations?' These were some of the questions motivating me to write, and I decided to explore them through the story of two friendships that helped me acclimate and adapt both to the United States and to teenagehood and the demands of femininity. The desire to tell this story was certainly enabled by a feminist attention to the personal, the permission to theorise from an autobiographical location. As I was writing the piece, however, I also saw that my questions were in fact not *just* personal but also cultural and political, as well as academic, and that I would be aided in addressing them by the work I knew how to do best – literary analysis. The piece became an act of autobiographical reading of Eva Hoffman's memoir *Lost in Translation,* which enabled me to tell my story in relation to and in dialogue with hers, analysing our very similar displaced girlhoods.

That essay, 'Pictures of a displaced girlhood', marks for me the moment in which I felt I was beginning to write 'otherwise', and it was, indeed, at once a personal and a relational, affiliative, turn.[7] In placing my voice in conversation with Eva Hoffman's, I was already acknowledging that the personal is but a vehicle for a collective and generational story. The stakes of this kind of writing, moreover, transformed me from an academic interested in ideas to a writer who is equally interested in the formal and generic choices, in the very texture of writing, and in what writing could explore and illuminate: individual stories, sometimes unknown, or forgotten stories that needed to be told; stories of girls and women, of the persecuted and the displaced.

In the personal, writing became compelling, pleasurable, addictive. It needed a plot. I began to revel in words, and in figuring out solutions to formal problems I had so far only analysed in the writing of others. It was lucky for me, of course, and certainly no coincidence, that this was the moment in which personal academic writing became more accepted. When Leo and I spent a year at the National Humanities Center in 1992–93, we formed a seminar on personal scholarly writing so as to analyse it as a phenomenon. Some who joined were sceptics and detractors; others were practitioners, or at least flirted with the idea of trying it. As we read and discussed examples, we became more and more aware of the pitfalls of personal writing – we found that the authors were invariably revealing either too much or not enough, being too self-congratulatory or too self-deprecating. As some of us shared our own work with the group, we realised how hard it was to get that balance right. This, however, was a writing challenge – how one fashions oneself as a character and an actor or thinker. And this self-fashioning, of course, would also determine the content of the writing, the questions that would and could be asked. I was hooked by these issues and by the practice, a new working practice for me, and although not all my subsequent writing has been autobiographical, it has all been anchored in the personal and, indeed, shaped by an attention to the craft of writing. Different projects have followed different trajectories and required different writing and analytic methods, and the challenge has been to define the genre appropriate for a given project. Even the more scholarly pieces I've written since, however, have been embodied even if not autobiographical. At the same time, some of my seemingly autobiographical work has ever steadily connected personal concerns to collective and generational ones.

Although both of us, in previous single-authored efforts, have experimented with personal writing and with the introduction of our personal voices into literary or cultural criticism and the writing of history, it is in our collaboration on *Ghosts of Home* that the challenges and potential pitfalls of our writing choices most pointedly come to the fore.

Why did we want to write this book together? In spite of the similarity of our backgrounds and early experiences as immigrant children, we each have a different relationship to the city of Czernowitz and to its history. Each of us was drawn into the project by a different pull.

MH: For me, the relationship is personal and familial. Born in Romania after my parents left their native Czernowitz under cover of night with false papers in 1945, following the Soviet takeover of the region, I grew up in a community of displaced 'Czernowitzers' who maintained a strong nostalgic relationship to the city of their birth, and who communicated to me the many traumatic events that they endured there. I never intended to make this history, or even the lively German and Yiddish literary culture of Czernowitz, part of my scholarly work. Nothing could have been further from my mind. It wasn't until Leo and I went to what was by then Ukrainian Chernivtsi with my parents in 1998 that the idea of a book emerged. And in spite of our different relationships to the story of Czernowitz Jews, the sense that that story was largely unknown and needed to be told emerged with equal force for us both. Equally strong was the sense that we needed to co-write it. I was the daughter of our main characters and had grown up with the postmemory of Czernowitz; I had known many of the people in the book since childhood and felt a special responsibility to represent them in a way that honoured them and my memories of them. And yet, although this work was unequivocally personal, I had chosen to work collaboratively.

LS: For me, the connection is less directly familial. I am a 'son-in-law' of Czernowitzers. I was born in Bolivia, far from the Eastern European place that we first visited with Marianne's parents, Lotte and Carl, in 1998. But I am the son of Austrian refugees who fled to South America from Vienna in 1939, and,

as a historian and child of participants, I had written about Jewish familial experiences with emancipation, acculturation, and exclusion in Austro-Habsburg
times and their aftermath – experiences akin if not exactly identical to that of
Czernowitz Jews – in two previous books.[8] Compared to Marianne's, my knowledge of Czernowitz was no doubt more academic, historical, more firmly situated
in the present of research and writing, than in my own personal past. I brought
to the project broad cultural understanding and historical skills that complement
hers.

As the son-in-law and daughter of these Czernowitz survivors who also became vivid informants and characters in our book, we both had a deep personal
stake in what we were writing: we were both participants in and scholars of the
story and place we wanted to study, recall and memorialise. And we were both
deeply intrigued by some of the paradoxes and contradictions that the story of this
city's Jewish community presented.

We came to think of *Ghosts of Home* both as an intergenerational memoir and
as an interdisciplinary and self-reflexive work of historical/cultural exploration.
We thus had to invent a hybrid genre to accommodate narrative, analysis and oral
history, as well as our own two voices grappling with a complex and contradictory
past. We wanted to tell it both as a history and as a story about how the past lives
on in the present. We will get to these generic and writing issues in a moment, but
let us first offer a bit of background.

It needs to be emphasised that Czernowitz actually no longer exists on any
present-day map. Its name now is Chernivtsi – a city located in the southwestern
region of the Republic of the Ukraine. The capital of a former province of the
Austro-Hungarian Empire until 1918, it was called Cernăuți after the First World
War when it fell under Romanian authority, and subsequently, under Soviet rule
after the Second World War, it was renamed Chernovtsy.

Our primary goal in *Ghosts of Home* was to illuminate the distinct culture of
this city and its Jewish inhabitants during the Habsburg years before the outbreak
of the First World War, and the persistent and paradoxical afterlife of that urbane
cultural ideal over subsequent decades. What we needed to convey was that for
many of the surviving Jews who lived there in the decade before the First World
War and in the interwar years – now scattered through the world – the place forever remained Czernowitz, the 'Vienna of the East', a city in which (in the words
of its most famous poet, Paul Celan) 'human beings and books used to live'. And
'Czernowitz' for them consisted of the German language, its literature, and the
social and cultural standards of the Austro-Germanic world which they embraced
as core constituents of their identity.

Even after Czernowitz's annexation into Greater Romania in 1918 and the
institution of a policy of 'Romanianisation', a predominant segment of the Jewish
population of the city and region remained devoted to the German language and
its culture. What our book needed to illuminate and explain was the continuing
vitality and strength of this identification – due, no doubt, to the positive connections so many of Czernowitz's Jews had drawn between Jewish emancipation and
assimilation in the imperial Habsburg realm, and the significant social, political

and cultural rewards that this process had yielded – rewards of full citizenship rights and professional and economic opportunities that were increasingly curtailed and that eventually disappeared under Romanian rule between the wars.

At the same time, however, Czernowitz/Cernăuți was also that place where Jews suffered anti-Semitism, internment in a Fascist Romanian/Nazi ghetto, and Soviet occupation. It was where they were forced to wear the yellow star, and where a fortunate number among them, managing to escape deportation, survived the Holocaust. Of the more than 60,000 Jews who inhabited the city at the start of Second World War, only slightly more than half were alive at its conclusion. When, after the war, the bulk of these survivors left the, by then again, Soviet-ruled Chernovtsy, they thought it was forever. They knew that the place they had considered their home had now definitively been taken from them. Czernowitz in the former Bukowina province, now twice lost to Jews, came to persist only as a projection – as an idea physically disconnected from its geographical location, and tenuously dependent on the vicissitudes of personal, familial and cultural memory. And yet, this *idea* of a pre-First World War multi-cultural and multi-lingual tolerant city and a modern, cosmopolitan culture persists and continues to evolve to this day in a lively and ever-growing internet community.

By focusing on how the inhabitants of this one city constructed their life worlds over time, we hoped to be able to trace the contradictions that defined this Jewish community, the exhilarating promises and shattering disappointments associated with the process of Jewish emancipation and assimilation. We could show how this one urban centre engaged and participated in some of the grand narratives of the European twentieth century: the intensity, reach, but also the tragedy, of the German-Jewish symbiosis; the encounter between Fascism and Communism; the rise of Zionism and modern Yiddishism; the displacement of refugees; and the shadow of Holocaust memory on the children and grandchildren of survivors. And we could ask how this small provincial Habsburg capital was able to produce such a rich and urbane cosmopolitan culture – one that would remain so vivid and powerful in the imagination of the generation of Jews who came of age in Romanian Cernăuți during the interwar years. What had made their identification with Habsburg Czernowitz so strong as to enable them to preserve and protect their positive memories of the city in the face of devastating negative and traumatic experiences? How, moreover, did nostalgia for the past, and negative memories of anti-semitic discrimination and persecution, co-exist and inflect each other, and how were these memories passed down over generations?

To get at these contradictions and complexities, we knew we needed to tell this history by way of the life narratives of ordinary people – those who are often hidden from history – to bring alive their dreams and aspirations, their varied individual responses to historical extremity and their ways of working through a painful past. We wanted to incorporate testimonies and oral histories, but we also wanted to insert ourselves as listeners, inheritors, mediators of this past, and to make palpable how we were affected and indeed constituted as tellers of this history by what we heard.

To do this, we decided to structure our narrative in *Ghosts of Home* along two temporal levels. On the level of the past, our book is an account of Jewish Czernowitz and key moments in its history over the course of the past 125 years. On the level of the present, it is fuelled by a collaborative quest, reflecting four journeys we made to Ukrainian Chernivtsi in 1998, 2000, 2006 and 2008, and to Transnistria, the region to which Jews were deported from Czernowitz, during two of these visits. The first of our trips inspired this project. We made it with Carl and Lotte Hirsch – their first return to the city of their birth since their hurried departure from Soviet-ruled Chernovtsy in 1945. With them as guides and mentors, we searched for physical traces of old Czernowitz and Cernăuți, for material connections to the places, residences and times that had been so central to their, and to their fellow exiles', sense of origin and identification. Subsequent trips were second-generation or group research trips, more centred on our own quest than on that of Marianne's parents or their generation.

The historical dimension of the book relies on a great range of traditional and less traditional source material – official and private contemporary documents, public and family archival materials, letters, memoirs, photographs, newspapers, essays, poetry, fiction and internet postings, as well as material remnants that we think of as testimonial objects that create a link between past and present. Central to our approach was the use of oral and video accounts from old Czernowitzers and their offspring – histories and narrations that we collected and taped in the course of our research in the Ukraine, Israel, Austria, Germany, France and the United States, or that we heard and watched in oral history archives in several places. But these materials were more than evidentiary sources for us. They focused our narrative around telling individual anecdotes, images and objects, serving as what we think of as 'points of memory' that open small windows to the past.

In taking this approach we were also able to reflect more theoretically on how memory and transmission work both to reveal and to conceal certain traumatic recollections, and how fragmentary, tenuous and deceptive our access to the past can be. In the effort to capture the effects of the past on the present and of the present on the past, and to trace the effects of the 'telling' on the witness and listener, our book exemplifies what James Young has called 'received history'. It explores 'both what happened and how it is passed down to us'.[9] And, in that process, it exposes the holes in memory and knowledge that puncture second-generation accounts – accounts motivated by needs and desires that, at times, rely on no more than speculative investment, identification and invention.

What is perhaps the most basic element of *Ghosts of Home* also posed its greatest writing challenge – the fact that it was co-authored. What voice would do justice to the project, to the history we wanted to tell and to our own investment in that history? The two of us were writing collaboratively, but at no time did we think we could write the book in the 'we' first person plural voice – a voice that is rhetorically weak and ineffective, as you can tell from the very sentence in which we are conveying this observation.

We agreed that both our individual voices and perspectives had to be present within the book, singly and in dialogue. And yet, we needed a *writing* voice that would hold the narrative together and that could be followed by our readers. After a great deal of discussion, experimentation and agony, we made the decision to write the book in the first person singular, in the 'I' voice. But we also had to contest the assumption that our distinct disciplinary training, or our biographical relationships to the story, was necessarily reflected in different sections of this book – that the 'I' we used in different chapters was in any way stable. On the contrary, what happened was that in the process of writing and rewriting, our voices began to merge and cross. Sometimes we identified the 'I' clearly, but at other points it was no more than a narrative voice, a device, perhaps even a 'character' in its own right, embodied but not directly corresponding to either of us in strict biographical sense. Sometimes we wrote our own 'I' sections, at others we wrote each other's. The same, of course, is true of this account of the writing.

All this, we realise, still sounds like *we*; each of us separately and the two of us together were at the centre of the story. But that is precisely what we needed to balance and to contest. We wanted, first of all, to give voice to our subjects, without, however, speaking for them, without pretending to understand and elucidate moments in the story that are so clearly distant from our own experiences. The book thus engages a number of individual voices in addition to our own within a web of narratives, recollections and analyses that connect with each other, and over time, through familial and communal relationships. Such a web of recollections and interconnections, together with our other historical and cultural source materials, allows, we believe, for the affective side of the afterlife of Czernowitz to emerge in fuller and richer dimensions.

Secondly, and related to this, we wanted to develop a writing voice that reflects the multiple dialogues (between us) and larger conversations with our other interlocutors and source materials that form the background of what we learned and what we knew, what we were able to tell. The writing 'I' had to be open, entangled in multiple relations and affiliations. In her recent writings, Nancy Miller has argued that memoir is always relational and not personal but rather transpersonal. 'The transpersonal domain', she writes, 'is a collective, generational experience.' It emerges from the belief that 'in the deliberate reattachment of self to others, private details take on public meaning'. 'The I of getting "personal" becomes "transpersonal" when it forges links,' Miller continues, describing links both to her own generation and to those who preceded her but to whom she felt deeply bonded. 'The transpersonal is a process through which the self moves into and out of the social, psychic and material spaces of relation.'[10]

For the two of us in this book, writing simply had to be transpersonal: our collaboration demanded it. And so did the genre of the intergenerational memoir. But it is the challenge of writing in the transpersonal, of finding the voice for it, that made the entanglements out of which the work emerged both palpable and impossible to obscure. Indeed, the 'I' voice that we forged in the book is already the transpersonal voice – the middle voice in which writing is also always already 'otherwise'.

But what of the *personal* remains in the *transpersonal*? Is the singular I no more than a pronoun, or a device? Is it submerged and superseded, or is it merely muted, moved from the centre to the edges of the narrative and the analysis? And what are the ethics and the politics of this move to the first person plural? This is indeed a question about collaboration: not just co-writing but a writing that foregrounds the dialogues and conversations that undergird it. It is a question that acquires particular resonance in the context of family stories and family archives such as those which comprise our book, and in the context, as well, of the kind of familial collaboration on which we embarked and that has raised so many eyebrows. And it acquires resonance as well in the context of stories of return to sites of past suffering such as the one we tell in our book.

Familial inheritance, such as the one motivating *Ghosts of Home*, goes beyond words and stories, taking the form of unconscious projections, obsessive patterns: symptoms rather than narratives.

> MH: It is in this sense that I see my own role in this work, and it is this that initially made me doubt my ability to do it. This is why Leo as a historian, and as someone less directly and immediately involved, as the in-law, in fact, promised to provide some necessary distance and balance. Dominick La Capra has written on historians' transferential relationship to the subjects they work on, on the personal investments they are not trained to acknowledge and reveal.[11] With two of us working together, we had a chance to acknowledge these investments, and to act as checks on one another's. At the same time, the deeply familial nature of the project makes it so overlaid with unconscious processes on every level that we often wondered how to manage them.

> LS: As a historian I have been trained to be suspicious of relying solely on the family archive as a basis for writing history. Most documents in family archives, including diaries and photographs, are personal and circumscribed – private and generally inaccessible to outsiders. They require explication and broader contextualisation. Without additional comparative and counterweighing evidence they reflect singular rather than collective experience. Their contents offer little that is generalisable. A broader focus beyond one family and beyond one generation is necessary if one wants to move from the personal to the transpersonal. In *Ghosts of Home*, Marianne's family provided only some of the numerous characters that allowed us to advance our story.

But what of the kind of familial collaboration that occurred between the two of us, within our domestic partnership? We encountered so many dangers in this family-based work – of being too self-congratulatory, too self-revealing and self-indulgent, of being too unaware of our own stakes, and our own power struggles. What room does co-writing a book leave for personal style and way of working, for individual ideas, for disagreements? Certainly, the two of us differ radically in our working and writing paces, and in our styles. One of us is a slower writer, more meticulous, more of a perfectionist; the other more impatient, eager to be done and to move on. Complementary styles, perhaps, but also styles that required a great deal of patience and negotiation on both our parts. Our collaboration demanded that we meld these different habits and styles – which has, in many ways resulted in a submersion of individuality. What has been lost in the melding, and what has been gained? And how has working together affected other aspects of our relationship? What are the erotics of academic collaboration?

In co-habitation, work cannot be compartmentalised or separated from other activities. Home offers no retreat: it is the office. It is great, on the one hand, that we can do things together and still be 'working'. We can 'work' as we take walks, go out for Sunday brunch, travel. We need not feel guilty about not working when we do these fun things. Work is less lonely and isolating. And we can get instant feedback.

At the same time, it is terrible that we are always 'working'. There is no time out, no possibility of taking a break. Isn't it unhealthy to be brainstorming all the time? When play and work blend, is play still play? And if work is not going well, will that affect our domestic interactions? Will inevitable arguments about 'the book' affect our negotiations about the children, the house, our vacations? And will we still be able to work together if we have domestic disagreements?

Above, the word 'work' appears in quotes. What kind of scholarship emerges from work done in the midst of the dailiness of domesticity? If we are working while walking the dog, or driving, or cooking, or having lunch, or weeding the garden, if we interrupt work to put in the laundry, or make the bed, can we still muster the necessary discipline and rigour required for scholarly production? Any couple deciding to write together should ask themselves these questions. Collaborators who are colleagues and friends can walk away from work. Domestic partners cannot.

As in any collaboration, one wonders, when done, whether the final product truly reflects all the contributing voices. As historians and critics, we are certainly sensitive to the power structures typical of nuclear and extended families that grant certain stories more weight while others remain less authoritative or believable.

Such structures operate even more powerfully in the context of stories of return to a painful past place, now inhabited by a different population, such as the one we evoke in our book. Whose voices are included in such a narrative, and whose are left out? What kind of communities are forged in the transpersonal and what boundaries get drawn? What archives and materials are readily available, and which population groups tend to be excluded from the historical record?

In stories of return, like ours, there is the question of how the past relates to the present and what place the present holds for returnees and researchers like us. And, here, what we found was that Czernowitz Jews and their descendants, including ourselves, 'returning' to Ukrainian Chernivtsi, showed very little interest in the present-day city and its inhabitants. And, beyond a few telling anecdotes, some critical if not dismissive, our book, also, deals little with life in present-day Chernivtsi and its Ukrainian population.

Is it, then, that transpersonal writing in the middle voice includes those who are 'like us' and excludes 'others'? Are we back to the limits of identity categories and the constraining parameters of their assumed politics? Certainly, language impairs dialogue, and so do the mutual suspicions and irreconcilable conflicts over space and history that animate such relationships. Although contemporary Chernivtsi residents, Jewish in tiny numbers and overwhelmingly non-Jewish, feel a claim and a sense of responsibility for the very place and its legacy, we must confess, with a shared sadness, that we cannot yet imagine a genuine dialogue between us. Our histories and our stakes are just too divergent. But trying to conceive a writing voice that would be broad enough to make space for such different perspectives offers one potential approach to an engagement that must and that will be possible in the future.

This paper was presented at two conferences: first at 'Academic Writing' at Emory University, Atlanta, on 7–8 May 2010; and then at 'Writing Otherwise' in Manchester on 28 June 2010. Although first published in this volume, it was initially written for the volume emerging from the Atlanta conference, to be published as *Rigor & Beauty: The Art of Scholarly Writing*, edited by Angelika Bammer and Ruth-Ellen Boetcher Joeres.

Notes

1   The tradition of personal academic writing has, of course, challenged these assumptions. See esp., Nancy K. Miller, *Getting Personal: Personal Occasions and Other Autobiographical Acts*; Jane Tompkins, 'Me and my shadow', in Linda S. Kauffman (ed.), *Gender and Theory: Dialogues on Feminist Criticism*; and Jane Gallop and Dick Blau, *Living With His Camera*.
2   Marianne Hirsch and Leo Spitzer, *Ghosts of Home: The Afterlife of Czernowitz in Jewish Memory*.
3   Roland Barthes, *S/Z: An Essay*.
4   Barthes, 'To write: an intransitive verb?' in *A Rustle of Language*, p. 19. For a discussion of Barthes' notion of the middle voice in the writing of history, see Hayden White, 'Historical emplotment and the writing of truth', in Saul Friedlander (ed.) *Probing the Limits of Representation: Nazism and the 'Final Solution'*.
5   See Spitzer, *Hotel Bolivia: A Culture of Memory in a Refuge from Nazism*.
6   George L. Mosse, *Confronting History: A Memoir*, p. 6.
7   Angelika Bammer (ed.), *Displacements: Cultural Identities in Question*.
8   See Spitzer, *Hotel Bolivia* and Spitzer, *Lives in Between: Assimilation and Marginality in Austria, Brazil and West Africa*.
9   James E. Young, 'Toward a received history of the Holocaust.'
10   Miller, 'Getting transpersonal: the cost of an academic life', p. 168.
11   Dominick La Capra, *Representing the Holocaust: History, Theory, Trauma*.

Bibliography

Bammer, Angelika (ed.), *Displacements: Cultural Identities in Question* (Bloomington, IN: Indiana University Press, 1994).
Barthes, Roland, *S/Z: An Essay*, trans. Richard Miller (New York: Hill and Wang, 1974).
Barthes, Roland, 'To Write: An Intransitive Verb?' in *A Rustle of Language,* trans. Richard Howard (Berkeley, CA: University of California Press, 1989).
Gallop, Jane, and Dick Blau, *Living With His Camera* (Durham, NC: Duke University Press, 2003).

Hirsch, Marianne, and Leo Spitzer, *Ghosts of Home: The Afterlife of Czernowitz in Jewish Memory* (Berkeley, CA: University of California Press, 2010).

La Capra, Dominick, *Representing the Holocaust: History, Theory, Trauma* (Ithaca, NY: Cornell University Press, 1994).

Miller, Nancy K., *Getting Personal: Personal Occasions and Other Autobiographical Acts* (New York: Routledge, 1991).

Miller, Nancy K., 'Getting transpersonal: the cost of an academic life', *Prose Studies*, 31:3 (December 2009), 166–80.

Mosse, George L., *Confronting History: A Memoir* (Madison, WI: University of Wisconsin Press, 2000).

Spitzer, Leo, *Hotel Bolivia: A Culture of Memory in a Refuge from Nazism* (New York: Hill and Wang, 1998).

Spitzer, Leo, *Lives in Between: Assimilation and Marginality in Austria, Brazil and West Africa* (Cambridge: Cambridge University Press, 1989).

Tompkins, Jane, 'Me and my shadow', in Linda S. Kauffman (ed.), *Gender and Theory: Dialogues on Feminist Criticism* (New York: Basil Blackwell, 1989).

White, Hayden, 'Historical emplotment and the writing of truth', in Saul Friedlander (ed.) *Probing the Limits of Representation: Nazism and the 'Final Solution'* (Cambridge, MA: Harvard University Press, 1992).

Young, James E., 'Toward a received history of the Holocaust', *History and Theory*, 36:4 (December 1997), 21–43.

Image credits

Janet Wolff Atlantic moves

- Lady Ottoline Morrell, *Mark Gertler*, photograph, 1918. ©National Portrait Gallery, London (p. 80).
- Leland Bell, *Standing self portrait,* 1979. Private collection, courtesy of Steven Harvey Fine Art Projects (p. 80).
- Map courtesy National Geographic Education (p. 86).
- *Windscale, 10 October 1957.* Photograph by Ivor Nicholas (p. 82).

Brenda Cooper If the shoe fits

- Family photograph, *c.* 1932. Possession of author (p. 122).
- Lubaina Himid, 'My Name is Kwesi', *Naming the money*, 2004. © Lubaina Himid (p. 127).
- Maud Sulter, *SYRCAS*, 1994, and *Jeanne Duval*, 2003. ©Lubaina Himid (pp. 121, 125, 128, 132).

Other images are printed with the permission of the authors.